ESSENTIAL METHODS IN SYMBOLIC INTERACTION

STUDIES IN SYMBOLIC INTERACTION

Series Editor: Shing-Ling S. Chen

Recent Volumes:

Volume 35:	Studies in Symbolic Interaction
Volume 36:	Blue Ribbon Papers: Interactionism: The Emerging Landscape
Volume 37:	Studies in Symbolic Interaction
Volume 38:	Blue Ribbon Papers: Behind the Professional Mask: The Self-Revelations of Leading Symbolic Interactionists
Volume 39:	Studies in Symbolic Interaction
Volume 40:	40th Anniversary of Studies in Symbolic Interaction
Volume 41:	Radical Interactionism on the Rise
Volume 42:	Revisiting Symbolic Interaction in Music Studies and New Interpretive Works
Volume 43:	Symbolic Interaction and New Social Media
Volume 44:	Contributions from European Symbolic Interactionists: Reflections on Methods
Volume 45:	Contributions from European Symbolic Interactionists: Conflict and Cooperation
Volume 46:	The Astructural Bias Charge
Volume 47:	Symbolic Interactionist Takes on Music
Volume 48:	Oppression and Resistance: Structure, Agency, and Transformation
Volume 49:	Carl J. Couch and the Iowa School: In His Own Words and in Reflection
Volume 50:	The Interaction Order
Volume 51:	Conflict and Forced Migration
Volume 52:	Radical Interactionism and Critiques of Contemporary Culture
Volume 53:	Studies in Symbolic Interaction
Volume 54:	Subcultures
Volume 55:	Festschrift in Honor of Norman K. Denzin: He Knew His Song Well

Volume 56: Festschrift in Honor of Kathy Charmaz
Volume 57: Festschrift in Honor of David R. Maines
Volume 58: Symbolic Interaction and Inequality
Volume 59: Essential Issues in Symbolic Interaction

STUDIES IN SYMBOLIC INTERACTION   VOLUME 60

ESSENTIAL METHODS IN SYMBOLIC INTERACTION

EDITED BY

SHING-LING S. CHEN
University of Northern Iowa, USA

United Kingdom – North America – Japan
India –Malaysia – China

Emerald Publishing Limited
Emerald Publishing, Floor 5, Northspring, 21-23 Wellington Street, Leeds LS1 4DL

First edition 2025

Editorial matter and selection © 2025 Shing-Ling S. Chen.
Individual chapters © 2025 The authors.
Published under exclusive licence by Emerald Publishing Limited.

Reprints and permissions service
Contact: www.copyright.com

No part of this book may be reproduced, stored in a retrieval system, transmitted in any form or by any means electronic, mechanical, photocopying, recording or otherwise without either the prior written permission of the publisher or a licence permitting restricted copying issued in the UK by The Copyright Licensing Agency and in the USA by The Copyright Clearance Center. Any opinions expressed in the chapters are those of the authors. Whilst Emerald makes every effort to ensure the quality and accuracy of its content, Emerald makes no representation implied or otherwise, as to the chapters' suitability and application and disclaims any warranties, express or implied, to their use.

British Library Cataloguing in Publication Data
A catalogue record for this book is available from the British Library

ISBN: 978-1-83662-019-8 (Print)
ISBN: 978-1-83662-018-1 (Online)
ISBN: 978-1-83662-020-4 (Epub)

ISSN: 0163-2396 (Series)

INVESTOR IN PEOPLE

CONTENTS

About the Contributors   *ix*

PART A
ESSENTIAL METHODS IN SYMBOLIC INTERACTION

Introduction   *3*
Natalia Ruiz-Junco

The New Iowa School and Generating Qualitative Research in the Laboratory   *9*
Michael A. Katovich

Experimenting With Social Order: Notes on Some Developments in Ethnomethodology and the New Iowa School   *25*
Dirk vom Lehn

Symbolic Interaction and the Grounded Theory Method   *49*
Antony Bryant and Carrie Friese

Qualitative Media Analysis   *79*
Christopher J. Schneider and David L. Altheide

Symbolic Interactionist Methods for Studying Music   *93*
Joseph A. Kotarba

Statistical Methods and Symbolic Interactionist Theorizing   *105*
Jeffery T. Ulmer

PART B
NEW INTERACTIONIST RESEARCH

Colonial Violence and the Chicago School: The Impact of Ellsworth Faris's Missionary Experiences in the Congo   *121*
Daniel R. Huebner

Ethnomethods of Increasing the Believability of Extraordinary Claims: Strategies for the Presentation of Self   *169*
David Aveline and Brant Downey

Index   *187*

ABOUT THE CONTRIBUTORS

David L. Altheide, PhD, is a Regents' Professor Emeritus on the faculty of Justice and Social Inquiry in the School of Social Transformation at Arizona State University, where he taught for 37 years. His work has focused on the role of mass media and information technology in social control. His most recent books are *Gonzo Governance: The Media Logic of Donald Trump* (Routledge, 2023), *Terrorism and the Politics of Fear* (2nd edition, Rowman and Littlefield, 2017), *The Media Syndrome* (Routledge, 2016), *Media Edge: Media Logic and Social Reality* (Lang, 2014), *Qualitative Media Analysis* (2nd edition, Sage, 2012), and *Terror Post 9/11 and the Media* (Lang, 2009). Dr Altheide received the Cooley Award three times, which is given to the outstanding book in symbolic interaction, and received the 2005 George Herbert Mead Award for lifetime contributions from the Society for the Study of Symbolic Interaction, as well as the society's Mentor Achievement Award in 2007. In fall 2012, he was a Fulbright Specialist in Germany (Zeppelin University) and a Distinguished Research Professor in Australia (Law Faculty, University of New South Wales). He also received a Fulbright Specialist Award at The Catholic University in Lisbon, Portugal in spring 2017.

David Aveline, PhD, is a Canadian born in London, England. He was raised in Montreal, Quebec, and currently lives in Calgary Alberta. He came to academics late in life after numerous jobs, including underground miner, racetrack groom, youth worker, and hotel manager. He is now an Associate Professor at Mount Royal University in Calgary and teaches such courses as the sociology of sexualities, sociology of religion, and sociology of the body. He obtained his Master's degree in Sociology at Concordia University in Montreal and PhD at Indiana University in Bloomington, Indiana. His areas of interest are human sexuality, 2SLGBT+ studies, interpretive theory, qualitative research, and most recently the sociology of the paranormal.

Antony Bryant is a Professor of Informatics at Leeds Beckett University, Leeds, UK; Chief Researcher, The Education Academy, Institute of Educational Research, Vytautas Magnus University, Kaunas, Lithuania. He has written extensively on qualitative research methods, being Senior Editor of *The SAGE Handbook of Grounded Theory* (2007) and *The SAGE Handbook of Current Developments in Grounded Theory* (2019); both co-edited with Kathy Charmaz. His writing on Grounded Theory includes *Grounded Theory and Grounded Theorizing* (Oxford, 2017), *The Varieties of Grounded Theory* (SAGE, 2019), and "Continual Permutations of Misunderstanding: The Curious Incidents of the

Grounded Theory Method", *Qualitative Inquiry*, May 2020. Other recent writings include "Liquid uncertainty, chaos and complexity: The gig economy and the open source movement," *Thesis Eleven*, FEB2020; "A Conversation between Frank Land and Antony Bryant," *Journal of Information Technology*, June 2020 Parts 1 & 2; "What the Web has Wrought," *Informatics* 2020, 7(2), 15.

Brant Downey holds a PhD in Sociology from Brandeis University. His disciplinary interests include the history of sociology and classical and contemporary theory. As an avid music fan, he recently started taking piano lessons, with the long-term goal of writing original music. He currently teaches in the Department of Sociology and Anthropology at Mount Royal University, in Calgary.

Carrie Friese is an Associate Professor in Sociology at the London School of Economics and Political Science. Her research is in medical sociology and science and technology studies. With Adele Clarke, she and Rachel Washburn have coauthored *Situational Analysis in Practice: Mapping Relationalities Across Disciplines* (2022), *Situational Analysis: Grounded Theory after the Interpretive Turn*, 2nd Edition (2018), and *Situational Analysis in Practice: Mapping Research with Grounded Theory* (2015).

Daniel R. Huebner is an Associate Professor of Sociology at the University of North Carolina Greensboro with research interests in social theory, the history of the social sciences, the sociology of knowledge, comparative-historical sociology, cultural sociology, and archival methods. Huebner is the author of *Reintroducing George Herbert Mead* (Routledge, 2022), coeditor with Hans Joas of George H. Mead's *Mind, Self, and Society: The Definitive Edition* (University of Chicago Press, 2015), and his recent work has appeared in *The Journal of the History of the Behavioral Sciences, Transactions of The Charles S. Peirce Society*, and *The American Sociologist*. His *Becoming Mead* (University of Chicago Press, 2014) received the 2016 Charles H. Cooley Award from the Society for the Study of Symbolic Interaction.

Michael A. Katovich is a Professor of Sociology in the Department of Sociology and Anthropology at Texas Christian University. He has written on diverse subjects, linked to the concepts and theoretical tenets that emerged within the new Iowa School of Symbolic Interaction.

Joseph A. Kotarba, PhD, is a Professor of Sociology at Texas State University, where he directs the *Music Across the Life Course Project*. He also serves as Lead Ethnographer and Evaluation Researcher for the Institute for Translational Sciences at the University of Texas Medical Branch-Galveston. He received the George Herbert Mead Award for Lifetime Achievement from the Society for the Study of Symbolic Interaction and the Society's Charles Horton Cooley Award for Best Book in the Symbolic Interactionist Tradition for *Baby Boomer Rock 'n' Roll Fans* (Rowman & Littlefield, 2013). He is currently studying the experience of music in the AI era and the culture of the translational science movement. His latest book is

ABOUT THE CONTRIBUTORS

Music in the Course of Life (Routledge, 2023). He received his doctorate from the University of California, San Diego.

Natalia Ruiz-Junco is an Associate Professor of Sociology at Auburn University. She works in the areas of social theory, social psychology, sociology of emotions, social movements, and qualitative methodology. She has a long-standing interest in interpretive and pragmatist theories. She is the coeditor of *Updating Charles H. Cooley: Contemporary Perspectives on a Sociological Classic* (Routledge, 2019), the *Routledge International Handbook of Interactionism* (Routledge, 2021), and *People, Technology, and Social Organization: Interactionist Studies of Everyday Life* (Routledge, 2024).

Christopher J. Schneider, PhD, is a Professor of Sociology at Brandon University. His research focuses on how developments in media and technology contribute to changes in social interaction and social control. Dr Schneider has written or collaborated on eight books and has published dozens of scholarly journal articles, book chapters, and essays. His most recent books are *Doing Public Scholarship: A Practical Guide to Media Engagement* (Routledge, 2024) and *Defining Sexual Misconduct: Power, Media, and #MeToo* (coauthored with Stacey Hannem) (University of Regina Press, 2022). *Defining Sexual Misconduct* received the 2024 Midwest Sociological Society's Distinguished Book Award and an Honorable Mention for the 2023 Cooley Award, given for notable book in symbolic interaction, from the Society for the Study of Symbolic Interaction. *Defining Sexual Misconduct* was also listed in *The Hill Times'* Best Books of 2022. Dr Schneider has received award recognition for his research, teaching, community service, and contributions to public scholarship. More recently, he is the 2024 recipient of Brandon University's Board of Governors Award for Excellence in Community Service and the 2022 recipient of Brandon University's Senate Award for Excellence in Research.

Jeffery T. Ulmer is a Professor of Sociology and Criminology at Penn State University and serves as the Director of the Criminal Justice Research Center. Ulmer's work has been shaped by symbolic interactionism since his undergraduate studies and was profoundly influenced by David Maines' mentorship in his early career. Ulmer's research has mostly focused on multi-method studies of inequalities in criminal prosecution and sentencing and the social organization of criminal courts. He has also published impactful research on the place of symbolic interactionism in criminological theory, religion and crime, and race, disadvantage, and violence rates. He was named a Fellow of the American Society of Criminology in 2021 and received the 2012 Distinguished Scholar Award and the 2001 Distinguished New Scholar Award from the American Society of Criminology's Division on Corrections and Sentencing. He and coauthors won the American Society of Criminology's 2012 Outstanding Article Award and the ASC's 2006 Hindelang Award for *Confessions of a Dying Thief: Understanding Criminal Careers and Illegal Enterprise* (2005, Transaction).

Dirk vom Lehn is a Professor of Organization and Practice at King's Business School, King's College London. His research primarily is concerned with examining the organization of action and interaction in museums and optometric practices using video-recordings as principal data and ethnomethodology as analytic attitude. He also conducts studies in the development of ethnomethodology. Dirk's latest publication are the monograph *Peopling Marketing, Organization, and Technology: Interactionist Studies in Marketing Interaction* (Routledge, 2024) and the edited collection *People, Technology, and Social Organization: Interactionist Studies of Everyday Life* (Routledge, 2023; with Will Gibson and Natalia Ruiz-Junco).

PART A

ESSENTIAL METHODS IN SYMBOLIC INTERACTION

INTRODUCTION

Natalia Ruiz-Junco

Auburn University, USA

ABSTRACT

This piece introduces the present volume in Studies in Symbolic Interaction. *It discusses each of the volume's contributions and provides an assessment of interactionism's current engagement with methods. The volume shows that interactionists are not limited to the use of methods informed by interactionist frameworks, while presenting a rich canvas of methods that are aligned with interactionism.*

Keywords: Interactionism; methodology; interactionist frameworks; sociology; history of knowledge

A markedly intense preoccupation with method has been characteristic of the modus operandi of sociologists for decades (Swedberg, 2012). Since the beginning of American sociology as an academic discipline, methodology has progressively become the critical pursuit of a discipline whose theoretical perspectives are fragmented and not unified (Ross, 1991; Turner & Turner, 1990). The present volume shows that improvements in methods do not have to come at the expense of advancement in theory when it comes to interactionism.

Interactionists have consistently sustained a strong interest in methodology, the most apparent manifestation of which is the enduring popularity of Herbert Blumer's (1969) statement about symbolic interactionism's "methodological position," a statement that has turned into a symbol of belonging for the interactionist community (see Ruiz-Junco et al., 2023).[1] This volume is thorough in its coverage of interactionist methods, even if, due to space limitations, not all relevant methodological approaches could be included.[2] This volume, however, constitutes a rich canvas of multiple interactionist engagements with methods, and invites us to study social life using qualitative and quantitative approaches.

In the first contribution, Michael A. Katovich promotes laboratory research from an interactionist and qualitative perspective. Katovich's point is that "examining social action, qualitatively, as simultaneously processual and

---

Essential Methods in Symbolic Interaction
Studies in Symbolic Interaction, Volume 60, 3–7
Copyright © 2025 Natalia Ruiz-Junco
Published under exclusive licence by Emerald Publishing Limited
ISSN: 0163-2396/doi:10.1108/S0163-239620250000060001

4   *Introduction*

structured, can occur in conjunction with creating dramatic scenarios in laboratory settings." Katovich traces the historical significance of laboratory studies in social psychology and discusses their limitations. By contrast, he describes the New Iowa School (NIS) as an interactionist approach that utilizes experiments and audio-visual data to examine how people in small groups coordinate their actions in purposive and emergent ways. His contribution contains valuable illustrations of laboratory research undertaken following NIS postulates, revealing the usefulness of such method for studying a plethora of research questions, including how the aligning of individual lines of action connects to consequential patterns of collective action.

Dirk vom Lehn offers us a brilliant investigation into the theoretical and methodological connections that exist between ethnomethodology, founded by Harold Garfinkel, and the New Iowa School (NIS), created by Carl Couch. These two research programs, vom Lehn argues, have in common their desire to explore how social order is constructed through social interaction. They share an aim to unearth "generic principles of social life" and the use of audio-visual data in their analyses. In addition, both programs are interactionist. Comparing these two research trends, vom Lehn notes that Garfinkel was influenced, among others, by Alfred Schutz's phenomenology, while Carl Couch was inspired by Manford Kuhn, Meadian pragmatism and Simmelian sociology. Despite the resemblances between ethnomethodology and NIS, vom Lehn expresses concern regarding the lack of fruitful engagement between them. As the author notes, NIS scholars were somewhat critical of ethnomethodology, and Garfinkel and his followers did not engage with NIS scholarship. Thus, vom Lehn's account suggests an image of two ships crossing paths at night. He believes both scholarly communities should consider changing this image, especially now that some ethnomethodologists are immersed in a move toward "the scientification of interactionist analyses," and a psychological laboratory research. In conclusion, vom Lehn urges ethnomethodologists and NIS scholars to fully embrace their common theoretical lineage, as well as the Society for the Study of Symbolic Interaction.

Tony Bryant and Carrie Friese pen the third contribution. These authors walk us through the history of Grounded Theory (GT), from the creation of the method to the discrepancies between two of the founders of the approach (Anselm Strauss and Barney Glaser) to the establishment of several recognizable branches of GT. In discussing the disagreements that led to the proliferation of GT approaches, the authors discuss how the different trainings of the founders, Strauss and Glaser (in Chicago and Columbia, respectively), may have been important factors contributing to the severance of their collaborative relationship. As Bryant and Friese note, the end of the Strauss–Glaser collaboration signified the subsequent creation of two distinctly different approaches to grounded theory, with "Classic Grounded Theory" renouncing the roots of the method in interpretive social science, and Straussian grounded theory, constructivist grounded theory, and situational analysis, affirming, with different degrees of explicitness, their solid theoretical affinity with interactionism. In fact, the authors consider interactionism and GT a theory-methods package, as GT adopts three distinct pillars of interactionism: denial of "the spectator view of knowledge" in favor of the social construction of knowledge; "open-mindedness" bolstered by a sort of phenomenological bracketing of one's assumptions; and abduction, introduced by C. S. Peirce and engaged by other interactionists, such as Anselm Strauss and Kathy Charmaz. Beyond providing a detailed historical account of the method's permutations and theoretical developments, this piece elaborates on three postulates of GT based on Blumer's (1969) famous three premises. Bryant and Friese argue that GT is intrinsically driven by an interactionist sensibility and by a pragmatist desire for liberation and social transformation. Indeed, as these authors put it, "A key feature of Pragmatism, and by implication SI, is the concern for knowledge to serve the project of emancipation."

The fourth contribution comes from Christopher J. Schneider and David L. Altheide, who introduce Qualitative Media Analysis (QMA) as a qualitative method to analyze documents (e.g., video and images) focused on meanings, processes, and symbolic phenomena. Schneider and Altheide provide us with helpful illustrations on how to conduct research using this approach. A significant takeaway of their chapter is an outline of 12 methodological activities that researchers should follow while doing QMA research projects. These activities, or "steps," include spotting a research problem, recognizing the idoneous media sources for the research question at hand (e.g., Facebook), choosing the unit of analysis (e.g., a post), and defining other key aspects of the research process (e.g., the "protocol" or "data collection sheet"). The authors demonstrate throughout their paper that this method cannot be understood without reference to three interactionist postulates: the emphasis on society as an interpretive process of people constructing definitions of the situation; the push for the dissolution of the subject/object dichotomy; and the focus on processual analysis. They also recommend researchers to develop "an open mind" in their systematic search for "relevant meanings and emphases."

Joseph A. Kaotarba contributes a methodological reflection on a specific subfield of sociology. Kotarba identifies a conceptual repertoire for the interactionist study of music, providing us with methodological insights about how to conduct research in this area. As Kotarba states, "Music is a ubiquitous feature of everyday life." In his repertoire of concepts, Kotarba integrates several interactionist ideas; among them, self, community, scene, and authenticity. Kotarba does not conceive of these concepts as mere ideas, but rather as interactionist tools coupled with interpretive methods used to study music in everyday life. As an illustration, he shows how he applied the concept of subculture in his ethnographic study of rave parties, collaborating with other researchers (graduate students) in an effort to use the "multi-perspectival approach." This emphasis on perspectival knowledge has its roots in George H. Mead's (2015 [1934]) interest in the organization of perspectives and is a central feature of interactionist ethnographic research (Prus, 1996).

Finally, Jeffery T. Ulmer completes this impressive showcase of interactionist methodological reflections. Ulmer offers a compelling portrait of interactionism as a perspective aligned with empiricism and scientific inquiry and opposed to positivism. He argues that quantitative methodology and statistical analysis have a considerable role in interactionist theorizing in general, and in abductive analyses in particular, because of their value in examining "outcomes of social interaction processes." He stresses how statistics can be a tool in explaining social context, thus moving beyond micro-sociology. For Ulmer, "using statistical analyses (...) to guide and inspire qualitative data collection to uncover causal mechanisms" can be paired with Peirce's abductive approach.

Readers can draw several lessons from this collection. I am going to mention only four. The first is that interactionists can improve their use of methods, and thus, their analysis of social life, by (re)engaging in productive dialogs with existing interactionist traditions (see Katovich, and vom Lehn, in this volume). The second is that interactionists can benefit from using and developing a diversity of methods, even if these have been extensively used by positivists and others whose epistemological stance is at odds with interactionist sensibilities (see Ulmer in this volume). The third is that interactionists must remain creative and open-minded throughout all phases of the research process, including engaging in casual, everyday conversations in the field (see Kotarba in this volume). Similarly, Kathy Charmaz (2004, p. 987), a well-known interactionist methodologist, encouraged us "to create a space where the unexpected can occur" (Charmaz, 2004, p. 987). The last one is that interactionists must re-pragmatize their research by adopting the pragmatist principle to use research to transform the social world, and to inform future action based on research findings (see Bryant and Friese, and Schneider and Altheide, in this volume).

In sum, interactionism is a tradition of multiple perspectives (vom Lehn et al., 2021). Interactionists are not committed to use a specific method; rather, they use a wide array of methods, and their interactionist frameworks shape the methods covered in these pages (e.g., grounded theory, laboratory research, qualitative media analysis). The present contributions help us (re)discover this exciting methodological legacy, and convincingly persuade us to develop it in the future.

NOTES

1. Of course, classic interactionists such as Charles Cooley (see Shalin, 1986) made substantial contributions to qualitative methodology before Blumer's foundational statement.

2. For instance, there are interactionist approaches to theorizing that contain important methodological lessons (see, e.g., Zerubavel, 2020), and methodological approaches that have been employed and even embraced by interactionists (Ruiz-Junco & Vidal-Ortiz, 2011; see also Ruiz-Junco & Vidal-Ortiz, 2023) that do not appear in this collection.

REFERENCES

Blumer, H. (1969). *Symbolic interactionism: Perspective and method.* University of California.

Charmaz, K. (2004). Premises, principles, and practices in qualitative research: Revisiting the foundations. *Qualitative Health Research, 14,* 976–993.

Mead, G. H. (2015 [1934]). *Mind, self, and society: The definitive edition.* Ed. C. W. Morris, annotated by D. R. Huebner & H. Joas. University of Chicago Press.

Prus, R. (1996). *Symbolic interaction and ethnographic research.* State University of New York Press.

Ross, D. (1991). *The origins of American social science.* Cambridge University Press.

Ruiz-Junco, N., Morrison, D., & McGinty, P. (2023). Interactionism and methodological individualism: Affinities and critical issues. In N. Bulle & F. Di Iorio (Eds.), *Palgrave handbook of methodological individualism* (Vol. II, pp. 551–572).

Ruiz-Junco, N., & Vidal-Ortiz, S. (2011). Autoethnography: The sociological through the personal. In I. Zake & M. DeCesare (Eds.), *New directions in sociology: Essays on theory and methodology in the 21st century* (pp. 193–211). McFarland Publishers.

Ruiz-Junco, N., & Vidal-Ortiz, S. (2023). W. E. B. Du Bois as interactionist: Reflections on the canonical incorporation of a marginalized scholar. *Symbolic Interaction, 46*, 332–348.

Shalin, D. N. (1986). Pragmatism and social interactionism. *American Sociological Review, 1*, 9–29.

Swedberg, R. (2012). Theorizing in sociology and social science: Turning to the context of discovery. *Theory and Society, 41*, 1–40.

Turner, S. P., & Turner, J. H. (1990). *The impossible science: An institutional analysis of American sociology*. Sage.

vom Lehn, D., Ruiz-Junco, N., & Gibson, W. (2021). Introduction. In D. vom Lehn, N. Ruiz-Junco, & W. Gibson (Eds.), *The Routledge international handbook of interactionism* (pp. 3–21). Routledge.

Zerubavel, E. (2020). *Generally speaking: An invitation to concept-driven sociology*. Oxford University Press.

THE NEW IOWA SCHOOL AND GENERATING QUALITATIVE RESEARCH IN THE LABORATORY

Michael A. Katovich

Texas Christian University, USA

ABSTRACT

Social psychological research created dramatic scenarios, demonstrating the potential to stimulate experimental subjects to act creatively. However, these experiments emphasized a positivistic reliance on quantitative outcomes, deception, and control of subjects. The researchers, while providing impressive creativity, deemphasized a more emergent and sequential way of using the laboratory to generate qualitative data. The new Iowa School (NIS) resonated to the creative and theatrical spirit of previous social psychological research while also creating a provocative stage that encouraged subjects to create novel plans of action. The NIS trusted that subjects would respect the intentions of the researchers and the broader order of the theatrical environment. Coupled with the use of audio-visual technology that allowed for "re-searching" social processes, the NIS generated qualitative data in laboratory settings that remained true to Mead's emphasis on how social acts become constructed and Simmel's notion of dyad and triads as real entities.

Keywords: Laboratory research; provocative stage; emergence; data generation; experimental subjects

INTRODUCTION

Qualitative research, especially in regard to symbolic interactionist endeavors, assumes, without much deliberation, studying social life in situ, or what some have called naturalistic settings (see Denzin, 1989; Molseed, 1994). The idea of coupling qualitative research in the laboratory, or what many assume as artificial settings, seems antithetical to interactionist research. How, one might ask, can an

---

Essential Methods in Symbolic Interaction
Studies in Symbolic Interaction, Volume 60, 9–23
Copyright © 2025 Michael A. Katovich
Published under exclusive licence by Emerald Publishing Limited
ISSN: 0163-2396/doi:10.1108/S0163-239620250000060002

interactionist describe and analyze actual behavior in a contrived and unilaterally scripted environment?

The notion of environments and interaction within contrived environments containing scripts on which interactors rely does have roots in dramaturgical studies (and, by extension, interactionist research), but a treatise on scripted behavior in preestablished and contrived settings is beyond the scope of this paper. Rather, the key focus of this paper is how symbolic interactionists can employ the laboratory to analyze social behavior and generate concepts applicable to Mead's (1932) notion of how the social act becomes established in the present and consequential in the future. In particular, this paper explores the spatial–temporal interest associated with qualitative interactionist research in laboratory environments. The paper asserts that examining social action, qualitatively, as simultaneously processual and structured, can occur in conjunction with creating dramatic scenarios in laboratory settings.

Concomitantly, this paper attempts to combine the interactionist endeavor, that is first and foremost a study of social action, with a particular school of thought, the new Iowa School (NIS—see Buban, 1986, pp. 26–28). The NIS emphasized analysis of social behavior generated in laboratory settings, simultaneously adopting and rejecting Manford Kuhn's dictums and suggestions (see Kuhn, 1964; Kuhn & McPartland, 1954). Kuhn's mandates became the foundations of the Iowa School of Symbolic Interaction (Meltzer & Petras, 1970). This School aimed to put Mead's theory of the self to the test and to stop what Kuhn considered the "unproductive debate" about what Mead "really meant" when he discussed the self (Katovich et al., 2003).

Specifically, the NIS accepted Kuhn's pragmatic notion to Mead, but rejected his pencil and paper (or point-in-time) methodology (Couch et al., 1987; Katovich et al., 2003). In the process, the NIS maintained a stolid commitment to an across-time, point-in-space methodology (emphasizing studying social processes as ongoing while making use of audio-visual technology that is placed in a static position). The data generated from this methodology often became structured in a value-added sequence (distinguishing necessary and sufficient conditions) and examined the inception and completion of social action (Couch et al., 1994). The key consequence of such a commitment (and the fundamental distinction between Kuhn's Iowa School and the NIS) shifted focus from an anchored (and relatively static) self to a dynamic process of coordinated social action that either implied or explicated a social objective. Whereas Kuhn regarded how the self is anchored as the key research question, the NIS asked how two or more people can accomplish a stated and mutually navigated purpose (Couch, 2017; Couch et al., 1994).

The organization of this paper is based on the premise that laboratory research established by the NIS is relevant to an interactionist agenda regarding the generation of qualitative data. First, I provide a brief examination of laboratory research in general, specifying some of the important imaginative groundwork that, unfortunately, did not inspire much in the way of qualitative research. Second, I attempt to clarify how laboratory research can be analogous to a promise associated with a sociological imagination (Mills, 1959, p. 3) and, in turn, a foundation for qualitative research. Third, I relate the basic premises of NIS laboratory research to its specific research endeavors that served as foundations of a sociological social psychology. Fourth, and extending previous arguments made by NIS researchers (see Couch, 1987; Katovich, 1984; Molseed, 1994), I elaborate on the theatrical and emergent interactional episodes that stimulate behaviors on provocative stages (I will discuss this stages as a meta-phorical and theatrical environment that challenged subjects to engage in creative play acting). Fifth, I re-examine and describe particular research studies by the NIS that appear emblematic of sociological (and qualitative) research in the laboratory. To conclude, I assess the dynamic nature of laboratory research as the grounds for creating qualitative data applicable to symbolic interaction.

LABORATORY RESEARCH AND THE SCIENCE OF SMALL GROUP RESEARCH

The creators of a sociological social psychology and their products, especially Sherif (1936), Lewin and White (1939), Lewin (1948), and Asch (1951), set out to study the scientific dynamics of individual decision making as it emerged in the context of groups. These researchers considered their studies as representing something new in social psychology, namely the systematic portrayal of the power of small social groups confronting an individual. Their intentions indicated that the goals of such research would provide precise descriptions of the processes associated with the formation and endurance of small social group life.

Despite noble intentions, the researchers assumed that information about the details of the experiments had to be selectively shared with subjects in the name of scientific inquiry (as understood by these researchers). Importantly, the selective sharing involved deception (see Mixon, 1972), or lying that became defined as necessary in the name of scientific inquiry. The deception involved the creation of identities, such as experimental confederates (or those paid by the experimenter to play specific roles and follow specific scripts) and naïve subjects (or those individuals who would provide substance to the dependent variables without being informed of the real purpose of the experiment). The end results displayed how, despite intentions, the researchers created environments that controlled subject behavior. In effect, the researchers set out to examine behavior in constraining environments based on deception of subjects that correlated with the disorientation of these subjects (Denzin, 1984; Zander, 1979).

By emphasizing control and strategically using deception, small group research established by the aforementioned researchers and those that followed their lead represented a science of social psychology that showed how subjects subordinated themselves to a superordinate group. However, the participants also subordinated themselves to the superordinate researchers and this process of subordination, arguably, contributed to the substance of the dependent variables (see Orne, 1962). Rather than emphasize how behaviors of subjects related, reciprocally, to the behaviors of other subjects, the researchers articulated the behavior of individuals as they reacted to contrived, authoritarian, and highly scripted scenarios. Such behavior, described as the "dissociated behavior of individuals" (Couch et al., 1987, p. 172), failed to examine the mutual responsiveness of individuals engaged in a conversation associated with minded behavior (Mead, 1934).

Further, the examination of results generated by small group researchers who conducted experiments in this paradigm appeared to rely (for the most part) on quantitative results. Emphasizing quantitative results provided a substantial basis for discussion, but did not advance scientific knowledge of how interactors created and maintained sequential action leading to social objectives. The sociological origins of small group research in laboratory environments then opted to reduce the activity in laboratory environments to a more reductionist (and statistical) approach.

While the aforementioned researchers and those influenced by their methodologies provided an imaginative way of transforming laboratory environments into dramatic and compelling settings (Couch et al., 1987), the specification of narrow, quantitative results begged the question of how small social group life is possible. The deceptive and quantitative approach also implied a lack of trust in relation to the experimental subjects. Instead of seeing the subjects as co-participants in the research environment, small group social psychologists viewed the experimental subjects as mere sources of a very refined data set.

Alternatively, the NIS examination of the importance of emergent interaction that takes place between subjects allows for a more expansive view of subjects. The environment, a controlled laboratory setting, remains, but sustained control of the environment is not the key objective. NIS laboratory researchers expressed confidence that subjects' behavior occurred in a controlled environment as the subjects altered the environment. The subjects behaved in relation to each other by creating unscripted programs of action as they honored the essential features of an interaction order (Goffman, 1983). The NIS viewed a controlled environment that allowed for creation of novel programs of action as similar to the boundaries of any game that would have durable "foul lines" in which nascent behaviors transpired. This view enabled NIS researchers to examine the emergent behavior of subjects. The subjects further behaved in direct relationship to other subjects, rather than to the experimenters or to a relatively static environment constructed by the experimenters.

LABORATORY RESEARCH AND A SOCIOLOGICAL IMAGINATION

One of the basic premises of the NIS connects decisions made by individuals inhabiting social environments with the sequences of events that contribute to how such environments become defined when such decisions emerge. In effect, considering the laboratory as a particular environment populated by a complex "subclass of groups" (see Glaser & Strauss, 1967, pp. 53–55) allows the laboratory researcher to emphasize the creative emergence of acts made by laboratory participants as they respond to environments into which they enter. Such inventiveness resembles

Goffman's (1959, pp. 30–33) notion of a "dramatic realization" by interactors who occupy, together, a particular setting in which their collective and cooperative behaviors correlate with shared assumptions of behaviors deemed appropriate within particular social settings. This realization can apply to the powerful metaphorical opportunities that laboratory research offers.

As stated earlier, social psychological uses of the laboratory provided metaphorical resonance to sociologically oriented processes. Regarding such use, I return to a focus on Asch (1951) and Sherif (1961) as well as the famous experiments conducted by Milgram (1974). Each of the researchers keyed on the sociological import of conformity to perceptions, obedience to authority, and distortions of judgment that accompanied subjugation. While the experiments conducted by these researchers relied on quantitative results and secretive practices that built ongoing closed awareness in the laboratory, they also provided glimpses into the possibilities of generating qualitative data in more open awareness environments (cf. Glaser & Strauss, 1964).

In particular, Sherif (1936) became interested in how normative orders emerged and examined individual reactions to experimental confederates who either promoted most, moderate, or least arbitrary norms. Asch (1951) also used confederates as the metaphorical wall of a monolithic opinion, paying specific attention to the behavioral responses of the naïve subject. Milgram's (1974) various experiments made use of audio-visual technology to record the responses of the naive subjects, not only to the scripted (and recorded) responses of the confederate learners but also to the rigidly scripted responses made by the confederate experimenter. While continuing to operate in a more positivistic realms and lacking emphasis on interaction between subjects, the aforementioned researchers nonetheless advanced the notion that transformation of behaviors in the laboratory can occur without disrupting an interaction order in general.

The emergence of unanticipated interaction that remained situated within the experimental framework occurred in the Milgram experiments. One of the key elements of the studies, which later became dramatized in Milgram's, 1963 educational film (*Obedience*) involved a negotiation of responsibility. This negotiation, occurring in a variety of the experiments, involved a combination of unscripted and scripted sequences of talk between recalcitrant and concerned subject/teachers and the confederate authority figure/scientist. The film captured subjects' inquiries regarding the health of the learners along with these same subjects' concerns related to the legal ramifications associated with doing harm to the learners. The dialog is instructive in that it portrayed the emergent aspects of interaction that could be possible within a laboratory – and became a notable sequence that influenced NIS researchers (Couch, 2017; Couch et al., 1987; Katovich, 1984).

As mentioned, neither Asch, Milgram, nor Sherif emphasized how subjects, explicitly, interacted with one another in the process of making decisions. Each did, however, show how experiments can resemble dramatic scenarios on provocative stages. In the process, they created a way of looking at subjects who would eventually deal with unpredictable inception of activity. Such unpredictability involved subjects making unscripted decisions that introduced unanticipated emotional responsiveness into the tightly scripted drama. Further, this phenomenon of unscripted decision making, in the presence of others, greatly influenced the surfeit of studies referred to, in general, as bystander intervention experiments.

Inspired by the 1964 gruesome stabbing and murder of Kitty Genovese, Darley and Latané (1968) hypothesized a social psychological explanation for the reluctance of witnesses (or those overhearing Ms. Genovese's cries for help) to come to the aid of Ms. Genovese. Instead of decrying the moral decay and subsequent indifference associated with urban atmospheres. Darley and Latané (1968, p. 378) proposed in inverse correlation between number of people present (or in the vicinity) during an emergency and decisions (along with subsequent speed in making decisions) to engage in helping behavior. To test their hypothesis, Darley and Latané created a dramatic stage that involved a seemingly real emergency to which naïve subjects respond. The subjects either believed they were alone or amid others (up to four).

While, in retrospect, the Genovese murder did not involve the apparent apathy or reluctance to intervene as originally reported and iterated in popular culture (Cook, 2014), the premise and results created and observed by Darley and Latané began a surfeit of social psychological studies that created a *genre*, culminating in perhaps the most studied phenomenon in social psychology (Manning et al., 2007). However, neither the helping study nor the Sherif, Asch, and Milgram studies, despite their popularity and place in the annals of laboratory research, provided direction into how qualitative research could be accomplished in the laboratory. Even so, and relevant to an interactionist perspective, the studies created the foundations for a provocative stage in the laboratory in which spontaneous affected responses become part of the experiment (Katovich, 1984). The responses on this stage invited improvisational interaction in which consequential sequences of social action occurred. Using video tape technology, researchers could also re-watch the sequences and engage in an iterative process of description and analysis that allowed qualitative researchers to establish necessary and sufficient behaviors that could put Mead's (1938) theory of social action to the test.

LABORATORY RESEARCH AND THE PREMISES OF THE NIS IN SYMBOLIC INTERACTION

The NIS emerged during the late 1960s and early-to-mid 1970s in the wake of the social psychological studies described. In particular, the NIS made an explicit commitment to generate qualitative data in a laboratory setting, while making use of the aforementioned audio-visual technology (see Buban, 1986; Couch, 2017; Katovich, 1984; Miller, 2011). The NIS commitment to audio-visual technology did not make their approach unique, per se (see, e.g., vom Lehn & Heath, 2016), but the precise use of such technology focused on small groups sharing the same space at the same time rather than acting alone as individuals. The basic premise involved designing experiments in which technology could key on two or three person groups (dyads and triads) engaged in present centered conversations or activities that required, at least hypothetically, commitment to a future (Couch, 1986, 1987; Miller, 2011).

As mentioned, the earlier experiments that had defined a more quantitative and positivistic approach, using hypotheses testing as the key to investigation, nevertheless demonstrated the metaphorical power of laboratory scenarios. As mentioned, Milgram's studies provided the possibility of creating theatrical drama with metaphorical power in the laboratory, asking, among other things, how using an authoritarian position can convince subjects to seriously harm others. Milgram's studies provided the impetus to create and study any scenario while considering the interaction under investigation as relevant to a variety of settings outside of the laboratory. NIS researchers, then, regarded their studies as capable of external validity on par with the findings of Sherif, Asch, Darley and Latané, and, specifically, Milgram (Buban, 1986, p. 29; Katovich, 1984, pp. 48–49).

While the NIS recognized its debt to previous social psychological research and advocated making observations in a controlled environment, it also made explicit arguments in contrast to positivistic social psychology. First, new Iowa School researchers avoided the "counting methods" advocated by prominent social psychologists, especially Bales (1950). As Miller et al. (1975, pp. 491–492) noted, the number of times a person says "Hi" is not nearly as significant as the interactional context in which "Hi" is said and to which it is responded. Taking the cue that Mead (1934) emphasized, the meaning and substantial importance of any act, gesture, or statement, emerges in the response on the part of another.

Second, NIS researchers committed themselves to "thick description" (Geertz, 1973), that not only signified the objective of providing evidence of complexity involved in conversations, but represented acute attentiveness to the timing and appreciation (among the subjects) of the content of their own and one another's pronouncements (see vom Lehn & Gibson, 2011). As implied above and will be noted later, the content of laboratory subjects' conversations, while not necessarily significant regarding quantity, becomes acutely exceptional at particular "high leverage" moments, or those particular times when crucial decisions or definitions of situations become evident. Thickness then not only implies the complexity of talk but the dramatic moments when such complexity helps define the group as its members either formulates decisions or deals with the consequences of their decisions.

The above indicates a distinctive approach to content in the laboratory, especially as practiced by the NIS. This School explicitly paid homage to Simmel (1950) and his famous distinction between forms of sociation (particular alignments structured by small groups – in particular dyads and triads) and content of talk that, however diverse, seemed subordinate to the group alignments (Couch, 1984, 1986, 2017). In the process of variegated appreciation of Simmelian forms of sociation, the NIS approach to qualitative sociology in the laboratory could be viewed as giving the impression that form transcended content regarding analytic importance.

However, the content of interactors' talk and expressions often became centerpieces of NIS analyses of interaction. The NIS went to great lengths to explore the content of action (making sure that the transcriptions corresponded to the spoken words). Such content indicated, at least on the surface, the importance of action to the participants. In this vein, the NIS did show a Blumerian-like (1980) interest in how interactors assessed and interpreted their own, and each other's actions. Also, the NIS approach to content served as an implicit "bow" to dramaturgy (Goffman, 1956, 1959) as the content supplied a plethora of spectacle and "show work" or efforts to make enduring impressions on the spot.

Despite the importance of content, the influence of Simmel's emphasis on social forms cannot be overestimated. From Simmel's perspective, the study of sociology lacked a distinct and explicit emphasis on social interaction – and especially, a focus on the small social group (Denzin, 1966). In this regard, Simmel viewed concepts such as society, social system, and social structure as far too general – and as demonstrative of (to borrow from Whitehead, 1929) an abstract equivalency – or mistaking a complex concept (e.g., society) for a physical/material reality. Simmel did believe in conceptualization, but asserted that this conceptualization be grounded in concrete equivalency – or correlating a hypothetical construct with actual and observable interaction within sensory reach. For instance, one of Simmel's more famous concepts, "the Stranger," showed how a particular social type could share significant characteristics despite possessing very different personal traits, making the concept complex and recognizable at the same time (Levine, 1971, pp. 331–333).

Regarding the small social group, Simmel's notion of the dyad focused on a fundamental human connection. The interactional dyad represents Simmel's version of a powerful, yet fragile connection (always on the verge of extinction). While dyads vary in regard to vitality, interactional depth, and the duration of a connection, particular elements of all interactional dyads can be observed – in particular, interactional dyads involve copresence, mutual responsiveness, and a shared focus (concepts articulated by Miller et al., 1975).

Simmel also regarded the addition of a person into the two-person group, forming a triad, as a key clue to answering the question: how is society possible? As mentioned, Simmel regarded the concept of society as too abstract and as used uncritically by sociologists. However, from Simmel's perspective, to actually see society one would have to, at the very least, see a potential for asymmetry in social interaction. Simmel viewed the most fundamental form of asymmetry as involving a contrast between a two-person bond acting in opposition to a singular individual without social support (Simmel, 1955).

The addition of one person to Simmel's conception of a dyad would create an altogether different dynamic that makes for a dramatic change in the structure of a small group and the elements of interaction that make up the group. Simmel, of course, regarded the transformation of a dyad to a triad as involving many more possibilities than conflict (e.g., the promotion of endurance of a group and its ability to survive departure), but the key point is that the group can be thought of as having its own distinct ontological reality. Keying on the group as a requisite entity established a fundamental premise of the NIS approach to qualitative research and social life. The two-or three-person group (dyads and triads) established, either on the surface or in great depth, a reality independent of any individual orientation.

REVISITING THE LABORATORY AS A PROVOCATIVE STAGE

NIS laboratory research resembled particular dynamics associated with dramatic productions involving subjects as method actors of sorts and researchers as flexible directors of the ongoing drama. The idea of such dramatization involved subjects as not only those who "played their parts" (as determined by the researchers) but appeared taken in by emergent spectacles that had consequential impacts on those involved in the experiment. Further, even though the NIS researchers created the scenarios and created the parameters to which subjects/ participants adhered, experimental subjects made on-the-spot decisions to transform the environments created by experimenters. Although the researchers initiated the broader framework and more narrow specifications for the occurrence of social action, such criteria served as opportunities for subjects to create their own agendas without disrupting the overarching premise of the general experiment (Katovich, 1984, p. 58).

Whereas the production extended the theatrical work established by previous social psychological researchers, the drama deviated from traditional and classic experimentation in three major ways. First, it avoided specific hypothesis testing (see also Couch, 1987, 2017). The purpose of the research did not set out to support or challenge particular suppositions or postulates. Rather, the research attempted to locate and demonstrate awareness of how particular processes, created by interactors, became possible through coordinated activity.

Second, as mentioned earlier, the laboratory subjects entered into an environment as co-participants of the theatrical production. Rather than being deceived or kept "in the dark" about the purpose of the research (see Mixon, 1972), researchers informed subjects of the intent of the experiment and requested the subjects to assume characterizations of the particular people or parts played in the process of coordination. The subjects would not be the naïve subjects as characterized by previous social psychologists. Instead, they would be agents within the laboratory who could, potentially, re-create their initial identities. While a few of the subjects (those that had participated in experiments conducted by sociologists and psychologists on campus) regarded the intentions of the NIS as "just another scam" (to use a phrase by one of the subjects), most expressed enthusiasm regarding the parts they would create.

Third, the provocative nature of the laboratory indicated that each participant/subject would immerse themselves in any particular characterization to make decisions "as if" such decisions would have an impact upon them beyond the interaction in the laboratory. Researchers not only asked participants to assume that they would not only make existential choices but to treat such choices as making immediate differences that would also make long-term differences (see Bateson, 1972). Subjects understood that they were indeed play acting, but that the immediate challenges of such acting occupied their time and interest at the moment and even, possibly, beyond the moment.

Symbolic interactionists had expressed a particular hostility toward using a laboratory as a setting (often referred to as an artificial environment) and providing "scripts" that not only pre-determined interaction but that strangled the life out of such interaction (Katovich, 1984, p. 49). The oft-used term "naturalism" assumed that authentic action occurred in situ (without any directorial influence by a researcher) and that any relegation of action in an environment structured to "force interaction" simply made such interaction falsely affected (Katovich, 1984, p. 51; Molseed, 1994, p. 242). However, most interactionists at the time wrote about interactional episodes that had become as (or even more) structured in extant environments and produced in accord with procedures that had as many, or more, constraints than what existed within the confines of a NIS laboratory setting (Katovich et al., 1986).

THE NIS AND QUALITATIVE RESEARCH IN THE LABORATORY

The generation of data in the laboratory by NIS researchers began in earnest after Couch (1970) identified particular generic concepts that, he imagined, could be sequentially related to represent the human construction of the what Mead (1938) construed as the social act (see also Couch, 1984, 1987; Katovich & Chen, 2014). One of the key assumptions associated with identifying sequences and conceptualizing these sequences involved the potential congruence between what occurred inside the laboratory and the everyday life worlds that endure outside of the laboratory (see Schutz & Luckmann, 1973). This basic premise denied the dichotomy between the so-called artificial life occurring within the laboratory and the more authentic-like activity that emerged outside of the laboratory (cf. Latour, 2016, pp. 142–143).

One of the key examples of the congruence between activity inside and outside of the laboratory, and the study that served as a working definition of the NIS generation of qualitative data in the laboratory, investigated how interactors construct social openings (Couch, 2017; Hintz & Miller, 1995; Miller et al., 1975). The Openings Study also demonstrated how the laboratory made use of the aforementioned powerful metaphorical possibilities of previous laboratory studies and the laboratory as a provocative stage. Specifically, the Study drew upon the descriptive data supplied by Schegloff (1968) and replicated the afore-mentioned Darley and Latané (1968) Bystander Apathy Study. This particular study, though, would also introduce a few twists – not the least of which was positioning two subjects together (physically copresent) rather than positioning single individuals who think they are either alone or amid others.

The Openings Study also introduced a "directorial strategy" of keeping a still camera on a targeted social group (in this case a dyad). Prior to the Openings Study, in what Carl Couch and Stan Saxton referred to as the "101 Studies" (Couch, 2017), the camera only included an individual as this individual responded to stimuli. This individualistic strategy belied the emphasis on dyads and triads, which, as mentioned, had become one of the foundations of the NIS. Further, the Openings Study also re-crafted Darley and Latané's study to reflect this changing emphasis from individualistic to dyadic (or in later studies, triadic).

MICHAEL A. KATOVICH

Whereas Darley and Latané indicated a sole interest in the behavior of one person leaving the room (in response to an emergency) alone, the Openings Study intended to analyze, systematically, how two people could coordinate behaviors so as to leave a room (also in response to an emergency) together.

One of the significant developments in the Openings Study involved the process of "re-searching" data, a process that Couch (1986, 1987, 1989, 2017) repeatedly asserted as a strength of using audio-visual recordings in the laboratory to analyze social life (Katovich & Chen, 2014, 2021). This "re-searching" activity, or the iterative examination of the same data at many different times, allowed for discovery through repetitive viewing (Katovich & Chen, 2021). While on the surface, the viewer is seeing the same behaviors at different times, on a deeper level, the viewer is recognizing behaviors that seemed obvious at one time, but that had a different emphasis and meaning at another time.

One simple, but significant example of this process of re-discovery involved two friends, with a shared history of behaving together, reacting to the emergency in a simultaneous fashion. The design of the Openings Study involved two strangers in contrast to two friends, both working on a project, side by side, prior to hearing an emergency. After considerable repetitive viewings, one of the viewers, Dan Miller, noted how the simultaneity exhibited by the friends actually encapsulated all of the "social elements" that strangers exhibited when responding to the emergency in concert (see Hintz & Miller, 1995). The response of the friends, seen many times, finally brought into clear focus how the friends, through their shared history, displayed an ability to truncate the sequences of behaviors that the strangers constructed in "step-by-step" fashion. Subsequent to this discovery, the researchers retraced their observations of each of the dyads without a shared history, noting a pattern that became the substantial elements involved in Openings (Couch, 2017; Hintz & Miller, 1995; Miller et al., 1975).

In a different experiment (Katovich et al., 1981), the same sort of discovery through repetition emerged. In this particular experiment, 34 groups of constituents, composed of triads, assumed the parts of partisans who would protest the decision of a University Dean to allocate money unevenly. The research positioners instructed all 34 groups to select a representative to negotiate with the Dean (who a positioner instructed to "play hardball" with representatives so as to "avoid bad publicity" for the University). The partisan groups, who had a shared history as friends prior to the experiment, expressed confidence in their mission and in the person selected as a representative. They did not imagine or anticipate a rough negotiation in which the representative would fail to achieve the planned-for results.

Half (17) of the constituents in partisan groups received a news report of the negotiation process prior to the representative's return (to give the group the bad news that their plans would not materialize). In turn, the other half (17) of the constituents received no such news. One of the initial objectives of the researchers involved a general appraisal of how groups process disappointing results and whether or not such processing involves reference to reception of news. The researchers anticipated that the groups would have distinct ways of processing information based upon whether or not such groups had access to information independent of the representative.

The aforementioned possibilities could be interpreted as hypotheses testing, but the researchers did not frame the study in this contingent way. Instead, the goal of the researchers had more to do with how the subsequent interaction emerged and what consequences, in general, could be different when comparing and contrasting the interactions after the negotiations. The researchers wished to examine how groups accepted or responded to unanticipated defeat (or the unanticipated consequences that defy expectations) rather than anticipate any specific process or sequence based upon the differences regarding access or no access to news. Rather than committing themselves to any specific expectations, the researchers adopted a willingness to be surprised by anything that could possibly arise.

As with the Openings Study, in which the researchers engaged in multiple viewings (and re-readings of transcripts), the process of discovery through repetitive viewing (and reading) emerged. While the researchers imagined several possibilities associated with the differences between groups that received news versus their no-news counterparts, an interaction that the researchers had viewed (and read in the transcripts) several times took on a fresh difference. The conflict occurred within a group in which the constituents heard a news report independent of the representative's summary of events. All of the researchers had taken notice of the conflict (owing to the colorful language used) reviewing it often and discussing its possible significance. But one particular viewing occurred in conjunction with a conversation about conflictual encounters. Specifically, the researchers took notice about how the different groups engaged in conflict. Such notice altered researchers' perceptions of the significance of the conflict. The specific interaction included the following content from a group that had received news about the negotiation:

> *Constituent A*: You could have said that (referring to excess money in the University's budget).
>
> *Constituent C*: You f***** up, Steve.
>
> *Representative*: I know.

The acquiescence of this particular representative, in the face of a blunt assessment by the constituents, struck the researchers during a particular reading/viewing. This particular specimen prompted one of the researchers to note that the constituents and representative seemed to resolve conflict in the news group much more quickly, even though the intensity of the conflict (and language used during the conflict) did not seem all that different from what occurred in the no-news groups. This observation prompted another time through the transcripts and recordings. The reviewing and re-reading that occurred led to a new discovery of a pattern in which the news group resolved conflict quickly and projected a political future (another plan to meet with the University Dean), whereas the no-news group kept the conflict personal, without projecting any political and collective future (Katovich et al., 1981, p. 438).

CONCLUSION: THE LABORATORY AS A SPACE FOR QUALITATIVE INQUIRY

Although laboratory research designed to study human behavior has traditionally emphasized the behavior of individuals and individualistic choices when confronted with scripted stimuli, the NIS created environments in the laboratory that invited and encouraged social interaction (among dyads and triads) on provocative stages. Such interaction on these provocative stages implies the creation, on the part of interactional subjects, of specific and unscripted programs of action based on broader parameters constructed by researchers. Rather than describing the laboratory as an artificial site, it more closely resembles the naturalistic settings associated with novel places in which experimental subjects can construct sequential programs of action, often independent of the general premises of the researchers (Molseed, 1994).

The laboratory, when viewed as a dynamic space for a context that allows for sequential interaction, becomes a place in which research subjects to fit together lines of action to construct novel objectives and unanticipated relations. The laboratory is also a present centered bounded place that allows subjects to project futures that give structure to this present. It is a temporal atmosphere in which the present is informed and arranged by references to past and future behaviors. Further, researchers ask the subjects to imagine a social context or third party by which emergent sociality can occur and endure for the length of the experiment.

Previous studies conducted by NIS researchers involve, as two examples indicate, a continuous and iterative examination of interactional data. Researchers view the same interactions and read transcriptions of these interactions continuously, preparing themselves for new ways of seeing what appears as the same activities. However, each viewing allows researchers to see and read the action with new perspectives that allow for seeing what occurs as not only different but different in a way that can reveal new patterns (Bateson, 1972). The laboratory, as a site for the generation and analysis of qualitative data, serves as a theater for interactionists by which imaginative dramas can become visible and audible.

REFERENCES

Asch, S. E. (1951). Effects of group pressure upon the modification and distortion of judgment. In H. Guetzkow (Ed.), *Groups, leadership and men* (pp. 177–190). Carnegie Press.

Bales, R. F. (1950). *Interaction process analysis: A method for the study of small groups.* Addison-Wesley Press.

Bateson, G. (1972). *Steps to an ecology of mind.* University of Chicago Press.

Blumer, H. (1980). Social behaviorism and symbolic interactionism. *American Sociological Review, 45*, 409–419.

Buban, S. (1986). Symbolic interaction: Studying social processes: The Chicago and Iowa Schools revisited. In C. J. Couch, S. L. Saxon, & M. A. Katovich (Eds.), *Studies in symbolic interaction: The Iowa School* (pp. 25–40). JAI Press.

Cook, K. (2014). *Kitty Genovese: The murder, the bystanders, the crime that changed America.* W. W. Norton.

Couch, C. J. (1970). Dimensions of association in collective behavior episodes. *Sociometry, 33*, 457–471.

Couch, C. J. (1984). Symbolic interaction and generic sociological principles. *Symbolic Interaction, 7,* 1–13.

Couch, C. J. (1986). Elementary forms of social activity. In *Studies in symbolic interaction. Supplement 2: The Iowa School (Part A)* (pp. 113–129).

Couch, C. J. (1987). *Researching social processes in the laboratory.* JAI Press.

Couch, C. J. (1989). *Social processes and relationships: A formal approach.* General Hall.

Couch, C. J. (2017). The romance of discovery. In M. A. Katovich (Ed.), *Studies in symbolic interactionism. Carl Couch and the Iowa School (his own words).* Emerald Publishing Limited.

Couch, C. J., Katovich, M. A., & Buban, S. L. (1994). Beyond Blumer and Kuhn: Researching and analyzing across-time data through the use of point-in-space laboratory procedures. In N. J. Hermann & L. T. Reynolds (Eds.), *Symbolic interaction: An introduction to social psychology* (pp. 121–138). General Hall.

Couch, C. J., Katovich, M. A., & Miller, D. (1987). The sorrowful tale of small groups research. *Studies in Symbolic Interaction, 8,* 159–180.

Darley, J., & Latané, B. (1968). Bystander intervention in emergencies: The diffusion of responsibility. *Journal of Personality and Social Psychology, 8,* 377–383.

Denzin, N. K. (1966). The significant others of a college population. *The Sociological Quarterly, 7,* 298–310.

Denzin, N. K. (1984). Retrieving the small social group. *Studies in Symbolic Interaction, 5,* 35–48.

Denzin, N. K. (1989). *Interpretive interactionism.* SAGE.

Geertz, C. (1973). Thick description: Toward an interpretive theory of culture. In *The interpretation of cultures: Selected essays* (pp. 3–30). Basic Books.

Glaser, B., & Strauss, A. (1964). Awareness contexts and social interaction. *American Sociological Review, 5,* 669–679.

Glaser, B., & Strauss, A. (1967). *The discovery of grounded theory: Strategies for qualitative research.* Aldine de Gruyter.

Goffman, E. (1956). The nature of deference and demeanor. *American Anthropologist, 58,* 473–502.

Goffman, E. (1959). *The presentation of self in everyday life.* Doubleday.

Goffman, E. (1983). The interaction order: American sociological association, 1982 presidential address. *American Sociological Review, 48,* 1–17.

Hintz, R. A., & Miller, D. E. (1995). Openings revisited: The foundations of social interaction. *Symbolic Interaction, 18*(3), 355–369. https://doi.org/10.1525/si.1995.18.3.355

Katovich, M. A. (1984). Symbolic interactionism and experimentation: The laboratory as a provocative stage. *Studies in Symbolic Interaction, 6,* 49–67.

Katovich, M. A., & Chen, S. L. (2014). New Iowa School redux: Second life as laboratory. *Studies in Symbolic Interaction, 43,* 63–84.

Katovich, M. A., & Chen, S.-L. S. (2021). Recent developments in the new Iowa School of symbolic interactionism. In D. vom Lehn, N. Ruiz-Junco, & W. Gibson (Eds.), *The Routledge international handbook of interactionism* (pp. 59–69). Routledge.

Katovich, M. A., Miller, D. E., & Stewart, R. L. (2003). The Iowa School. In L. T. Reynolds & N. J. Herman-Kinney (Eds.), *Handbook of symbolic interactionism* (pp. 119–139). Rowman & Littlefield.

Katovich, M. A., Saxton, S. L., & Powell, J. O. (1986). Naturalism in the laboratory. In C. J. Couch, S. L. Saxton, & M. A. Katovich (Eds.), *Studies in symbolic interaction supplement 2 (Part A)* (pp. 79–88). JAI Press.

Katovich, M. A., Weiland, M. W., & Couch, C. J. (1981). Access to information and internal structures of partisan groups. *The Sociological Quarterly, 22,* 432–446.

Kuhn, M. H. (1964). Major trends in symbolic interaction theory in the past twenty-five years. *The Sociological Quarterly, 5,* 61–84.

Kuhn, M. H., & McPartland, T. S. (1954). An empirical investigation of self-attitudes. *American Sociological Review, 19,* 68–76.

Latour, B. (2016). Give me a laboratory and I will raise the world. *Science, Technology & Human Values, 41,* 613–634.

Levine, D. (1971). *Georg Simmel: On individuality and social forms.* University of Chicago Press.

Lewin, K. (1948). *Resolving social conflict.* Harper & Row.

Lewin, K. R. L., & White, R. K. (1939). Patterns of aggressive behavior in experimentally created social climates. *The Journal of Social Psychology*, *10*, 271–299.

Manning, R., Levine, M., & Collins, A. (2007). The Kitty Genovese murder and the social psychology of helping: The parable of the 38 witnesses. *American Psychologist*, *62*, 555–562.

Mead, G. H. (1932). *The philosophy of the present*. University of Chicago Press.

Mead, G. H. (1934). *Mind, self, and society*. University of Chicago Press.

Mead, G. H. (1938). *The philosophy of the act*. University of Chicago Press.

Meltzer, B. N., & Petras, J. W. (1970). The Chicago and Iowa Schools of symbolic interactionism. In T. Shibutani (Ed.), *Human nature and collective behavior* (pp. 3–17). Routledge.

Milgram, S. (1963). Behavioral study of obedience. *Journal of Abnormal and Social Psychology*, *67*(4), 371–378.

Milgram, S. (1974). *Obedience to authority: An experimental view*. Tavistock Publications.

Miller, D. E. (2011). Toward a theory of interaction: The Iowa School. *Symbolic Interaction*, *34*, 340–348.

Miller, D. E., Hintz, R. A., & Couch, C. J. (1975). The elements and structure of openings. *The Sociological Quarterly*, *16*, 479–499.

Mills, C. W. (1959). *The sociological imagination*. Oxford University Press.

Mixon, D. (1972). Instead of deception. *Journal for the Theory of Social Behavior*, *2*, 145–177.

Molseed, M. J. (1994). Naturalistic observation in the laboratory. *Symbolic Interaction*, *17*, 239–251.

Orne, M. T. (1962). On the social psychology of the psychological experiment. *American Psychologist*, *17*, 776–783.

Schegloff, E. A. (1968). Sequencing in conversational openings. *American Anthropologist*, *70*, 1075–1095.

Schutz, A., & Luckmann, T. (1973). *The structures of the life world*. Northwestern University Press.

Sherif, M. (1936). *The psychology of social norms*. Harper & Row.

Sherif, M. (1961). Conformity-deviation, norms, and group relations. In I. A. Berg & B. M. Bass (Eds.), *Conformity and deviation* (pp. 159–198). Harper and Brothers.

Simmel, G. (1955). *Conflict and the web of group affiliation*. The Free Press.

Simmel, G. (1950). *The sociology of Georg Simmel* (Kurt Wolff, Trans. and Ed.). Free Press.

vom Lehn, D., & Gibson, W. (2011). Interactionism and symbolic interactionism. *Symbolic Interaction*, *34*, 315–318.

vom Lehn, D., & Heath, C. (2016). Actionat the exhibit face: Video and the analysis of social interaction in museums and galleries. *Journal of Marketing Management*, *32*, 1441–1457.

Whitehead, A. N. (1929). *Process and reality*. Harper Brothers.

Zander, A. (1979). The study of group behavior during four decades. *The Journal of Applied Behavioral Science*, *15*, 272–282.

EXPERIMENTING WITH SOCIAL ORDER: NOTES ON SOME DEVELOPMENTS IN ETHNOMETHODOLOGY AND THE NEW IOWA SCHOOL

Dirk vom Lehn

King's College London, UK

ABSTRACT

In the 1960s, sociologists began to challenge the dominant structural-functionalist paradigm by imagining alternative sociologies. Interactionist sociologies, such as ethnomethodology and symbolic interactionism, emerged as theories and methods to investigate social order. When developing ethnomethodology in the 1950s and 1960s, Harold Garfinkel deployed "incongruity procedures," today often known as "breaching experiments," to elicit actions that make "observable-and-reportable" features of the social order. A little later, in the 1960s and 1970s, the social psychologist and symbolic interactionist Carl Couch developed a program today known as The New Iowa School that promotes the use of laboratory experiments and audio-visual recordings as principal data to reveal the generic principles of social order. In this paper, I first explore Garfinkel's incongruity procedures and Couch's laboratory experiments, before discussing some of the critical responses to these two interactionist sociologies. I also touch on the relationship of ethnomethodology and the New Iowa School to symbolic interactionism. In the concluding section, I make a case for the re-embedding of both programs within the Society for the Study of Symbolic Interaction and its work to promote and support interactionist research.

Keywords: Audio-visual recordings (video); experimentation; incongruity procedures; social order; sociation

---

Essential Methods in Symbolic Interaction
Studies in Symbolic Interaction, Volume 60, 25–48
Copyright © 2025 Dirk vom Lehn
Published under exclusive licence by Emerald Publishing Limited
ISSN: 0163-2396/doi:10.1108/S0163-239620250000060003

INTRODUCTION

The 1960s have been a decade of experimentation. Popular media at the time as well as publications discussing this period today highlight people's experimentations with new forms of living and working. The authors of these articles and books often point to the use of psychoactive drugs and to new cultural forms in theater, dance, art, film, journalism, and radio. They also refer to political activism and "happenings" that challenged public and social order (Cottrell, 2017). Much of this activism and new cultural forms emerging in the 1960s and 70s were inspired by contemporary developments in the sciences, with developments related to the Apollo program being of particular importance. This is reflected not only in well-known 1960s science fiction being preoccupied with space travel and alien arrivals but also in novelists' use of concepts arising in the sciences when developing new story structures (Darlington, 2021).

1960s Sociology has also been influenced by these developments in the sciences and wider society. For example, with the growing deployment of computer systems, sociological questions were increasingly pursued by using statistics as well as positivist and quantitative approaches. The validity of interpretive approaches, including that of naturalistic research, was called into question and challenged by those promoting positivist social sciences, often alongside an analytic orientation to the structural functionalist theory. Some suggested that because of sociology's emphasis on methods and techniques rather than societal and social issues, the discipline was heading for crisis (Gouldner, 1970; Vaughan, 1993).

Harold Garfinkel's ethnomethodology was one development in sociology that was subject to such criticism. Gouldner (1970) likened Garfinkel's often so-called "breaching experiments" that used the disruption of the everyday to shed new light on questions in sociological theory to the "happenings" organized by political activists.

> Behind both the 'happening' and the ethnomethodological demonstration there is a common impulse: to bring routines to a halt, to make the world and time stop. Both rest on a similar perception of the conventional character of the underlying rules, on a view of them as lacking in intrinsic value, as arbitrary albeit essential to the conduct of routine. And both are forms of hostility to the 'way things are', although the ethnomethodologist's is a veiled hostility, aimed at less dangerous targets. (Gouldner, 1970, p. 394)

Garfinkel (1963, 1967b) conceived his demonstrations in light of his "misreading" (Eisenmann & Lynch, 2021; Lynch, 2004) of Husserl's (Farber, 1943; Husserl, 2012/1913) phenomenology and Alfred Schütz's (1945; 1972) social phenomenology. The demonstrations stand in the beginning of Garfinkel's operationalization of the "sociological attitude" he (2006/1948) developed since the 1940s and later called "ethnomethodology" (Garfinkel, 1967b). Today, they sometimes are wrongly equated with ethnomethodology, ignoring the development of Garfinkel's much larger program over the past 60 years.

Another strand of research developing since the late 1960s is Carl Couch's particular kind of symbolic interactionist research that became institutionalized and managed at the Center for Research on Interpersonal Behavior (CRIB) at the University of Iowa. Couch differentiated his project from that of his teacher

Manford H. Kuhn at the University of Iowa and from the program of research promoted by Herbert Blumer and Everett Hughes at the University of Chicago. Kuhn had challenged the naturalistic approach to sociology pursued at Chicago that at the time pervaded symbolic interactionism. He developed the Twenty-Statement-Test (TST) as a scientific, positivist instrument to measure people's self-conceptions and orientations to others. At the same time, at the University of Chicago, Herbert Blumer and Everett Hughes argued for the study of social processes by using naturalistic, observational research methods, such as participant observation. Couch criticized Kuhn for his lack of interest in social processes and Blumer and Hughes for proposing the use of research methods that would not allow the uncovering of generic principles of social processes. In the 1960s, Couch (1970), therefore, began to develop his own program of research whose studies used laboratory experiments to investigate "the elementary forms of social activity" (Couch, 1986). This program has become known as "The New Iowa School," following the original "Iowa School" setup by Manford H. Kuhn in the 1950s.

In the following, I briefly discuss these two interactionist sociologies developed to uncover generic principles or ethnomethods underlying the organization of social action. I begin with Garfinkel's "breaching experiments" and the experimental and quasi-experimental research that has become an important part of ethno-methodological studies of interaction (Section "Disrupting the Social Order: Garfinkel's Experiments With Social Order"). In the Section "Discovering Forms and Elements of Interaction: The New Iowa School", I turn to Couch's laboratory experiments and his team's use of video-recordings as principal data to examine "the structure and elements of social order" (Couch, 1989b). In the Section "Responses to Couch and Garfinkel", I explore the resistance these two (experimental) approaches to investigating social order encountered, in symbolic interactionism and in sociology more widely. Finally, in the Section "Discussion: Interactionist Futures", I explore the affinities current developments in interactionism have with the two discussed interactionist programs.

EXPERIMENTING WITH SOCIAL ORDER

Both Garfinkel and the ethnomethodologists on the one hand and Carl Couch and the New Iowa School on the other hand pursue the sociological question regarding the possibility of social order. They are principally interested in uncovering the foundations of social order and investigate their manifestations in concrete situations. Both, Garfinkel and Couch, at least in some stage in their academic career, used an experimental approach for their research endeavors. In this section, I begin my investigation into Garfinkel's and Couch's interactionist programs to studying social order by examining, first, how Garfinkel deployed an experimental approach to make visible the "seen but unnoticed backgrounds of everyday activities" (Garfinkel, 1967b, p. 37), before, second, turning to Couch and his laboratory experiments designed to explore how people engage in cooperative action.

Disrupting the Social Order: Garfinkel's Experiments With Social Order

Garfinkel's research began when he joined the Department of Social Relations for Interdisciplinary Social Science Studies Talcott Parsons had begun to setup at Harvard since 1946. By that time, he had become enthused with sociology after having read, amongst others, Parsons's (1968/1937) "The Structure of Social Action" and studied at Newark with Howard Odum who had founded the Department of Sociology and the Institute of Research in the Social Sciences at the University of North Carolina in the 1920s. After arriving at Harvard, Garfinkel began to develop a PhD proposal that was shaped by his analysis of Talcott Parsons's sociological theory, the phenomenology of Edmund Husserl, and Alfred Schütz's social phenomenology.[1] He had come to know Schütz after Aron Gurwitsch had recommended him to the Austrian-American sociologist who in the 1950s worked at the New School for Social Research after having had to flee the Nazis from Austria. In the development of his research proposal, Garfinkel drew on Schütz's essays "On Multiple Realities" (Schütz, 1945) and "Common-Sense and Scientific Interpretation of Human Action" (Schütz, 1953). In these essays, Schütz distinguishes several "finite provinces of meaning," i.e., dream, phantasm, world of art, the world of religious experience, the world of scientific contemplation et al. He (1945) arrives at the concept of "finite provinces of meaning" through his critical examination of William James's concept of "subuniverses" that in his view is too "psychologistic" (p. 551) to capture the intersubjective constitution of the social world.

For Schütz the world of the everyday or "the world of working" stands out from these finite provinces of meaning as "paramount" (Schütz, 1945, p. 549). It is the world that impacts people's actions and experiences, and that they modify through their practical actions. As they inhabit the world, they select the objects in reach they orient to and use as means to achieve their aims. Schütz conceptualizes actions as being driven by motives and as future-oriented. In his view, therefore, when producing their actions people are "passionately interested in the results of [their] action and especially in the question whether [their] anticipations will stand the practical test" (Schütz, 1945, p. 549). Garfinkel's (2006/1948, pp. 180–181) notion of "experiments in miniature" reflects Schütz's concept of the temporal organization of action. He argues that with each action a participant tests their hypothesis about the next action an interlocutor would produce in response to their action. And in turn their own action embodies their orientation to the interlocutor's prior action; it fulfills or does not fulfill the interlocutor's expectation regarding the participant's action. Garfinkel (2006/1948, p. 181) suggests that sociality arises from participants' mutually monitoring and orienting to each other's actions.

Schütz (1945) is further interested not only in what people anticipate when planning their action but also in why they anticipate certain results from their actions. He describes the reasons for orienting to the world in particular ways as "system of relevances." The assumption that interlocutors orient to the social world by applying the same system of relevances is the second-half of the idealization of the "general thesis of the reciprocity of perspectives." Schütz (1953) develops as a concept to capture the possibility for sociality. The first-half

DIRK VOM LEHN

is "the idealization of the interchangeability of standpoints," i.e., that in principle interlocutors perceive the world in the same way when they would take the (geographical) place of the other. In the natural attitude of the everyday people take-for-granted that they inhabit a world in common. They mutually assume that everybody acting around them orients to the scene in the same way as they do. "It needs a special motivation, such as the upshooting of a 'strange' experience not subsumable under the stock of knowledge at hand or inconsistent with it to make us revise our former believes" (Schütz, 1945, p. 550).

When developing the proposal for his PhD, Garfinkel drew on the Schützian idea of the possibility of intersubjectivity. Yet, he went beyond the phenomenologist's conception of sociality by "radicalizing" (Eberle, 1984; Eickelpasch, 1982; Zimmerman & Wieder, 1970) the practical and material underpinnings of intersubjectivity. In his view, Schütz's phenomenological analysis of the social world focuses all too much on the subjective experience of the everyday, while being unable to explain the emergence of social interaction from individual perspectives. For Schütz "the Social" appears to be lodged in participants' heads, while Garfinkel argues that participants render "the seen but unnoticed" features of the social world observable through their actions. When working on his PhD dissertation, Garfinkel (1952) designs laboratory experiments to foster situations in which participants will make these unnoticed features observable.

The laboratory experiment involved medical students in conversations about their assumptions and expectations regarding conduct in interviews of applicants striving to join their medical faculty. As the students had previously themselves been interviewed before becoming members of the faculty, they had the knowledge and competency to assess what would be expected from applicants. They then were asked to listen to recordings of job interviews and to assess the performance of interviewees who by conventional standards conducted themselves in inappropriate ways and should have performed badly. After the students had submitted their assessments of the applicants though the person leading the experiment contradicted their assessment by praising the applicants' conduct and use of language and stated that the panel had decided to appoint them. Thus, the students were told that they had completely misjudged the applicants' performance and that they would need to reflect on the criteria they use to assess interview performances. Through their participation in the interviews, the participants were unsettled in their orientation to the situation they found themselves in. Having participated in such interviews themselves not long ago they initially felt confident they would be able to judge applicants' performance. But when they were told they had misjudged the applicants' performance and the outcome of the interview, they were bewildered and some displayed anxiousness as they reflected on their orientation to the situation. After it was revealed that they had been misled in the experiment, some participants were relieved and laughed, while others took longer to be persuaded about the deception (Garfinkel, 1952, 1963; cf. Ayaß, 2021).

In his well-known "Trust-paper," Garfinkel (1963) used the term "experiments" for the procedures designed to unsettle participants in ordinary circumstances, such as the home, in restaurants, or in shops. Later in the very same paper and in subsequent publications he avoided this term and instead described the activities as "tutorials" (Garfinkel, 2002), "demonstrations" (Garfinkel, 2002), or "expectancy breaching procedures" (Garfinkel, 1967a, p. 58). Authors of textbooks and publications who propose to use such activities as teaching tools often prefer to describe them as "breaching experiments" (Braswell, 2014; Loyal & Maleševic, 2020; O'Byrne, 2011; Rafalovich, 2006). Like the experiments Garfinkel conducted for his PhD research, the procedures he used in subsequent years served him to uncover participants' "seen but unnoticed" presuppositions in the social world. They are not "experiments" in the (natural-)scientific sense of the word but "incongruity-inducing procedures" (Garfinkel, 1963, p. 198) designed to disrupt and have people question the ordinary social world.

Garfinkel (1956) used these "experiments" as "lecture demonstrations" when "teaching undergraduates some important concepts of sociological theory." Yet, we would be mistaken to consider them as mere teaching tools because for Garfinkel the breaching procedures have been critical in the development of ethnomethodology as a program of research designed to respecify sociological concepts and theories (Heritage, 1984; Lynch, 2023; Sormani & vom Lehn, 2023a; vom Lehn, 2014). With these "breaching procedures" (Ayaß, 2021) Garfinkel directly addresses Schütz's (1953) "general thesis of the reciprocity of perspectives." Schütz turns the problem of social order into a cognitive issue that is resolved by participants mutually assuming that in principle they orient to the situation in the same way (Heritage, 1984; vom Lehn, 2014). Rather than trying to uncover participants' assumptions about each other's orientation to situations, Garfinkel (1963, p. 187) asks "what can be done to make for trouble." He designed procedures through which the assumptions about the "congruency of relevances" and the "interchangeability of standpoints" were called into question. For example, he asked his students to interpret questions of their friends and family members in unexpected ways, such that when a husband asked his wife, "Did you remember to drop off my shirts today?" the wife questioned what shirts he meant and what he meant by "dropping off." In her reflections about the conversation with her husband the student wrote that in the course of the exchange the husband grew increasingly indignant and frustrated with her until eventually treating her like a child (Garfinkel, 1963, pp. 221–223). Another example is the procedure in which Garfinkel asked his students to treat customers in a shop like sales personnel or guests at a restaurant like waiting staff. In these cases, the subjects to the procedure displayed puzzlement and later said that they had felt "shaken" by the experience (Garfinkel, 1963, pp. 223–226).

For Garfinkel breaching procedures were means to uncover "how social structures are ordinarily and routinely being maintained" (Garfinkel, 1963, p. 187). Yet, they not only disrupt the foundations of social order but also challenge "social-theoretic conceptions of those foundations as orders of rules, norms, and possible sanctions underpinning immediate actions" (Lynch, 2023, p. 8). From more recent discussions of Garfinkel's breaching procedures (Eisenmann & Rawls, 2023), we know that later in his career he used them to render observable and respecify social scientific phenomena. Thus, there is a continuity in his use of breaching

DIRK VOM LEHN

procedures as "a way of exhibiting recognizable phenomena as an experimental praxeology" (Lynch, 2023, p. 17). For him the breaching procedures can reveal aspects of social life that formal analytic approaches necessarily miss (Eisenmann & Rawls, 2023).

Discovering Forms and Elements of Interaction: The New Iowa School

The origins of the New Iowa School (NIS) is often traced back to Carl Couch's (1970) article "Dimensions of Association in Collective Behavior Episodes." In this article Couch states the parameters of his approach to sociology. He presumes that "the primary task of sociologists is to explain social behavior by examining how interacting persons align themselves with each other" (p. 458). Over the following two decades he developed a program of research that he anchored in the social psychology of his teacher at Iowa, Manford H. Kuhn, Mead's pragmatist sociology, and Simmel's formal sociology.

Since the late 1940s, Kuhn developed an empirical program of research that was in alignment with the strong empirical orientations of his colleagues in the social and behavioral sciences at the University of Iowa. In textbooks devoted to symbolic interactionism the Iowa School is often positioned against the Chicago School whose "members" conducted naturalistic research stressing the need for insightfully "feeling one's way inside the experience of the actor" (Blumer in Meltzer et al., 1975, p. 57).[2] Kuhn and his colleagues appreciated the work of Blumer, Hughes and others at Chicago as important and worthwhile but were dissatisfied with the naturalistic approach to studying social relationships. Kuhn argued that participant observation and naturalistic observations might be suitable to uncover social rules but would "produce nothing but 'high-class journalism'" (Kuhn in Weckroth, 1989, p. 213). Therefore, Kuhn proposed experiments as a method to find "generic principles of human behavior, this is social laws" (Kuhn in Weckroth, 1989, p. 213).

In contrast to symbolic interactionists at Chicago who used observational methods, Kuhn and his colleagues at the Iowa School "sought to 'empiricize' Mead's ideas, reconceptualizing or abandoning those he deemed 'non-empirical' and developing observational techniques that were consistent with this aim" (Meltzer et al., 1975, p. 58; cf. Kuhn, 1964). He, therefore, followed Mead (1967b/1936) in suggesting that scientific knowledge had to be based on observations that "satisfy the scrutiny of empirical test, demonstration, or pragmatic test – the 'so what' test of the usefulness of research" (Hickman & Kuhn, 1956; Katovich et al., 2003, p. 119). By combining Mead's pragmatic approach with scientific methods Kuhn aimed to develop a theory of the self "that was both testable and useable" (Katovich et al., 2003, p. 120). It, however, moved away from the process view that contemporary symbolic interactionists primarily pursued and developed a structural theory of the self (Reynolds, 1993). Together with Thomas McPartland (1954) he introduced the "Twenty Statements Test" (TST) to measure the self that within social psychology has been well received, used and discussed (Katovich et al., 2003; cf. Spitzer et al., 1966; Spitzer & Parker, 1976). Through the TST Kuhn and his students found

> "that the self is a set of statuses and identities, plans of action, values and definitions; that the self is acquired and maintained in symbolic interaction and is a function of the social relationships in which it is acquired and maintained; that the self is instrumental in organizing social conduct; and that the self can be known and articulated to others. (Miller, 2011, p. 341)

Kuhn was convinced that over time the scientific approach to studying the social world would prevail and "replace the more esoteric and sensitizing expressions of prevailing interactionist ideas" (Miller, 2011, p. 341). And indeed, in the 1960s his theory of the self and its operationalization through quantitative measurements has been somewhat influential within symbolic interactionism. It "cemented the perception that the core focus of the Iowa school was on the self as a static and a stable object anchored in social structures" (Katovich et al., 2003, p. 121). His student, Carl Couch, aligned with the argument for the development of rigorous research methods as a basis for the development of a science of social interaction (Couch, 2017c; Katovich et al., 2003; Katovich & Chen, 2021). As a student of Kuhn Couch was certain that by virtue of measures like the TST social psychologists would be able to identify general principles of human conduct and thus to "transform symbolic interactionism into a true science" (Couch, 2017b, pp. 9–10). Yet, Couch did not agree with Kuhn's structural view on the self and was interested more in social processes.

He and his colleagues at CRIB, therefore, diverted from Kuhn in at least two ways. First, they developed a program of research concerned not with the self but with "the systematic study of the processes and structures of coordinated social behavior" (Katovich et al., 2003, p. 121). They considered these structures as "interconnections developed, maintained and destroyed by persons acting toward, with and against one another" (Buban, 1986, p. 35). And second, the experimental approach they adopted for their research was not "scientific" in the same sense as proposed by Kuhn and those pursing a scientific sociology. Fine (1993: 72), therefore, describes the experiments conducted at CRIB as "laboratory simulation [...] that serves in effect as an ethnographic site" where the researchers examine the social action to "extract universal principles."

For the study of social processes, Couch turned to Mead and his theory of emergence (Mead, 2002/1932) and Simmel's (2009b/1908) "formal sociology." Both Mead and Simmel strove to develop a science of society. Mead (2002/1932) highlights the importance of time for social relationships. He suggests that while "reality exists in a present" (p. 1), it always "implies a past and a future" (p. 1) which both do not exist, one not anymore, and the other not yet. Simmel's (2009/ 1908) book "Sociology" begins with a chapter where he discusses the importance of interaction as a means through which people relate to and influence each other. In his view, it is the task of sociologists to investigate the different "social forms" through which people engage with each other. While neither Mead nor Simmel had developed a research program to explore the issues they had theoretically identified, Couch and the members of the NIS take their concepts and theories as starting points for the development of a research program devoted to a version of Simmel's (2009a) question of "How is society possible?" by asking "How do people produce cooperative acts?" (Couch, 2017b, p. 22).

DIRK VOM LEHN

By pursuing this question and focusing on investigating "Forms of Social Processes" Couch (2017a) diverted from Kuhn's concern with the self without aligning the Iowa School's program of research with that of the symbolic interactionists at Chicago. He proposed conduct laboratory experiments that involved the audio-visual recording of interactions between participants who engaged in loosely predefined tasks.[3] The members of the NIS differentiated their *laboratory experiments* from those conducted by behavioral scientists and from the naturalism promoted by their interactionist colleagues at the University of Chicago. In the behavioral sciences laboratories are used to control for external influences that could interfere with participants' responses to given stimuli. Symbolic interactionists have been critical of such kind of research arguing "that laboratory experimentation murders social life in order to dissect it" (Katovich, 1984, p. 49). Regarding many symbolic interactionists' demand for social research to be "naturalistic" Couch and his colleagues suggested that traditional interactionists had "produced their own fetish of naturalism" (Katovich, 1984, p. 49). They suggested "that experimental research is in principle, and potentially in practice, the epitome of symbolic interaction principles" (McPhail, 1979). McPhail (1979) provocatively proposed that the distinction between "natural(istic)" and "artificial/experimental" is an artificial construct that cannot be maintained. As one of the foundational principles of symbolic interactionism is that there are neither inherent meaning nor immaculate perception talk about an "natural" untouched world was misguided. "Symbol manipulating human beings construct and interdependently sustain the interpretations and responses (the instructions and the meanings) which establish the order of things. Such is the social construction of reality" (p. 90).

The experiments conducted by members of the NIS markedly differ from those undertaken in the behavioral sciences. Within the NIS laboratory "researchers actively control and manipulate selected social worlds and participants actively transform these worlds" (Katovich, 1984, p. 50). They argued that through careful socialization of the subjects into the experimental situations research could create naturalistic conditions could be undertaken in laboratory settings (Katovich et al., 1986). Therefore, "[I]n the laboratory setting actors mutually construct situated activity and relationships just as people do in settings outside of the laboratory" (Molseed, 1994, p. 242). The researchers create a social environment within the laboratory "that retains fidelity to social life while simultaneously allowing for the control of the observer's observations" (Katovich, 1984, p. 50). Katovich (1984, p. 51), therefore, describes the NIS laboratory as a "provocative stage" or a "metaphorical behavior setting" (1984, p. 52), "wherein features constructed by experimenters precede the drama, but the social objective of the drama must be created by participants." Similarly, Molseed (1994, p. 242) likens the laboratory to a naturalistic setting where "the researcher provides participants with a situation in which they are invited to interact and form, transform, and even terminate relationships just as they would in other settings." At the start of such experiments, participants are carefully socialized into the situation they will inhabit and develop, thus facilitating a suspension of disbelief that they "consider the researcher's environment on his [sic] terms, as an occasion for particular action" (Katovich, 1984, p. 51). Within the laboratory then the researcher gives the participants, mostly dyads or triads, a task, instructions and a time limit, then switches the video-camera on to record the task and leaves the room. While undertaking the task, the participants in these experiments actively and creatively contribute to the production of the laboratory context through their actions. They are not constrained in how to fulfill the task but decide themselves how to proceed in order to complete the task (Maines, 1986). Thus, the NIS researchers observe and reveal how the participants produce the social act under scrutiny.

The design of the NIS laboratory experiments is informed by "sensitizing concepts" (Blumer, 1931) helping the researcher "to organize a social scene that will yield data that will allow for the detection of elements and structures of forms of social action" (Katovich, 1984, p. 54). The reason for gathering data through laboratory experiments is that these settings coupled with carefully prepared tasks aimed to understand sociological phenomena reduces "clutter" (Couch, 1987, p. 8). The quality of the data collected depends on the researchers' sociological imagination and not on the quality of the technical equipment. Rather than concentrating on the design of the laboratory and its furnishings it is more important the researchers think carefully about the study and its objective. In his book "Researching Social Processes in the Laboratory" Couch (1987) provides detailed information on how to design laboratory environments. His key arguments relate to the relationship between control and the possibility of creative actions. The researchers cooperate with their research subjects rather than deceiving them. They orchestrate actions in the laboratory like theater directors and use instructions "as aids given to participants in order to encourage them to visualize a way of interacting with another in relation to an environment" (Katovich, 1984, p. 61). Couch and his colleagues (1986), therefore, argue against hiding cameras and microphones for moral reasons.

The principal data collected by NIS scholars are audio-visual recordings. They compare the impact of video technology on the social sciences to that of the invention of the microscope and telescope in biology and astronomy. The reason for the importance of video-recordings for the social sciences is, they suggest, that they can be "'re' 'searched'" (Couch, 1987, p. 8) and "examined again and again" (Couch, 1987, p. 8) which allows the researcher to transcribe the action and identify its elements. "With the opportunity to view detailed interaction systematically and repeatedly, we could forge more detailed, explicit, and decisive descriptions of micro-sociological social life" (Couch, 2017b, p. 14). Moreover, video-recordings that capture the processes of social action are highly shareable and therefore, in comparison to fieldnotes allow other researchers to examine the same data, and to uncover the social processes that unfolded in front of the camera.

With their research, Couch (1987, p. 90) aims to explore "how the simultaneous actions of individuals fit together to produce social acts." Couch and his colleagues at CRIB investigate different forms of sociation and are concerned with establishing, maintaining, and destroying the elements of sociation through participants' interaction (Couch, 1986, 1987). The elements of sociation, therefore, are conceived as "collective accomplishments" (Couch, 1989b, p. 464). To talk of sociation, it is not enough for two participants to both orient to the same object but also it is required that they orient to each other (See Fig. 1).

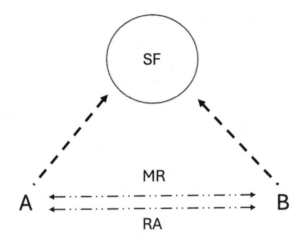

Notes:
RA = Reciprocal Attention
MR = Mutual Responsiveness
SF = Shared Focus
— — = Attentiveness
— · - = Responsiveness

Fig. 1. Elements of Sociation (cf. Couch, 1987).

Let us briefly turn to an example that Couch together with two of his doctoral students conducted in the 1970s. In this experiment, the researchers investigate the emergence of cooperative action. They pursue the question, "How is coordinated action achieved?" (Couch, 1987, p. 7). They derived the research question from Mead's (1967a/1934) and Blumer's (1969) discussion of the social act that Manford Kuhn (1962) and Frank Miyamoto (1959) further specified, as well as Schegloff's (1968) conversation-analytic investigation of the sequential organization of openings. In the laboratory, the researchers created a situation in which two participants independently from each other completed a questionnaire. While they were engaged in these independent activities, they were disturbed by an alarm going off in the neighboring room. The disturbance let to the transformation of independent activities – completing a questionnaire – to cooperative actions – attending to the events in the neighboring room. The analysis of the video-recordings of the incidence was concerned with the emergence of cooperative actions from independent activities. They then were further interested in the temporal organization of the emergence of cooperative action and in how social pasts influence the emergence of cooperative action. They observed that the two participants involved in the experiment "simultaneously evidenced a startled or freezing response, turned to each other and established eye contact, rose from their chairs and simultaneously moved toward the door together" (Miller et al., 1975).

Their examination of the video-recording revealed that the emergence of a cooperative act includes six elements: (1) establish co-presence, (2) acknowledge reciprocal attention, (3) create mutual responsiveness, (4) produce congruent functional identities, (5) establish a shared focus, and (6) move toward a social objective (Couch, 1984b, p. 8; Miller et al., 1975, p. 479).

Although NIS scholars show quantifications of observations in their publications, tables detailing the number of occurrences of particular actions appear to be mere rhetorical devices. "The number of times a person says 'O.K.' within an encounter is far less important than how a given 'O.K.' fits in with the preceding and following actions of the other person" (Couch, 1987). With their research they aim "to note and characterize the nature of the relatedness established between persons as they act toward and with each other and respond to each other" (Couch, 1987, p. 91). Through the analysis they strive to identify the nature and intensity of the relationships between participants. Thus, they differentiate their research, for example, from interaction process analysis developed by Bales (1976), as well as from ethnomethodological conversation analysis as developed by Schegloff and Sacks (Schegloff, 1968; Schegloff & Sacks, 1973). They note that conversation analysts focus only on talk and highlight that the "universes of communication" are made up of different dimensions: appearance (Stone, 2009/1962), touch (Leichty, 1975), and discourse (Mead, 1967a/1934). The analysis of video-recordings of situations provides access to all these dimensions of these universes of communication and can reveal how these dimensions are intertwined with each other.[4]

RESPONSES TO COUCH AND GARFINKEL

Couch (2017b) was convinced that the experiments revealing the elements of openings were a "breakthrough" that "will have an impact on the social sciences equal to that of Mendel's impact on the biological sciences" (p. 3). Although he was warned by colleagues that it was up to the academic community to decide if the findings of the NIS were to be considered a "breakthrough" he stuck to his claim. Yet, the manuscript where he was most vocal about this has remained unpublished until 7 years ago (Couch, 2017b). The reason for his seemingly embellished and self-aggrandizing characterization of NIS's successes might lie in the fragile situation of CRIB that relied on funding from the University of Iowa to support the maintenance of the laboratories and the researchers' studies. If so, Couch's fears were confirmed when in the early 1980s, CRIB lost its funding and had to close.

Couch and the NIS scholars published their research primarily in journals like Symbolic Interaction and the Sociological Quarterly as well as in the annual publication Studies in Symbolic Interaction. They also published a small number of monographs, such as Couch's (1987) book on research methods, his monograph discussing NIS's findings on social processes and relationships (Couch, 1989a), and his studies on the relationship between media of communication and cultural development (Couch, 1984a, 1996), as well as various volumes of Studies in Symbolic Interaction (Couch et al., 1986; Couch & Hintz, 1975; Denzin, 1989; Maines & Couch, 1988). Only a few of these books have been reviewed; thus far, I have only found Matthews (1988) review of Couch's (1987) "Researching Social Processes in the Laboratory," Weckroth (1989) review of the supplement to the 1986 publication of Studies in Symbolic Interaction that focuses on The Iowa School (Couch et al., 1986), Poster's (1997) review of "Information Technologies and Social Orders" (Couch, 1996), and most recently Ploder's (2019) review of "Carl Couch and the Iowa School" edited by Michael Katovich (2017b). NIS research also has been discussed in handbooks of symbolic interactionism (Couch et al., 1994; Katovich & Chen, 2021; Katovich et al., 2003). These review chapters primarily written by students and collaborators of Couch highlight the innovative nature of the research undertaken at CRIB. This view also is confirmed by articles about the relevance of symbolic interactionism for sociology. Fine (1993, p. 72), for example, describes studies undertaken at CRIB as "the most compelling and ambitious on-going research program within interactionism, specifying the generic principles of collective action." Other than this, thus far I have not been able to find any indication of much impact or even controversy about the NIS program, at least not in sociology or symbolic interactionism. Instead, recently published chapters discussing the theory of symbolic interactionism barely, if at all, mention the (New) Iowa School (Dingwall, 2022; Salvini, 2022), or see relationships between NIS research and communication studies (Chen, 1995). Research based on studies undertaken at CRIB, however, does continue and currently explores, for example, how NIS methods and concepts can be used to investigate social relationships mediated by screens (Johns, 2012) and in virtual environments (Katovich & Chen, 2014).

Although the program of the NIS developed almost at the same time when Garfinkel and Sacks created ethnomethodology and conversation analysis, Couch and his team made few references to EMCA. They acknowledge the innovative research examining audio-recorded talk undertaken by Sacks, Schegloff, Jefferson, and Zimmerman and West (Sacks et al., 1974; Schegloff, 1968; West & Zimmerman, 1977) and ascribe it "high fidelity." Yet, they criticize that ethnomethodology concerns itself primarily with very short sequences of interaction while ignoring the impact of larger time-frames on the organization of action (Hardesty, 1982). They also question the "robustness" of ethnomethodological theory (Couch, 1995), challenge the "one party at a time rule" that in the 1970s was one of the key findings conversation analysts had made, and criticize conversation analysis for being "descriptive" and for neglecting "the more fundamental question" (Hintz & Miller, 1995, p. 367, Fn. 1), i.e., how do people achieve cooperation?[5] Still, it has sometimes been argued that the differences between symbolic interactionism and ethnomethodology are not insurmountable (Denzin, 1969), a suggestion that, at least in the 1970s, was rebuked by ethnomethodologists (Zimmerman & Wieder, 1970). As far as I can see, Garfinkel and the ethnomethodologists have not acknowledged the research undertaken by the NIS, even though there are touch-points, for example in the use of audio-visual recordings as principal data.

Garfinkel and the breaching procedures have received plenty of response. Some refer to them as curious methods of investigation or introduce them as an interesting teaching tool (Braswell, 2014; Loyal & Maleševic, 2020; O'Byrne, 2011; Rafalovich, 2006). Other authors describe "breaching experiments" as "social breaching" and mistake "breaching" for "ethnomethods" (Rafalovich, 2006, p. 156). They suggest that breaching experiments are a technique teachers can use to enhance students' understanding of sociological concepts and the value of studying mundane situations. Teachers can deploy breaching experiments as research exercises for students to learn about the research process, gather and analyze data, and write-up research reports (Rafalovich, 2006).

In this way, sociologists and social psychologists use breaching experiments as aids for the presumed "sluggish imagination" of their students. They, for example, use them to sensitize students to participants' moral entanglement with others in public places. Halnon (2001) asked her students "to stand unobtrusively by themselves in a public place as a 'somewhat relaxed statue'" (p. 425). When discussing their experience of the task students suggested that "the experiment challenged them to take a step into the world of a stigmatized person" (Halnon, 2001, p. 428). Displaying being disengaged from the events and actions around them, created unexplained experiences of nervousness and anxiety in the students and encouraged them to develop techniques that allowed them to avoid being recognized by friends and family and to blend in with those present in the situation. Moreover, students felt the need to explain themselves to others while taking part in the task because "when someone is in a stigmatizing situation you feel the need to try and explain yourself, because with that explanation you provide a sense of comfort to your-self and those around" (Halnon, 2001, p. 436).

Breaching experiments have been particularly popular in the teaching of deviance (Rafalovich, 2006). Cheatwood et al. (1978), for instance, report a teaching exercise in which the course convenor adopts the persona of a professor at a 1938 large German university. Students responded positively to this teaching technique that encouraged them to reflect on sociological concepts like labeling. In a related way, Jones (1998) asked her students to perform 12 "random acts of kindness" over the course of a semester and reflect on their experiences in a journal (p. 181). In their reports students differentiated responses to their act from different audiences, such as family members and strangers. In class, students also noted that certain acts of kindness, such as female students offering men help with their cars, were not always positively received. Yet, the breaching experiments undertaken by the students enabled them to learn about the social construction of deviance, reflect on their own place in society – "ethnocentrism" – and positively influences students' opinion about sociology.

Apart from using breaching experiments for teaching purposes, sociologists also use them as an "aid for [their own] sluggish imagination" (Garfinkel, 1967b, p. 38). Stanley et al. (2020), for example, use a breaching experiment to learn about the subtle organization of behavior in public places. They explore how passers-by turn doing nothing in public places into "something" by bodily and visually turning to people who in a public space just stand still. In their analysis, they also find that the standing still in public places was treated as suspicious behavior by the authorities who monitored the researchers' conducting presuming it might be "the beginning of an anarcho-syndicalist protest" (p. 18).

The use of breaching procedures for teaching and research purposes is complemented by research of the impact these interventions have on participants. Braswell (2014) argues that the deployment of breaching experiments can negatively impact students and research subjects as well as researchers themselves. Students and researchers may be confronted with hostility (Braswell, 2014), their research activities may be costly to the researchers (Rafalovich, 2006) as they may be confronted with protestations by unwitting research subjects (Braswell, 2014). Research also has examined accounts students give regarding their experience of breaching experiments. Encouraged by reports of anxiety among students participating in some of the experiments conducted by Stanley Milgram, Gregory (1982) explored students' emotional response to breaching experiments undertaken as part of a seminar in ethnomethodology.[6] He found that students' anxiety was caused by their difficulties to account for their actions that disrupted others' lives.

A different strand of research pursues the intellectual origins of breaching experiments. Emirbayer and Maynard (2011), for instance, contextualize ethnomethodological breaching experiments within the development of pragmatist philosophy. They suggest that pragmatist scholars describe human conduct in the everyday as characterized by habits, i.e., "unreflective forms of action" (p. 227; cf. Dewey, 2024/1918). As long as people act in the everyday uninterrupted and without facing disruption, they take the world as it happens unquestioned for granted (p. 226). Doubt and perplexity only arise when they face unexpected resistance. "Thinking is what occurs most especially in situations where regular channels of action no longer suffice, where conflicts or ruptures in practice cause perplexity" (p. 228). This notion of "perplexity" was further explored by Jane Addams who considered it as "emotional and existential, not merely a problem 'out there', objective and actual, but an experience of internal strain, bafflement, and puzzlement" (p. 228). Emirbayer and Maynard argue that Garfinkel worked to differentiate his program of research from pragmatism and symbolic interactionism by instead drawing on the European tradition of phenomenology. Yet, they propose that there are "fundamental commonalities" (p. 255) between pragmatism and ethnomethodology as they are principally concerned with people's practices in the everyday, both exploring how people creatively deal with disruption to the anticipated social organization of action (Joas, 1996), and how language-use contributes to the social production of the everyday. Breaching procedures that Garfinkel developed as a research technique already when working on his doctoral dissertation are a manifestation of such commonalities between pragmatism and ethnomethodology pointed to by Emirbayer and Maynard (2011). While pragmatist philosophers discuss people's responses to disruptions to anticipated courses of actions as perplexities, Garfinkel (1963, 1967a) asked his students to conduct themselves deliberately in ways that will evoke such perplexities.

A slightly different view on the origins of breaching experiments, "tutorial exercises" or "demonstrations" (Garfinkel, 1963; 1967a, 2002) has been proposed by Eisenmann and Rawls (2023). Based on their analysis of materials housed in the Garfinkel Archives in Newbury Park they found that rather than being an oddity in the development of the ethnomethodological program, the teaching practices (Garfinkel, 1956), his "experiments with 'trust'" (Garfinkel, 1963) and the tutorial demonstrations related to perception show the "continuity between various approaches Garfinkel took to trouble/trust, indexicality and embodied practices over many years" (Eisenmann & Rawls, 2023, p. 20).

Other scholars use the idea of studying people orientation to disrupted taken-for-granted social situations underlying in the vein of Garfinkel's procedures. Mondada and Svensson (2023), for example, explore how everyday practices were undercut by the measures introduced regarding behavior in public places during the COVID-19 pandemic, and Yamazaki and Arano (2023) investigate how unassuming customers interact with a robotic sales assistant. These and other studies (Sormani & vom Lehn, 2023b) show the continued interest in and the relevance of Garfinkel's program that is concerned with the uncovering of the generic principles underlying social order.

DISCUSSION: INTERACTIONIST FUTURES

I have discussed two programs of research that emerged in the USA since the 1960s. Despite being developed roughly in parallel I have found few interchanges between the two programs. In my view Garfinkel's and Couch's programs have some interesting commonalities: (1) both Garfinkel and Couch are interested in uncovering "generic principles of social life," (2) later developments of these programs prioritized the use of audio-visual recordings as principal data, and (3) scholars following these programs examine these recordings in great detail by using transcripts of talk and bodily action.

- Couch and the NIS scholars who collaborated at CRIB for a period of about 15 years – 1970 to (about) 1985 – highlight their interest in revealing the generic principles underlying social processes. They are in alignment with interactionist scholars who since the 1950s argued for "processual analyses of emerging organizations [...] that will facilitate the isolation of primitive elements of social structure" (Couch, 1989b, p. 446). Garfinkel's (1967b, 2002) program stretching over a longer period – 1940s until his death in 2011 and continued by others – has been methodologically more diverse. It includes ethnographic studies (Sudnow, 1967; Wieder, 1974) as well as the analysis of audio- and video-recorded interaction (Heath et al., 2010; Sacks, 1992). It aims to uncover the "ethnomethods" people use in their everyday to continually produce the coherence of an intersubjective world. The experience of incongruity has been a fundamental part of Garfinkel's life and work (Eisenmann & Rawls, 2023), and he has used incongruity procedures throughout his academic career. They serve him as "an aid to sluggish imagination" (Garfinkel, 1967b, p. 38), a resource to help him uncover the generic principles of the ordinary organization of action by eliciting unordinary "observable-and-reportable" actions (Garfinkel, 1967b, p. 1).

- The use of audio-visual recordings has been pioneered by NIS scholars since the 1970s. Couch (1987) describes in detail the opportunities and challenges of this type of data, including the importance of transcription. He and colleagues at CRIB had shown, for example, that bodily and material action are of critical importance for the accomplishment of collective action (Couch & Hintz, 1975). Similar points, although in a different way, have been made also by those promoting the use of video as principal data for the ethnomethodological analysis of interaction since the 1980s (Goodwin, 1981; Heath, 1986; Heath et al., 2010). Today, in ethnomethodology the use of video as principal data has all but replaced the analysis of mere audio-recordings that lack access to people's bodily, visual and material action that is so important to understand the organization of interaction (Heath et al., 2010; Mondada, 2016).
- CRIB research and the ethnomethodologists both highlight the importance of transcripts as tools for the researcher when aiming to uncover the fine details of the organization of action (Couch, 1987; Heath et al., 2010). In my analysis of CRIB research I was surprised to find that NIS scholars did not use the system developed by conversation analysts to transcribe talk. Despite emphasizing the importance of uncovering the details of actions, their transcriptions are far less detailed than those produced by ethnomethodologists who also include elongations of letters, minute pauses between utterances, the emphasis of syllables and other characteristics of talk (see Jefferson, 1984), as well as the on- and offset of bodily action such as gesture, head-movements, and shifts in bodily orientation (Heath et al., 2010).

Apart from these commonalities, there also are important and interesting differences between the two programs. Garfinkel's original program as he developed it in the 1950s and 1960s has been strongly informed by his analysis of phenomenology and Alfred Schütz's (1972) writings. Although he is interested in uncovering generic forms of social action, that he calls ethnomethods, there is no evidence that he has read Simmel's formal sociology much. By taking a position strongly influenced by phenomenology, ethnomethodologists take the perspective of the actor, work to reveal how participants in interaction orient to each other's actions, and use actions as evidence for their arguments about how an action orients to an immediate prior action and foreshadows a next action. Thus, they unpack the sequential organization of actions by analyzing the immediate, interactional context of an action, such as an utterance or a bodily action. Couch and his colleagues at the NIS highlight that they see their work closely related to Simmel's formal sociology. Titles, such as "Elementary Forms of Social Activity" (Couch, 1986) and "Forms of Social Processes" (Couch, 2017a), exhibit this relationship to Simmel and the NIS's concern with the development of a sociology that understands generic principles of social life. In their analysis, therefore, they adopt "a third party standpoint" (Couch, 2017b, p. 112) that, in their view, allows them to "reveal structures of social activities and social relationships" (Couch, 2017b, p. 113).

CONCLUSION

My interest in the research undertaken at CRIB has been motivated by the observation that some research in EMCA currently moves some way into the direction Couch has criticized, namely the scientification of interactionist analyses. In EMCA, there is a growing interest in studying the organization of action and interaction in laboratories (Kendrick & Holler, 2017). The experiments conducted in these laboratories follow the frameworks developed in psychology and the cognitive sciences (de Ruiter & Albert, 2017). In these settings, researchers use complex technologies to precisely measure, for example, changes in the tone of voice and gaze direction, and provide quantitative indicators to disseminate their findings (Kendrick et al., 2023). Thus, they create intellectual relationship with researchers in experimental psychology (de Ruiter & Albert, 2017) while "traditional" ethnomethodologist distance themselves from these pursuits; if Couch was here and ethnomethodologically inclined seeing these developments he may have said, "[T]hey are trying too damn hard to be scientific" (Maines, 1986, p. 416).

At the same time, ethnomethodologists conduct research using methods some describe as "naturalistic experiments" (Heath & Luff, 2018). While some of these experiments have been undertaken in public places like museums (Heath et al., 2002; Hindmarsh et al., 2005), others are undertaken in laboratories and laboratory-like environments (Kuzuoka et al., 2004). These naturalistic experiments aim to reveal the principles underlying the social organization of action in settings where people's everyday activities are "disrupted" by the deployment of novel technologies. In a way, therefore, they combine Garfinkel's breaching procedures and Couch's conception of laboratories as "provocative stages" (Katovich, 1984) or "naturalistic settings" (Molseed, 1994) without considering NIS scholars' use of laboratory experiments to reveal the structure of collective action. Maybe, the experiments undertaken at CRIB could serve these ethnomethodologists to inform the design of their naturalistic experiments.

Most surprising for me has been the lack of interest in Couch and his program by symbolic interactionists. Over the past 15 years or so, I have never met an interactionist who is undertaking research following Couch's program at the annual meetings of the Society for the Study of Symbolic Interaction (SSSI). And publications in Symbolic Interaction, SSSI's flagship journal, related to Couch's program have become rare (Miller, 2011; Ploder, 2019). Similarly, ethnomethodologists only occasionally publish their research in Symbolic Interaction and do not consider the annual meetings of SSSI as relevant for their research. Both, the disaffiliation of interactionists from Couch's program and from ethnomethodology and vice versa the disengagement of scholars pursuing Couch's program or ethnomethodologists from SSSI is unfortunate. Carl Couch and to some extent also Manford Kuhn have played important roles in the founding of the Society for the Study of Symbolic Interaction and its flagship journal Symbolic Interaction (Katovich, 2019); and as an interactionist program of research Garfinkel's ethnomethodology has plenty of touch points with the intellectual and political direction of symbolic interactionism.[7]

DIRK VOM LEHN · 43

Maybe this paper makes a small contribution to rekindling the interactionist interest in Couch's program and to encouraging ethnomethodologists to (re-) engage with SSSI and Symbolic Interaction as well as with Couch's methodological proposals. The long-term continuance of research programs like ethnomethodology, the NIS program, and interactionism more widely are achieved through collective action. Investigations into and reflections on the past symbolic interactionists and ethnomethodologists share may encourage such collective action and thus help create and ensure interactionist futures that include a variety of interactionist sociologies, such as ethnomethodology and the NIS program. Here, I have started such investigations.

ACKNOWLEDGMENTS

I would like to thank the participants in the sessions organized at the 2024 meetings of the Pacific Sociological Association: Black Hawk Hancock, Robin James Smith, Morana Alač, Terry Au-Yeung, Timothy Halkowski, Phil Hutchinson, Patrick Watson, for their critical questions and comments. I also would like to thank Christian Heath for making me aware of and kindling my interest in the NIS many years ago. Very many thanks also to Michael Katovich for his detailed comments on an earlier version of this chapter.

NOTES

1. Edited and introduced by Anne W. Rawls, the proposal was published as "Seeing Sociologically" (Garfinkel, 2006/1948). This proposal outlines a theoretical orientation rather than a planned research project. The PhD research project Garfinkel eventually undertook, incorporates parts of this outline but principally is an empirical endeavor.
2. In this regard, see the debate between Blumer (1980) and McPhail and Rexroat (1980). It is also worthwhile considering Blumer's discussion of experimentation in his PhD (1928) where he highlights the unsuitability of the format of scientific experiments for the study of human conduct and points to experiments naturally undertaken by people in the everyday to test the environment's response to their actions, actions that can be observed by the social psychologist; "Nature performs experiments – man observes them" (Blumer, 1928, p. 28).
3. In the following, I will use just the terms "video-record" and "video-recordings."
4. These arguments were made by NIS scholars in the 1970s, before ethnomethodologists took up the analysis if interaction using video-recordings as principal data (Goodwin, 1981; Heath, 1986; Heath et al., 2010).
5. I leave this critique uncommented but wish to add that over the past 20 years several studies of openings have been undertaken, for example by Pillet-Shore (2018a, b, 2021).
6. For a recent discussion of Milgram's experiments see recent publications by Hollander and Turowetz (2017, 2024).
7. Even if ethnomethodologists differentiate themselves from symbolic interactionism (Turowetz & Rawls, 2021), ethnomethodology is an interactionist research endeavor.

REFERENCES

Ayaß, R. (2021). Der dünne Boden der natürlichen Einstellung. Harold Garfinkel's 'breaching procedures'. In J. R. Bergmann & C. Meyer (Eds.), *Ethnomethodologie reloaded. Neue Werkinterpretationen und Theoriebeiträge zu Harold Garfinkels Programm* (pp. 57–77). Transcript.

Bales, R. F. (1976). *Interaction process analysis*. University of Chicago Press.

Blumer, H. G. (1928). *Method in social psychology*. University of Chicago.

Blumer, H. (1931). Science without concepts. *American Journal of Sociology, 36*(4), 515–533.

Blumer, H. (1969). *Symbolic interactionism: perspective and method*. Prentice Hall.

Blumer, H. (1980). Mead and Blumer: The convergent methodological perspectives of social behaviorism and symbolic interactionism. *American Sociological Review, 45*(3), 409–419.

Braswell, M. (2014). Once more unto the breaching experiment: Reconsidering a popular pedagogical tool. *Teaching Sociology, 42*(2), 161–167. https://doi.org/10.1177/0092055X14521021

Buban, S. L. (1986). Studying social processes: The Chicago and Iowa school revisited. In N. K. Denzin (Ed.), *Studies in symbolic interaction* (Vol. 8, pp. 25–40). JAI Press.

Cheatwood, D., Corzine, J., & Glassner, B. (1978). Techniques in teaching deviance. *Teaching Sociology, 5*(2), 171. https://doi.org/10.2307/1317063

Chen, S.-L. S. (1995). Carl Couch: Bridging sociology and communication. *Symbolic Interaction, 18*(3), 323–339.

Cottrell, R. C. (2017). *Sex, drugs, and rock 'n' roll: The rise of America's 1960s counterculture*. Rowman & Littlefield Publishers.

Couch, C. J. (1970). Dimensions of association in collective behavior episodes. *Sociometry, 33*(4), 457–471.

Couch, C. J. (1984a). *Constructing civilizations* (Contemporary Studies in Society). JAI Press Inc.

Couch, C. J. (1984b). Symbolic interaction and generic sociological principles. *Symbolic Interaction, 7*(1), 1–13. https://doi.org/10.1525/si.1984.7.1.1

Couch, C. J. (1986). Elementary forms of social activity. In C. J. Couch, S. L. Saxton, & M. A. Katovich (Eds.), *Studies in symbolic interaction, supplement 2: The Iowa school (Part A)* (pp. 113–129). JAI Press.

Couch, C. J. (1987). *Researching social processes in the laboratory*. JAI Press Inc.

Couch, C. J. (1989a). *Social processes and relationships: A formal approach*. General Hall.

Couch, C. J. (1989b). Toward the isolation of elements of social order. In N. K. Denzin (Ed.), *Studies in symbolic interaction* (Vol. 10 Part B, pp. 445–469). JAI.

Couch, C. J. (1995). Presidential address: Let us rekindle the passion by constructing a robust science of the social. *The Sociological Quarterly, 36*(1), 1–14.

Couch, C. J. (1996). *Information technologies and social orders*. Aldine Transaction.

Couch, C. J. (2017a). Forms of social processes. In M. A. Katovich (Ed.), *Studies in symbolic interaction* (Vol. 49, pp. 111–139). Emerald Publishing Limited. https://doi.org/10.1108/S0163-239620170000049019

Couch, C. J. (2017b). The romance of discovery. In M. A. Katovich (Ed.), *Studies in symbolic interactionism. Carl Couch and the Iowa school. In his own words* (pp. 3–107). Emerald Publishing Limited.

Couch, C. J. (2017c). Carl Couch and the Iowa School. In his own words. In M. A. Katovich (Ed.), *Studies in symbolic interaction* (p. 49). Emerald Publishing Limited.

Couch, C. J., & Hintz, R. A. (1975). *Constructing social life: Readings in behavioral sociology from the Iowa school*. Stipes Publishing, LLC.

Couch, C. J., Katovich, M. A., & Buban, S. (1994). Beyond Blumer and Kuhn: Researching and studying across-time data through the use of point-in-space laboratory procedures. In N. J. Herman-Kinney & L. T. Reynolds (Eds.), *Symbolic interaction: An introduction to social psychology* (pp. 121–138). General Hall.

Couch, C. J., Saxton, S. L., & Katovich, M. A. (1986). *Studies in symbolic interaction: Iowa school suppt. 2*. JAI Press.

Darlington, J. (2021). The 1960s: Experimentalism in the space age. In J. Darlington (Ed.), *Christine Brooke-Rose and post-war literature* (pp. 33–55). Palgrave Macmillan. https://doi.org/10.1007/978-3-030-75906-3_3

de Ruiter, J. P., & Albert, S. (2017). An appeal for a methodological fusion of conversation analysis and experimental psychology. *Research on Language and Social Interaction, 50*(1), 90–107. https://doi.org/10.1080/08351813.2017.1262050

Denzin, N. K. (1969). Symbolic interactionism and ethnomethodology: A proposed synthesis. *American Sociological Review, 34*(6), 922–934.

DIRK VOM LEHN

Denzin, N. K. (1989). *Studies in symbolic interaction* (Vol. 10). JAI Press.

Dewey, J. (2024). *Human nature and conduct—An introduction to social psychology*. Adventure Booking.

Dingwall, R. (2022). The historical foundations of symbolic interactionism. In W. H. Brekhus, T. DeGloma, & W. R. Force (Eds.), *The Oxford handbook of symbolic interactionism* (1st ed., pp. 27–48). Oxford University Press. https://doi.org/10.1093/oxfordhb/9780190082161.013.2

Eberle, T. S. (1984). *Sinnkonstitution in Alltag und Wissenschaft: Der Beitrag der Phänomenologie an die Methodologie der Sozialwissenschaften*. P. Haupt.

Eickelpasch, R. (1982). Das ethnomethodologische Programm einer "radikalen" Soziologie. *Zeitschrift für Soziologie, 11*(1), 7–27.

Eisenmann, C., & Lynch, M. (2021). Introduction to Harold Garfinkel's ethnomethodological 'Misreading' of Aron Gurwitsch on the phenomenal field. *Human Studies, 44*(1), 1–17. https://doi.org/10.1007/s10746-020-09564-1

Eisenmann, C., & Rawls, A. W. (2023). The continuity of Garfinkel's approach: Seeking ways of 'Making the Phenomenon Available Again' through the experience and usefulness of 'Trouble'. In P. Sormani & D. Vom Lehn (Eds.), *The Anthem companion to Harold Garfinkel* (pp. 19–41). Anthem Press. https://doi.org/10.2307/jj.4418210

Emirbayer, M., & Maynard, D. W. (2011). Pragmatism and ethnomethodology. *Qualitative Sociology, 34*(1), 221–261. https://doi.org/10.1007/s11133-010-9183-8

Farber, M. (1943). *The foundation of phenomenology: Edmund Husserl and the quest for a rigorous science of philosophy*. Aldine Transaction.

Fine, G. A. (1993). The sad demise, mysterious disappearance, and glorious triumph of symbolic interactionism. *Annual Review of Sociology, 19*, 61–87.

Garfinkel, H. (1952). *The perception of the other: A study in social order*. PhD. Harvard University.

Garfinkel, H. (1956). *Some classroom demonstrations of sociological concepts: An essay in sociological theory*. Garfinkel Archive.

Garfinkel, H. (1963). A conception of and experiments with 'Trust' as a condition of stable concerted actions. In O. J. Harvey (Ed.), *Motivation and social interaction* (pp. 187–238). Ronald Press.

Garfinkel, H. (1967a). Common-sense knowledge of social structures: The documentary method of. In ibid. *Studies in ethnomethodology* (pp. 76–103). Polity Press.

Garfinkel, H. (1967b). *Studies in ethnomethodology*. Polity Press.

Garfinkel, H. (2002). *Ethnomethodology's program: Working out Durkheim's aphorism*. Rowman & Littlefield Publishers.

Garfinkel, H. (2006). *Seeing sociologically: The routine grounds of social action*. Paradigm.

Goodwin, C. (1981). *Conversational organisation: Interaction between speakers and hearers*. Academic Press.

Gouldner, A. W. (1970). *The coming crisis of western sociology*. Basic Books.

Gregory, S. W., Jr. (1982). Accounts as assembled from breaching experiments. *Symbolic Interaction, 5*(1), 49–63. https://doi.org/10.1525/si.1982.5.1.49

Halnon, K. B. (2001). The sociology of doing nothing: A model 'Adopt a Stigma in a Public Place' exercise. *Teaching Sociology, 29*(4), 423. https://doi.org/10.2307/1318944

Hardesty, M. J. (1982). Ethnomethodology and symbolic interactionism: A critical comparison of temporal orientations. *Symbolic Interaction, 5*(1), 127–137.

Heath, C. (1986). *Body movement and medical interaction*. Cambridge University Press.

Heath, C., Hindmarsh, J., & Luff, P. (2010). *Video in qualitative research*. SAGE Publications Ltd.

Heath, C., & Luff, P. (2018). The naturalistic experiment: Video and organizational interaction. *Organizational Research Methods, 21*(2), 466–488. https://doi.org/10.1177/1094428117747688

Heath, C., Luff, P., vom Lehn, D., Hindmarsh, J., & Cleverly, J. (2002). Crafting participation: Designing ecologies, configuring experience. *Visual Communication, 1*(1), 9–33. https://doi.org/10.1177/147035720200100102

Heritage, J. (1984). *Garfinkel and ethnomethodology*. Polity Press.

Hickman, C. A., & Kuhn, M. H. (1956). *Individuals, groups, and economic behavior*. Dryden.

Hindmarsh, J., Heath, C., vom Lehn, D., & Cleverly, J. (2005). Creating assemblies in public environments: Social interaction, interactive exhibits and CSCW. *Journal of Computer Supported Collaborative Work (JCSCW), 14*(1), 1–41.

Hintz, R. A., & Miller, D. E. D. (1995). Openings revisited: The foundations of social interaction. *Symbolic Interaction, 18*(3), 355–369. https://doi.org/10.1525/si.1995.18.3.355

Hollander, M. M., & Turowetz, J. (2017). Normalizing trust: Participants' immediately post-hoc explanations of behaviour in Milgram's 'obedience'experiments. *British Journal of Social Psychology, 56*(4), 655–674.

Hollander, M. M., & Turowetz, J. (2024). *Morality in the making of sense and self: Stanley Milgram's obedience experiments and the new science of morality*. OUP.

Husserl, E. (2012). *Ideas: General introduction to pure phenomenology*. Routledge.

Jefferson, G. (1984). Transcript notation. In J. M. Atkinson & J. Heritage (Eds.), *Structures of social action* (pp. ix–xvi). Cambridge University Press.

Joas, H. (1996). *The creativity of action*. Polity Press.

Johns, M. D. (2012). Two screen viewing and social relationships. Exploring the invisible backchannel of TV viewing. In M. Strano, H. Hrachovec, F. Sudweeks, & C. Ess (Eds.), *Proceedings cultural attitudes towards technology and communication* (pp. 333–343). Murdoch University.

Jones, A. L. (1998). Random acts of kindness: A teaching tool for positive deviance. *Teaching Sociology, 26*(3), 179. https://doi.org/10.2307/1318831

Katovich, M. (1984). Symbolic interactionism and experimentation: The laboratory as a provocative stage. In N. K. Denzin (Ed.), *Studies in symbolic interaction* (Vol. 5, pp. 49–67). JAI Press.

Katovich, M. (2019). Carl J. Couch. In C. T. Conner, N. M. Baxter, & D. R. Dickens (Eds.), *Forgotten founders and other neglected social theorists* (pp. 173–190). Rowman & Littlefield.

Katovich, M. A., & Chen, S.-L. S. (2014). New Iowa school redux: Second life as laboratory. In *Symbolic interaction and new social media.* (Vol. 43, pp. 63–84). Emerald Publishing Limited.

Katovich, M., & Chen, S.-L. S. (2021). Recent developments in the new Iowa school of symbolic interactionism. In D. vom Lehn, N. Ruiz-Junco, & W. Gibson (Eds.), *The Routledge international handbook of interactionism* (pp. 59–69). Routledge.

Katovich, M., Miller, D. E., & Stewart, R. L. (2003). The Iowa school. In L. T. Reynolds & N. J. Herman-Kinney (Eds.), *Handbook of symbolic interactionism* (pp. 119–139). Rowman & Littlefield.

Katovich, M., Saxton, S. L., & Powell, J. O. (1986). Naturalism in the laboratory. In C. J. Couch, S. L. Saxton, & M. A. Katovich (Eds.), *Studies in symbolic interaction supplement 2 (Part A)* (pp. 79–88). JAI Press.

Kendrick, K. H., & Holler, J. (2017). Gaze direction signals response preference in conversation. *Research on Language and Social Interaction, 50*(1), 12–32. https://doi.org/10.1080/08351813.2017.1262120

Kendrick, K. H., Holler, J., & Levinson, S. C. (2023). Turn-taking in human face-to-face interaction is multimodal: Gaze direction and manual gestures aid the coordination of turn transitions. *Philosophical Transactions of the Royal Society B: Biological Sciences, 378*(1875), 20210473. https://doi.org/10.1098/rstb.2021.0473

Kuhn, M. H. (1962). The interview and the professional relationship. In A. M. Rose (Ed.), *Human behavior and social processes. An interactionist approach* (pp. 193–206). Routledge & Kegan Paul Books.

Kuhn, M. H. (1964). Major trends in symbolic interaction theory in the past twenty-five years. *The Sociological Quarterly, 5*(1), 61–84.

Kuhn, M. H., & McPartland, T. S. (1954). An empirical investigation of self-attitudes. *American Sociological Review, 19*(1), 68–76.

Kuzuoka, H., Yamazaki, K., Yamazaki, A., Kosaka, J., Suga, Y., & Heath, C. (2004). Dual ecologies of robot as communication media: Thoughts on coordinating orientations and projectability. *6*(1), 8.

Leichty, M. G. (1975). Sensory modes, social activity and the universe of touch. In C. J. Couch & R. A. Hintz (Eds.), *Constructing social life: Readings in behavioral sociology from the Iowa school* (pp. 65–79). Stipes Publishing Company.

Loyal, S., & Maleševic, S. (2020). *Contemporary sociological theory*. SAGE Publications Ltd.

Lynch, M. (2004). Misreading Schutz: A response to Dennis on 'Lynch on Schutz on science. *Theory & Science, 5*(1), 1–9.

DIRK VOM LEHN 47

Lynch, M. (2023). Garfinkel's praxeological 'experiments'. In P. Sormani & D. vom Lehn (Eds.), *The Anthem companion to Harold Garfinkel* (pp. 3–18). Anthem Press.

Maines, D. R. (1986). Researching form and process in the Iowa tradition. In C. J. Couch, S. L. Saxton, & M. A. Katovich (Eds.), *Studies in symbolic interaction. Supplement 2: The Iowa school (Part B)* (pp. 415–429). JAI Press.

Maines, D. R., & Couch, C. J. (Eds.). (1988). *Communication and social structure.* Charles C Thomas Pub Ltd.

Matthews, B. A. (1988). Review of 'Researching Social Proceses in the Laboratory' by Carl J. Couch. *Social Forces, 67*(1), 270–271.

McPhail, C. (1979). Experimental research is convergent with symbolic interaction. *Symbolic Interaction, 2*(1), 89–94. https://doi.org/10.1525/si.1979.2.1.89

McPhail, C., & Rexroat, C. (1980). Ex cathedra Blumer or ex libris Mead? *American Sociological Review, 45*(3), 420–430.

Mead, G. H. (1967a/1934). *Mind, self, and society from the perspective of a social behaviorist.* University of Chicago Press.

Mead, G. H. (1967b/1936). *Movements of thought in the nineteenth century.* The University of Chicago Press.

Mead, G. H. (2002/1932). *The philosophy of the present.* Prometheus.

Meltzer, B. N., Petras, J. W., & Reynolds, L. T. (1975). *Symbolic interactionism: Genesis, varieties critics.* Routledge & Kegan Paul Books.

Miller, D. E. (2011). Toward a theory of interaction: The Iowa school. *Symbolic Interaction, 34*(3), 340–348.

Miller, D. E., Hintz, R. A., & Couch, C. J. (1975). The elements and structure of openings. *Sociological Quarterly, 16*(4), 479–499.

Miyamoto, S. F. (1959). The social act: Re-examination of a concept. *Pacific Sociological Review, 2*(2), 51–55.

Molseed, M. J. (1994). Naturalistic observation in the laboratory. *Symbolic Interaction, 17*(3), 239–251. https://doi.org/10.1525/si.1994.17.3.239

Mondada, L. (2016). Challenges of multimodality: Language and the body in social interaction. *Journal of SocioLinguistics, 20*(3). https://doi.org/10.1111/josl.1_12177

Mondada, L., & Svensson, H. (2023). A natural breaching experiment? Interactional troubles during the Covid19 pandemic. In P. Sormani & D. vom Lehn (Eds.), *The Anthem companion to Harold Garfinkel.* Anthem Press.

O'Byrne, D. (2011). *Introducing sociological theory.* Routledge.

Parsons, T. (1968). *The structure of social action (2 volumes).* The Free Press.

Pillet-Shore, D. (2018a). Arriving: Expanding the personal state sequence. *Research on Language and Social Interaction, 51*(3), 232–247. https://doi.org/10.1080/08351813.2018.1485225

Pillet-Shore, D. (2018b). How to begin. *Research on Language and Social Interaction, 51*(3), 213–231. https://doi.org/10.1080/08351813.2018.1485224

Pillet-Shore, D. (2021). When to make the sensory social: Registering in face-to-face openings. *Symbolic Interaction, 44*(1), 10–39.

Ploder, A. (2019). Tragedy of a breakthrough: The Iowa school of symbolic interaction in autobiographical narratives. *Symbolic Interaction, 42*(2), 332–335. https://doi.org/10.1002/symb.368

Poster, M. (1997). Information technologies and social orders. *Contemporary Sociology, 26*(4), 516–518.

Rafalovich, A. (2006). Making sociology relevant: The assignment and application of breaching experiments. *Teaching Sociology, 34*(2), 156–163. https://doi.org/10.1177/0092055X0603400206

Reynolds, L. (1993). *Interactionism: Exposition and critique* (3rd ed.). Altamira Press.

Sacks, H. (1992). *Lectures on conversation* Eds. G. Jefferson & E. A. Schegloff (2 Volumes). Wiley-Blackwell.

Sacks, H., Schegloff, E. A., & Jefferson, G. (1974). A simplest systematics for the organization of turn-taking for conversation. *Language, 4*(1), 696–735.

Salvini, A. (2022). Symbolic interactionism and social research. In W. H. Brekhus, T. DeGloma, & W. R. Force (Eds.), *The Oxford handbook of symbolic interactionism* (1st ed., pp. 49–69). Oxford University Press. https://doi.org/10.1093/oxfordhb/9780190082161.013.33

Schegloff, E. A. (1968). Sequencing in conversational openings. *American Anthropologist, New Series*, *70*(6), 1075–1095.

Schegloff, E. A., & Sacks, H. (1973). Opening up closings. *Semiotica*, *8*(4), 289–327.

Schütz, A. (1945). On multiple realities. *Philosophy and Phenomenological Research*, *5*(4), 533–576.

Schütz, A. (1953). Common-sense and scientific interpretation of human action. *Philosophy and Phenomenological Research*, *14*(1), 1–38.

Schütz, A. (1972). *Phenomenology of the social world* (Walsh, G., & Lehnert, F., Trans.). Northwestern University Press.

Simmel, G. (2009a). Excursus on the problem: How is society possible? In A. J. Blasi, A. K. Jacobs, & M. J. Kanjirathinkal (Eds.), *Sociology* (pp. 40–52). Brill.

Simmel, G. (2009b). In A. J. Blasi, A. K. Jacobs, & M. J. Kanjirathinkal (Eds.), *Sociology: Inquiries into the construction of social forms*. Brill.

Sormani, P., & vom Lehn, D. (2023a). Introduction: Rediscovering Garfinkel's 'Experiments,' renewing ethnomethodological inquiry. In P. Sormani & D. vom Lehn (Eds.), *The Anthem companion to Harold Garfinkel* (pp. ix–xxvii). Anthem Press.

Sormani, P. & vom Lehn, D. (Eds.). (2023b). *The Anthem companion to Harold Garfinkel*. Anthem Press.

Spitzer, S. P., & Parker, J. (1976). Perceived validity and assessment of the self: A decade later. *The Sociological Quarterly*, *17*(2), 236–246. https://doi.org/10.1111/j.1533-8525.1976.tb00976.x

Spitzer, S. P., Stratton, J. R., Fitzgerald, J. D., & Mach, B. K. (1966). The self concept: Test equivalence and perceived validity. *The Sociological Quarterly*, *7*(3), 265–280. https://doi.org/10.1111/j.1533-8525.1966.tb01693.x

Stanley, S., Smith, R. J., Ford, E., & Jones, J. (2020). Making something out of nothing: Breaching everyday life by standing still in a public place. *The Sociological Review*. https://doi.org/10.1177/0038026120940616

Stone, G. (2009). Appearance and the self: A slightly revised version. In D. Brissett & C. Edgley (Eds.), *Life as theater: A dramaturgical sourcebook* (pp. 141–162). Transaction Publishers.

Sudnow, D. (1967). *Passing on, the social organization of dying*. Prentice Hall.

Turowetz, J., & Rawls, A. W. (2021). Ethnomethodology and conversation analysis: The other interactionism. In D. vom Lehn, N. Ruiz-Junco, & W. Gibson (Eds.), *The Routledge international handbook of interactionism* (pp. 82–95). Routledge.

Vaughan, T. R. (1993). The crisis in contemporary American sociology: A critique of the discipline's dominant paradigm. In T. R. Vaughan, G. Sjorberg, & L. T. Reynolds (Eds.), *A critique of contemporary American sociology* (pp. 10–53). General Hall Inc.

vom Lehn, D. (2014). *Harold Garfinkel: The creation and development of ethnomethodology*. Left Coast Press.

Weckroth, K. (1989). Review of 'Carl J. Couch, Stanley L. Saxton & Michael A. Katovich (eds.): studies in symbolic interactionism'. In N. K. Denzin (Ed.), *Studies in symbolic interaction* (Vol. 10, pp. 213–215). JAI Press.

West, C. D., & Zimmerman, D. H. (1977). Women's place in everyday talk: Reflections on parent-child interaction. *Social Problems*, *24*(5), 521–529. https://doi.org/10.2307/800122

Wieder, D. L. (1974). *Language and social reality: The case of telling the convict code*. Mouton.

Yamazaki, K., & Arano, Y. (2023). Breaching and robot experiments: The spirit of experimentation of Harold Garfinkel. In P. Sormani & D. vom Lehn (Eds.), *The Anthem companion to Harold Garfinkel* (pp. 139–160). Anthem Press.

Zimmerman, D., & Wieder, D. L. (1970). Ethnomethodology and the problem of order: Comment on Denzin. In J. D. Douglas (Ed.), *Understanding everyday life* (pp. 285–298). Routledge & Kegan Paul Books.

SYMBOLIC INTERACTION AND THE GROUNDED THEORY METHOD

Antony Bryant[a] and Carrie Friese[b]

[a]*Leeds Beckett University, UK*
[b]*London School of Economics, UK*

"*ex nihilo nihil fit*" – Parmenides; "nothing comes from nothing"

ABSTRACT

Barney Glaser and Anselm Strauss, together with Jeanne Quint, collaborated on a research project in the 1960s that resulted in the highly innovative and now widely used Grounded Theory Method [GTM]. The pioneering characteristics of the method drew on the different backgrounds of Glaser and Strauss; respectively, the work of Lazarsfeld and Merton based at University of Columbia, New York, and Chicago School sociology. This latter influence encompassed Symbolic Interactionism and Pragmatism, although Glaser later sought to downplay or even deny the importance of this. In what follows we outline the trajectory leading through Strauss from the Chicago School to GTM, and the ways in which later developments in the method – e.g., Constructivist GTM and Situated Analysis – build specifically on these antecedents to the method itself.

Keywords: Grounded theory; symbolic interactionism; pragmatism; abduction; Chicago School of Sociology; Anselm Strauss

INTRODUCTION

In the 1960s, Anselm Strauss and Barney Glaser challenged the methodological orthodoxy of the US sociological academy with their publications on Grounded Theory, particularly *Awareness of Dying* (Glaser & Strauss, 1965), the first example of a grounded theory, and *The Discovery of Grounded Theory* (Glaser & Strauss, 1967), a book-length manifesto for the method (hereafter GTM; Grounded Theory Method).

Essential Methods in Symbolic Interaction
Studies in Symbolic Interaction, Volume 60, 49–78
Copyright © 2025 Antony Bryant and Carrie Friese
Published under exclusive licence by Emerald Publishing Limited
ISSN: 0163-2396/doi:10.1108/S0163-239620250000060004

50   *Symbolic Interaction and the Grounded Theory Method*

These two books, together with *Time for Dying* (1968) and *Status Passage* (1971), were the culmination of a major research project that began in 1960, centered around The University of California, San Francisco (UCSF). Strauss had moved there from the Department of Sociology at the University of Chicago, recruiting Glaser who had recently completed his PhD at The University of Columbia, New York. They were joined in their project by Jeanne Quint, a practising nurse and nurse-researcher.

Strauss was the oldest of the group, but only 3 years older than Quint, and 11 years older than Glaser. Quint had extensive experience in nursing, including time in the Army Nurse Corps during WW2 and various post-graduate qualifications in nursing, statistical analysis, and physiology. Glaser was a student of Paul Lazarsfeld and Robert K Merton at Columbia, although he always maintained that Hans Zetterberg was the main influence on his doctoral work.

Strauss's background was firmly in the Chicago School of Sociology, having obtained both his Masters and PhD from that department. The Chicago School in its earliest manifestation, *the first* Chicago School, centered on the work of GH Mead and Herbert Blumer. This was followed by the *second* Chicago School centered on the work of Erving Goffman and Howard Becker as well as Strauss.[1]

The early work on what became GTM was the product of these three distinctive researchers, drawing on their backgrounds, formations, and experiences. Quint's nursing background was crucial given the context of the research project itself, and it appears she did most if not all the data gathering. Some of the early papers listed all three as authors, but *Awareness* and the subsequent canonical texts were co-authored only by Glaser and Strauss. Quint published *The Nurse and the Dying Patient* in 1967 (Quint, 1967), and her subsequent work focused largely on what we would now term hospice and palliative care, practices in which she was a pioneer. When she died in 2012, *The Journal of Hospice and Palliative Nursing* included this tribute.

> She was a strong voice for nurses as professionals whose clinical expertise, knowledge, and scholarship should be valued. What many nurses remember most is that Jeanne taught us that, as nurses, we need to care for each other...To the core of her being she was committed most to the needs of seriously ill patients and families. (Ferrell, 2012)

The impact of the research project of which *Awareness* was one noteworthy outcome cannot be overstated. Not only did it encompass a series of methodological innovations and challenges to academic orthodoxy but it was also key to the re-characterization of dying as a social process. The final paragraph of *Awareness* makes the point that a substantive grounded theory "is often of great practical use long before the theory is tested with great rigor" (p. 293). The collaborative research of Quint, Strauss, and Glaser, that led to publication of *Awareness*, was certainly the basis for "great practical use," specifically in the pioneering work of Jeanne Quint on what we now recognize as hospice and palliative care.

Glaser undertook his doctoral studies at Columbia. Merton was ostensibly his supervisor, but Glaser claimed that their relationship was at best arms-length. He was, however, influenced by Lazarsfeld, a key figure in American sociology at the

ANTONY BRYANT AND CARRIE FRIESE

time, making key contributions to teaching and implementing empirical methods in social research. In his native Austria Lazarsfeld and his wife, Marie Jahoda, had led the team behind the detailed study of the town of Marienthal, published as a "sociography of an unemployed community" in the 1930s (Jahoda et al., 1932). This large-scale and participative study of the effects of unemployment on a small Austrian community became a classic of sociological research, and it led to Lazarsfeld being invited to the United States on a fellowship in the mid-1930s. The study used a range of different methods, including surveys, statistical analyses, participant observation, and action research. The report was notable for its narrative style and innovative ways of integrating data from different sources and in different formats, although it relied predominantly on quantitative data and associated forms of analysis. Lazarsfeld later felt that this reliance was misplaced or over-played, at the expense of the data itself.

Glaser (2008) credited Lazarsfeld with several key methodological insights which, in the light of later developments, can be seen as intimations of GTM, albeit with a considerable leap from Lazarsfeld's insights to GTM itself. Alvin Gouldner (1973) shed further light on Lazarsfeld's position at the time. Gouldner noted that Lazarsfeld was "surely the dean of social science methodologists in the United States today," but his (Lazarsfeld's) position was that social scientists should not be guided first and foremost by "formal canons of science" but by "the *implicit* rules and procedures which successful social scientists *tacitly* employ and embody in their researches" (emphasis in original). Gouldner went on to argue that Lazarsfeld viewed social science research proceeding "on the basis of (at first) *inarticulate* operational rules and often *ineffable* information or experience" (emphasis added). The "inarticulateness of the creative ... needs to be rendered articulate." Glaser and Strauss's writings can then be seen as the paradigm example of how the *creative* aspects of research can be rendered articulate.

Gouldner's article is noteworthy in many regards. Although not a direct colleague of Strauss, they would surely have known of each other in the 1950s as Strauss was based at the University of Chicago, Gouldner nearby at the University of Illinois. Gouldner certainly knew about what he termed "data-grounded theory," characterizing it as a continuation of the Chicago School project of aligning scientific and imaginative investigation.[2]

Gouldner noted that GTM in its early form sought to encompass the paradoxical but abiding affinity of certain forms of Positivism and Romanticism. These two perspectives seem to be diametrically opposed; the former espousing an accessible and knowable external world, amenable to objective investigation by neutral observers, the latter emanating from individual insights, predilections, and idiosyncrasies. But Gouldner argued that they shared a motivation to challenge and undermine traditional forms of authority: Positivism doing this via explicit norms and procedures, Romanticism through imagination and narrative.

GTM in its earliest form developed from and encompassed this uneasy combination. The later development of Constructivist GTM took the rigor of GTM but challenged and dispensed with the positivist idea of investigators having direct access to "data" as the basis for objective and neutral observations. Glaser's self-styled "Classic GTM" held onto positivist ideals, while Strauss and

Corbin's 1990s writings largely avoided the issue – primarily focusing on providing insights for doctoral researchers looking for guidance in using GTM.

THE CHICAGO AMALGAM – PRAGMATISM AND SYMBOLIC INTERACTION

While it is crucial to stress that both Glaser and Strauss made significant contributions to the development of GTM, it is also important to counter Glaser's later assertions that he was really the principal if not sole progenitor of the method. *The Grounded Theory Review* included the introduction to Glaser's book *Applying Grounded Theory* in 2014, in which he states:

> In this book I am writing about only the application of classic GT *as I originated it in 1967* in which the concepts of a GT theory are abstract of time, place, and people. (Glaser, 2004, emphasis added)

In fact before collaborating with Glaser, Strauss had worked with Chicago School colleagues, producing key studies such as *Boys in White* (Becker et al., 1961), now widely regarded as an embryonic example of GTM. Furthermore, in *Continual Permutations of Action* (1993 [CPoA]) Strauss refers to *Psychiatric Ideologies and Institutions* (Strauss et al., 1964) as "virtually a grounded theory" (p. 12).

Boys in White is now rightly valued as a classic text, the output from a definitive collaborative qualitative research project. The four authors are listed alphabetically rather than in order of importance to the study itself. Indeed, Becker admitted later on that

> [W]hen I showed up at the school that fall, I knew I was supposed to study medical students and medical education; but, to be truthful, I had very little idea of what I was going to do beyond 'hanging around with the students,' going to classes and whatever else presented itself. (Becker, 1998, p. 151)

This seems to exemplify the issue referred to by Lofland (see below) of *analytic interruptus*, a qualitative case study that results in nothing more than "the kind of descriptions that can be produced by conscientious journalists or literate laymen" (Lofland, 1970, p. 37).

Before the study commenced Blanche Potter Geer already had extensive experience in education research, and this was an important factor in the collaborative study. Geer went on to publish several further works with Becker. Her background in anthropology and her immersion in the research contexts she studied were key aspects of the project.

More critically, Strauss himself was key in taking the study to a more conceptual level, emanating from the "constant concern to join the level of individual actor and social micro-process" with "organizational phenomena in the macro-social structural level that influence action" (Baszanger, 1992, quoted in Nunes & Barros, 2014)

Strauss largely confirmed this in an interview given in 1994, reflecting on the period in which he was involved in the *Boys in White* project, also publishing *Mirrors and Masks*.

> I was trying to put together these viewpoints for the first time [social organization and structure], stressing on the one hand the complexity and fluidity of the interrelated collective and individual aspects that form identity, without ignoring the significance of external factors, imprecise structural limitations, and the breadth of the different forms of organization and interaction. The conception of a connection between the micro and macro levels is, you might say, the central thread of that book [Mirrors and Masks]. At that time I wasn't yet aware that the ideas expressed were obviously grounded in the mode of action of the Chicago School. Certainly, the impression I had was that what I was writing was in contact with the 'reality out there.' Today, I'm aware that this book anticipated many of the concepts I expressed and elaborated in later works. (Legewie & Schervier-Legewie, 2004)

Baszanger (1992) has argued that it was Strauss's theory of action that constituted the cornerstone for the research on medical students and later medical residents. A concern that stayed with him throughout his writing and research. The emphasis placed on work in this scholarship, and in Strauss's own, shows the influence of Everett Hughes – another University of Chicago graduate and, later, faculty member. Baszanger (1998, p. 355) has argued that if Strauss's first phased at the University of Chicago as a graduate student was primarily shaped by Blumer, Strauss's second phase at the University of Chicago as an assistant professor was primarily shaped by Hughes. Hughes is recognized for his pragmatist approaches to the sociology of work, and he initiated the research resulting in *Boys in White*.

> In 1952, Strauss returned to Chicago as an assistant professor and was, this time, "ready for Everett Hughes and all those people." "Those people" were, for the most part, former students of Hughes, a group that included Howard Becker, Erving Goffman, Fred Davis, and Eliot Freidson. At the time, they had all embarked on a program of research dealing with occupations and professions, supervised by Hughes. (Baszanger, 1998, p. 355)

The focus on work in Strauss's pragmatist sociology, a focus that persisted in his student's work, including Adele Clarke's and Susan Leigh Star's historical sociologies of science as work, is heavily informed by Hughes's interactionist approach to work as a field of inquiry (see Star, 1991).

Boys in White can then be seen as an exemplary collaborative research project, drawing on the wide range of expertise and experience of all four researchers. Much of the literature on research seems to assume that the activity is carried out by individual researchers, whereas, apart from doctorial research, it often is a team activity. Becker's book *Tricks of the Trade* fails to address this aspect in anyway. Similarly in much of the GTM literature implies that a lone researcher carries out investigation and analysis. Yet even in the original studies this was not the case. Glaser and Strauss, together with Quint, must have performed the coding across the data as a team, although the monographs that form the canonical trilogy of their early GTM works – *Awareness*, *Discovery*, and *Time* – give little or no clue regarding the details of this process. What was Quint's involvement in addition to gathering the data? Did Glaser and Strauss do all the coding? If so, was it done in concert, studying the notes and extracts together, or did each one peruse the same extract individually, later bringing their respective accounts together for a further stage of comparison, discussion, and resolution? A close reading of *Awareness* and *Time* fails to offer much clarification, given that most of the text uses the passive voice, thereby evading the issue of using the first or third person. *Discovery* uses the term "the researcher" (singular) throughout, although at one point (pp. 107–108) the following assertion is made:

> If one is working on a research team, it is also a good idea to discuss theoretical notions with one or more teammates. Teammates can help bring out the points missed, add points they have run across in their coding and data collection... (Glaser & Strauss, 1967, p. 108)

In all their joint works Glaser and Strauss only offer one brief discussion of how they worked, and even here it is only in regard to their development of the formal GT – Status Passage – not to their other research.

> Because so much relevant data and theory was "in" us from our previous work, the principal mode used to generate theory was to talk out our comparisons in lengthy conversations, and either record the conversation or take notes. We talked through virtually everything we could remember, and studied relevant literature for more data and theory. These conversations went on almost five days a week for three months. At this time we gave up in exhaustion, and with the realization that we could begin to write it all up. We achieved writing about one third of our material, as mentioned earlier. (1971, pp. 192–193)

A further account of how teamworking can facilitate the development of GTM-based conceptualization can be found in Carolyn Wiener's chapter in the Handbook (Wiener, 2007). In general, however, the issue of collaborative qualitative research is largely ignored in the methodological literature.

> Accounts and insights into how research is actually carried out are few-and-far-between, which is unfortunate since it gives free rein to the stereotype of the lone, usually male, researcher, reinforced in films, books, plays, awards of international prizes, and so on. (Bryant, 2017, p. 22)

Early-career researchers, and PhD students in particular, often feel isolated and in need of guidance, not only from experienced advisors and supervisors but also from those who are only a few steps ahead of them in their development. In recent years, students' accounts have appeared (e.g., Bryant, 2017, Chapter 19), and various forms of research workshop provide a forum for such interactions.[3]

Strauss was a key figure in the Chicago School and was influenced by the work of G. H. Mead, Robert Park, and Herbert Blumer. Mead was a pivotal figure, albeit an enigmatic one. He published very little in his lifetime but is widely regarded as a crucial link between the Pragmatism of Peirce, Dewey, and James, and the Symbolic Interactionism of Blumer and others.

Pragmatism was first articulated by C. S. Peirce, then taken up by William James (1902, 2000) and John Dewey (1927, 1931). Although Peirce later distanced himself from these two, they shared several core ideas which then became central to SI, and eventually to constructivist GTM. The first of these was a rejection of what Dewey termed "the spectator view of knowledge."

This epistemological position saw the knower as essentially passive, coming to know the world through neutral, objective observation, and reception of sensory data. The mind is a receptacle into which knowledge is poured. Our knowledge claims about the world are to be judged in terms of their accuracy in reflecting reality. Richard Rorty referred to this as the fallacy of "the mirror of nature" in his restatement of Pragmatism, *Philosophy and the Mirror of Nature* (1979), where he took aim at the philosophical idea of knowledge as representation, as a mental mirroring of a mind-external world.

The Pragmatist position in contrast sees knowledge, or rather *knowing*, as an active and interactive process; construction rather than reception or discovery. Furthermore, the process is never complete, statements about the world are *fallible*, open to revision and even rejection in the light of further investigation or experience. The key criterion for knowledge claims is that they are useful, offering practical avenues for action and understanding.

Although there are now numerous epistemological positions, Rorty's simple and eloquent distinction serves well enough: There is either the view that "knowledge is discovered" – e.g., positivism, post-positivism – or there is the view that "knowledge is constructed as part of a social process" – e.g., constructivism, interpretivism, pragmatism.[4]

Peirce rejected the concept of reality as brute existence in favor of a view of reality as something that to some extent we construct, but critically as something "that constructs us": Ultimately a theory of what he termed "concrete reasonableness." Dewey extended this line of thought, seeing society as an active communicative process, with individuals both subordinate to and mutually dependent on one another and their surroundings. In effect this encapsulates and anticipates Giddens' concept of structuration (Giddens, 1984, also Joas, 1989).

It is only a short step from this to the basic tenets of SI as will be explained below. But there are also other aspects of these developments that relate to the foundations of GTM which Strauss took up throughout his work, including both his GTM and non-GTM writings.

The problem of reconciling agency with structure has been a perennial one in the social sciences. To some extent it has been resolved with Giddens' concept of structuration, a term he introduced in the 1980s to characterize the process by which social structures are dynamically generated by social actions, simultaneously conditioning and constraining those practices and actions. This was anticipated by Dewey and is a key topic of Strauss's final work *Continual Permutations of Action* (1993). The ideas developed in this book, together with his writings on GTM, form the basis of Adele Clarke's *Situational Analysis* – see below.

Another key issue is the idea, given some prevalence in Glaser and Strauss's work, and continued by Glaser, that the GTM researcher had to shed all preconceptions at the outset of any investigation. In *Discovery* this is hinted at early on

> To generate theory ... we suggest as the best approach an initial, systematic discovery of the theory from the data of social research. Then one can be relatively sure that the theory will fit and work. (Glaser & Strauss, 1967, p. 3)

This orientation is in contrast to "theory generated by logical deduction from a priori assumptions."[5] Yet the quote above has a footnote that immediately undermines or at least qualifies this position. "Of course, the researcher does not approach reality as a tabula rasa. He (sic) must have a perspective that will help him see relevant data and abstract significant categories from his scrutiny of the data" (footnote 3, p. 3).

This anticipates and parallels a similar discussion between Blumer and some critics of Pragmatism and SI encapsulated in Blumer's response to a critical article on SI in *American Sociological Review*.

Professor Huber cannot be serious in asserting that pragmatism and symbolic interactionism treat the act of scientific inquiry as beginning with a "blank mind." Neither Mead nor I ever advanced such an absurd position. Mead's view on the matter is stated unequivocally in his classic article, "Scientific Method and the Individual Thinker": mine is given in the article, "The Methodological Position of Symbolic Interactionism." As a reading of these articles should show beyond question, both Mead and I see the act of scientific inquiry as beginning with a problem. Any reasonable consideration of what is involved in the experience of the investigator when he perceives, poses and addresses a scientific problem should show how ridiculous it is to characterize this experience as starting with a "blank mind." (Blumer, 1973)

A third aspect of this Pragmatist/SI context which was influential in the development of GTM is *abduction*. The concept of abduction was coined by C. S. Peirce, distinguishing it from induction and deduction. He defined it as "the process of forming explanatory hypotheses. It is the only logical operation which introduces any new idea" (CP 5.172). Moreover, abduction encompasses "all the operations by which theories and conceptions are engendered" (CP 5.590). For Peirce abduction was the core process in the "context of discovery," as we seek to develop new theories and explanations. It precedes deduction and induction, which only apply to the subsequent stages of the "context of justification" when theories are assessed, confirmed, or refuted. Deduction is used to derive testable consequences from explanatory hypotheses conceived through abduction, induction then assists the process of arriving at a verdict on any hypothesis based on a verdict that is dependent on the number of testable consequences that have been verified. The way in which GTM draws on this foundation is developed below.

Through Strauss GTM inherited a rich tradition based on Pragmatism and SI, albeit that in several key respects the full impact of this was only fully understood and articulated later, and not by Strauss or Glaser (see below). This overall orientation to knowledge, agency, and conceptualization encompassed the process of social co-construction propounded by Peirce and Dewey, initiation of research from a position of open-mindedness but not "a blank mind" or *tabula rasa*, and recognition and incorporation of abduction in the context of discovery. In addition, there is also Dewey's idea of "problem finding" as the initial stage of inquiry, Mead's "problematic situation," and the basic tenets of SI and Blumer's argument for the importance of sensitizing concepts in research. Taken together these formed a significant foundation for GTM, and the basis for arguing that SI and GTM form a "theory-methods" package.

A further aspect of the relationship between SI and GTM was highlighted by Lofland (1970) in his critical overview of SI, *Analytic Interruptus*

> ... we interactionists have been too "hung up" on our general imagery and have not seriously gotten on to the main work that we have set for ourselves. As a result, at least one variety of interactionism is conceptually impoverished. One way in which this impoverishment might be corrected is for those of us who use an implicit paradigm of strategic analysis to stop engaging in what I shall call "analytic interruptus" and get on with the hard work. (Lofland, 1970, p. 35)

Lofland specifically referred to the paucity of empirical detail in much SI research. The issue as he saw it was that the "qualitative case study has become identified as the research method of that variety of interactionism that here concerns us" (p. 37) Such studies only go so far, remaining at an abstract level that often "seemed little better than the kind of descriptions that can be produced by conscientious journalists or literate laymen" (p. 37).

Lofland argued that there have been some glimpses of ideas that go beyond these limitations, singling out the work of "Blumer and Hughes ... Anselm Strauss, Howard S. Becker, Alfred Lindesmith... and even C. Wright Mills in his early social psychological phase." He footnotes the book by Lindesmith and Strauss on Social Psychology (1968).

He then went on to single out Glaser and Strauss's *Discovery* with its innovative procedure of constant comparative analysis, which offers the "means by which they (Glaser and Strauss) apparently hope the conceptual landscape of interactionism (and sociology more generally) can be made more lush. They attempt to provide us with something like a manual for the germination and care of concepts in our intellectual garden. They are, in a sense, agricultural extension agents bringing help to us interactionist farmers." (pp. 38–39)

Lofland located the move from overly abstract case studies to more detailed and empirically based ones as having been signposted by Goffman's "emergence as the champion inventor of the mini-concept ...in part explicable as a response to the barrenness of the conceptual landscape of interactionist sociology." Interestingly Lofland contended that there was a sense in which "Goffman has been to Chicago interactionism what Robert K. Merton was to Harvard functionalism. The latter made a loud call for 'middle-range theory' in a similarly impoverished context, and propounded a few such theories." (p. 38)

Although he did not make the link between these two trends and the emergence of GTM, Lofland unwittingly referenced the way in which Chicago School sociology, specifically SI and its Pragmatist influences, combined with the Columbia School of Merton and Lazarsfeld, to provide the intellectual bases for GTM in the joint work of Strauss and Glaser, respectively.

"SI INSTITUTIONALIZES GT AS ITS OWN!"

We have now indicated the ways in which certain key issues of Pragmatism and SI are crucial in the context of the development of GTM. These observations will be developed as we move to demonstrate how this amalgam forms a symbiotic

58   *Symbolic Interaction and the Grounded Theory Method*

relationship with the method; one that has grown and matured in the decades since publication of the canonical GTM texts. Before going into the details of this process of methodological maturation and growth, however, we need to mention and contend with Glaser's vigorous rejection of this view.

It is now common knowledge that Glaser and Strauss diverged in their writings on GTM in the 1980s and 1990s. Glaser took specific exception to *Basics of Qualitative Research* [BQA] by Strauss and Juliet Corbin (1990), thereafter increasingly claiming that GTM was largely or even solely his idea; coining the term "Classic Grounded Theory" to refer his one, true version, directly emanating from the canonical texts and thereafter articulated in his writings. Initially this was done to distinguish his approach from the work of Strauss and Corbin, but later it also served to demarcate GTM from what he referred to as "jargonized GT," specifically the constructivist variety introduced by Kathy Charmaz in the 1990s.

The redoubt that Glaser built around "Classic GT" incorporated a strong and sustained attack on the idea that SI and GTM constituted a theory-methods package. Glaser repeatedly claimed that SI-oriented researchers were trying to take over GTM, institutionalizing it as their own. He discussed this at some length in 2005 in a chapter from *Grounded Theory Perspectives III*, later placed on-line on The Grounded Theory Review website.

> Researchers, especially in nursing, just want a theoretical perspective. SI institutionalizes GT as its own! Researchers like it because it gives them an ontology (what is data) and an epistemology (a philosophy of research). The takeover becomes structurally induced by researchers, especially nursing, in their research, since they want a theoretical perspective in advance. It gives them a feeling of power, while they do not realize that the SI takeover reduces the general method power of GT. The writers on GT as a SI method use as their legitimating source because of Strauss's (my co-author of discovery of GT) training in SI. They ignore the roots of GT in my training in concept-indicator index construction in quantitative survey research. (Glaser, 2005)

Glaser's somewhat incoherent argument does not amount to much more than a series of repeated assertions that GTM is more than SI; hardly a contentious statement. He argued that "the takeover of GT by Symbolic Interaction (SI)" amounts to "the remodeling of GT," a phrase he used repeatedly when admonishing anyone making statements about GTM with which he disagreed, but the nature of this remodeling was far from clear. Glaser's criticisms conflated data, method, and philosophical orientations regarding ontology and epistemology. His use of the latter terms in the extract above are confused and confusing.

There is reference to something termed "SI type data," which is never clarified, and Glaser then continues;

> ... GT can use SI type data and its perspective, but as a general method it can use any other type data, even other types of qualitative data, as well as quantitative, visual, document, journalistic and in any combination, and any other theoretical perspective, such as e.g. systems theory, social structural theory, structural functional theory, social organization theory, cultural theory etc. Thus, the takeover of GT as an SI perspective methodology is just discipline-perspective dominance, as discussed above, and nothing more. It, of course,

ANTONY BRYANT AND CARRIE FRIESE

dominates with a set of TCs (process, strategies, conditions, context etc) I have considered at length in chapters above. (Glaser, 2005) NB TCs refers to Theoretical Codes.

This is at best opaque: What is SI data? How could GTM incorporate structural functionalism given that GTM is oriented around social actions, whereas the latter is oriented around structures? Moreover, Glaser asserts that this institutional takeover or "discipline-perspective dominance" undermines GTM as "a general inductive method." We will explain the ways in which these criticisms miss the point, but it can be argued that Glaser's attempts to distance GTM from SI stem largely from his yearning to push Strauss as far out of the picture as possible, rather than offering any persuasive logical basis. As such we can now move on to explain the ways in which GTM and SI form a symbiotic basis for social inquiry.

GTM AND SI "A THEORY-METHODS PACKAGE"

Glaser and Strauss proposed an approach to social research that began with an open-ended, exploratory phase. Rather than seeking to prove or disprove a hypothesis, or propose one or more specific research questions, GT research should start by posing questions such as "what is going on?," "what are people doing?," "what are people saying?" This is clearly aligned with Blumer's claim above that scientific inquiry starts with "a problem." Unfortunately, in stressing that GTM research must begin in this open-ended manner, Glaser and Strauss could be understood to insist on the researcher beginning with a "blank mind," just as Huber had mistakenly claimed regarding Pragmatism and SI. We have already alluded to the opening pages of *Discovery* which hint at something akin to a "blank mind," also to the admonition in the accompanying footnote that begins "Of course, the researcher does not approach reality as a *tabula rasa.*"

Unfortunately, this caveat was largely ignored in their subsequent writings, particularly so for Glaser who, as part of his vigorous defense of what he termed "classic" GTM, persisted with the claim that GT researchers should "avoid all preconceptions," simply letting the theory "emerge from the data." The implication being that the researcher was little more than a conduit channeling the data from its specific context through to a conceptual outcome. Glaser's sustained refusal to acknowledge the active role of the researcher in *constructing* theories and concepts was somewhat perplexing, particularly given that his most important solo GTM book was *Theoretical Sensitivity* (Glaser, 1978), an extended discussion of the term introduced in *Discovery* specifically referring to the development of a researcher's ability to generate and refine conceptual insights.[6]

Why Strauss failed to develop this insight in a more interpretive and constructivist manner is somewhat baffling. His background in The Chicago School would have made him aware of the constructivist position through familiarity with Pragmatism and particularly the teaching of Mead and those who developed his ideas. Moreover, he was invited to spend time teaching in Germany by Thomas Luckmann, co-author of one of the most significant sociology texts of the 20th century, *The Social Construction of Reality* (Berger & Luckmann, 1966). Despite all this Strauss never developed this facet of GTM in his GTM writings, particularly failing to do so in the first two editions of *Basics of Qualitative Research* co-authored with Corbin. It was only with Kathy Charmaz's avowedly constructivist re-articulation of GTM in the 1990s that the full relationship between GTM and SI became overt.

The term "theory/method package" was coined by Susan Leigh Star (1989, 1991, 1995, 2007) who argued for the co-constitution of theory and method, whereby the methods we use encompass certain ideas about the nature of social life, and conversely our theories of social life orient us toward certain methods of inquiry. In the case of SI and GTM, the basic premises of SI provide an orientation that GTM builds on.

Blumer argued that SI was based on "three simple premises";

> (1) "that human beings act toward things on the basis of the meanings that they have for them" – including physical objects, activities and encounters with other human beings, institutions and other collectivities, and concepts and ideals; (2) "that the meaning of such things is derived from, or arises out of, the social interaction that one has with one's fellows"; (3) "these meanings are handled in, and modified through, an interpretative process used by the person dealing with [these] encounters". (Blumer, SI 1969, p. 2)

Although these may not be at the forefront of every GT researcher's mind, they clearly come into play once the research begins; seeking possible answers to the "what is going on?," "what are people saying and/or doing?" questions. The process of a researcher asking these questions necessarily involves the researcher as an active participant. The metaphor of "data gathering" is not appropriate, rather the metaphor should be couched in terms of the researcher(s) being "in dialog with their data" (see below).

Researchers have a proprietorial relationship with "*their* data." Each researcher will have their own distinctive relationship. If researchers work as part of a team, they will need to negotiate their perspectives which may diverge to some extent but may also reinforce one another. On the other hand, researchers working on their own need to be aware of the inevitability of partiality, taking care to couch their findings appropriately, also finding ways of gaining confirmation or confidence in analytic outcomes. GTM offers clear guidance on this specific aspect, particularly stressing the process of "constant comparison." Indeed, GTM was initially termed "the method of constant comparison."

Glaser and Strauss were at pains to offer GTM as a *rigorous* method for generating theory, hence their different forms of coding, sampling, and generating of theoretical insights and conceptualizations. Given that their original research was done in concert with one another, plus Jeanne Quint, it would have been useful to know how they worked as a team, but nowhere do they offer any real insights into how this process unwound. In *Status Passage* they offer a few hints of how they worked together in "Generating Formal Theory" (Glaser & Strauss, 1971, Chapter 9, pp. 192–193).

> Because so much relevant data and theory was 'in us' from our previous work, the principal mode used to generate theory was to talk out our comparisons in lengthy conversations, and

either record the conversation or take notes. We ... studied relevant literature for more data and theory. These conversations went on almost five days a week for three months. At this time we gave up in exhaustion, and with the realization that we could begin to write it all up.

Rigorous GTM research, whether conducted solo or as a team, involves "lengthy conversations" comprising the researcher(s) and the data. In this sense SI provides the orientation for GTM. Blumer's outline of SI can be rephrased for GTM as follows:

(1) GTM researchers acting toward all aspects and actors in the research context on the basis of the meanings that they have for them – i.e., the researchers and the other actors, including physical objects, activities, and encounters with others, institutions and other collectivities, and concepts and ideals;
(2) GTM researchers recognizing that the meaning of such things is derived from, or arises out of, the social interaction that they have with all those acting and interacting within the research context;
(3) These meanings being handled in, and modified through, a complex series of interpretative processes emanating from this range of interactions and encounters between researchers, other actors, institutions, collectivities, and so on.

This is not to say that all GTM researchers must necessarily address and account for these aspects in their research outputs. Indeed, those who adhere to Glaser's "classic" variant will likely reject or avoid any such claims. But we would argue that many of the central precepts of GTM can only be understood as emanating from the SI perspective and orientation to research and characterization of social processes. Further, that a full appreciation of the historical development of GTM can only be accounted for by recognizing the influence of the Pragmatist and SI tradition that came through Strauss. Again, this is not to downplay the importance of Glaser's contribution and the tradition represented by those working at Columbia, particularly Lazarsfeld. Indeed, Lazarsfeld was himself concerned with the practices of interpretation as distinct from discovery.

PRAGMATISM AND GTM

The initial reception of GTM in academic sociology and research practices was rather limited, but by the 1980s it had begun to spread largely through the teaching Strauss offered in USA and Europe. The notes that Strauss produced in Germany formed the basis for *Qualitative Analysis for Social Scientists* [QASS], incorporating large sections of Glaser's *Theoretical Sensitivity* (Strauss, 1987, pp. 22–23).

This was followed by the first edition of *BQA* co-authored with Corbin. A second edition followed in 1998, two years after Strauss's death, and two further substantially revised editions were published in 2007 and 2014 (Corbin & Strauss, 2008, 2015). The 1998 edition was for many years the most widely read GTM

62 *Symbolic Interaction and the Grounded Theory Method*

text, and even today it is still the preferred source for the Strauss-Corbin version of GTM, rather than the later editions.

As was mentioned earlier, Glaser took exception to the book, charging the authors with departing from the fundamental tenets of GTM. The Strauss and Corbin version was certainly distinct from the initial GTM writings by Glaser and Strauss. Although in many regards *BQA* drew on ideas already explicated in *QASS* which did not elicit any critical response from Glaser.

QASS developed from Strauss's teaching in Germany. He had been invited to spend time at the University of Konstanz by Thomas Luckmann in 1975. While there he met, among others, Hans Georg Soeffner. In 1982, Soeffner and others invited Strauss to Germany for a study visit. During this visit he produced a Study Letter for the students of sociology of the Fern Universität Hagen with the title: *Qualitative analysis in social research: Grounded theory methodology: Study Letter, University Hagen*. It was an early version of *Qualitative Analysis for Social Scientists* (Strauss, 1987).

Strauss was already well known in Germany, albeit not for GTM. A German translation of *Mirrors and Masks* (Strauss, 1959) was widely read. In the English-speaking world it was largely eclipsed by Goffman's *Presentation of Self in Everyday Life* (Goffman, 1959), but in Germany the relationship was reversed.[7]

Although Strauss did not draw on Pragmatism in his GTM writings, he must have done so in his teaching in Germany. This is exemplified in the Handbook of Grounded Theory (Bryant & Charmaz, 2007) where the contributions from Kelle, Reichertz, Strübing, and Hildenbrand all draw on Pragmatism in their respective contributions (Kelle; Reichertz: Strübing; Hidenbrand, 2007). This *Straussian* form of GTM – not to be confused with the Strauss-Corbin version – was largely unknown outside Germany until publication of the Handbook in 2007. Kathy Charmaz was key in this regard, since she was fully aware of their work and its importance for GTM as a whole.

In *QASS* Strauss was unequivocal regarding the importance of both Pragmatism and Chicago School SI in the development of GTM.

> Contributing to [GTM] development were two streams of work and thought: first, the general thrust of American Pragmatism (especially the writings of John Dewey, but also those of George H. Mead and Charles Peirce) and including its emphases on action and the problematic situation, and the necessity for conceiving of method in the context of problem solving; second, the tradition in Chicago Sociology at the University of Chicago from the 1920s through the mid-1950s, which extensively utilized field observations and intensive interviews as data-collecting techniques, and furthered much research on the sociology of work. Both the Kelle, 2007 philosophical and the sociological traditions assumed that change is a constant feature of social life but that its specific directions need to be accounted for; they also placed social interaction and social processes at the center of their attention. (Strauss, 1987, pp. 5–6)

QASS introduced the coding paradigm, conditional matrix, and axial coding, but it was only publication of *BQA* that provoked the angry response from Glaser. Recent commentators (e.g. Kelle, 2007) have, however, pointed out that Strauss and Glaser were in part responding to a common issue; how best to move from a plethora of codes to key concepts or categories with explanatory reach

ANTONY BRYANT AND CARRIE FRIESE

and power. The coding paradigm was intended to facilitate this for doctoral and early-career GT researchers. Glaser saw this as *forcing* the process of moving from data to conceptualizations; the subtitle of his rejoinder *Basics of Grounded Theory* was *Emergence* versus *Forcing* (Glaser, 1992). Yet Glaser himself had already recognized that this process could be problematic, offering what he termed 18 Theoretical Coding families in his 1978 book *Theoretical Sensitivity* (Glaser, 1978, chapter 4).

Whatever the rights and wrongs of these two approaches, the conditional matrix can be understood as an attempt to couple GTM with pragmatist theory. Here the coding that lies at the heart of GTM is put in a context of structural influences that range from the micro-level to the macro-level. Developing these conditional matrices involves locating the basic social process derived from the coding process in social space. For Strauss, social space was largely understood through the interactionist concepts of reference groups (Shibutani, 1955) and the concepts of social worlds/arenas that Strauss contributed to the development of separately from his work on the GTM. In *QASS* Strauss introduced the concepts of social worlds and arenas to GTM audiences. He defined them as follows:

> A social world is a community, not necessarily spread out or contiguous in space, which has at least one primary activity (along with related clusters of activity); sites where the activities occur; technology for implementing the activity; and organizations to further one or another aspect of the world's activities. Unless very small, there are also subworlds, segments of the larger world. Within each social world, various issues are debated, negotiated, fought out, forced, and manipulated by representatives of implicated subworlds. Arenas involve political activity but not necessarily legislative bodies and courts of law. Issues are also fought out within subworlds by their members. Representatives of other subworlds (the same and other ones) may also enter into the fray. (Strauss, 1987, pp. 230–231)

Here he sought to demonstrate how GTM could contribute to the development of social theories that span actions, processes, and structures. He developed this aspect of his work in his final book *CPoA*, which makes only passing mention of GTM. Adele Clarke's Situated Analysis [SA] develops this perspective.

SA AND GTM

Situational Analysis is a methodological extension of Grounded Theory. It is often used alongside Grounded Theory, supplementing the coding processes that are a key feature of GTM. SA involves construction of different kinds of maps while using memos to reflect analytically upon those maps. It inherits and builds upon the same roots of The Chicago School of Sociology as GTM. It is designed to take place alongside GTM, supplementing the coding practices of the latter, allowing for an exploration of basic social processes with techniques that map social spaces.

Messy maps lay out all the major actors and actants, discourses and spaces, temporalities and organizations and political–economic and social–cultural elements that come together in the situation of inquiry.

Relational maps provide a space to consider where and how those elements (which constitute the situation of inquiry) come together, or do not.

Social worlds/arenas maps continue to delineate these relations but focus on where and how different elements are bound together through patterns of commitment, partially overlap and/or diverge in the situation of inquiry or the arena. Social worlds/arenas maps frame the organizational and institutional structures and their interrelations in the broader arenas of commitment in which they are situated. These are meso-level maps, linking local practices to more general social processes.

Positional maps create discursive grids of debates arising in or forming from the situation of inquiry, asking not (at first) who is articulating what position but rather *how* the positions themselves are articulated in discourses.

Strauss's development of GTM, on the one hand, and his development of social worlds/arenas as an interactionist theory, on the other hand, inspired Adele Clarke in her creation of SA as a theory/method package. Clarke notes that while Strauss developed his theories of social life through social worlds/arenas and related concepts such as negotiated orders, he developed GTM as a method for conducting social research. Strauss rarely brought social worlds/arenas and GTM together. Situational Analysis pushes on the methodological implications of social worlds/arenas and develops the situational and positional maps from this mapping activity. It is through an expansion of Strauss's social worlds/arenas maps that Clarke brings the action-oriented focus of GTM around "the interpretative turn" in a manner that links action with meaning, and that resists the positivist assumptions that can be seen in Glaser's classic GTM.

Conditional matrices, as developed by Strauss and Corbin (1998) as part of the GTM, assumed conditions to be the context for action. SA instead understands action to be an element of the situation itself. People, things, and actions can only be interpreted and have meaning in relation to the situation in which they are found to occur. From this quite Deweyan perspective, the world itself can be viewed as a highly fluid "mosaic of situations," constantly shifting and morphing into new situations with and through other situations. This is why SA makes the situation the unit of analysis, wherein action is one of many elements. The goal of these maps and memos is to understand the situation of action as the focus of the research instead of as "context" or "conditions of action."

> The conditions *of* the situation are *in* the situation. There is no such thing as 'context'. The conditional elements of the situation need to be specified in the analysis of the situation itself as *they are constitutive of it*, not merely surrounding it or framing it or contributing to it. They *are* it. Regardless of whether some might construe them as local or global, internal or external, close-in or far away or whatever, the fundamental question is: 'How do these conditions appear – make themselves felt as consequential – *inside* the empirical situation under examination?'. At least some answers to that question can be found through doing situational analyses. (Clarke, 2005, pp. 71–72)

In effect SA extends and enhances Strauss's work, drawing both on his collaborative work on GTM and his ideas – derived from both Pragmatism and SI – seeking to encompass both social action and social structures.

GTM AND SOCIAL JUSTICE

A key feature of Pragmatism, and by implication SI, is the concern for knowledge to serve the project of emancipation. Strauss understood this, which can be seen in his introduction to the collection of works by G.H. Mead, which themselves encompass Pragmatist philosophy and SI. Here Strauss argued that through Mead we can understand the ways in which Romanticism can be reconciled with a scientific perspective, anticipating one of the key points of Gouldner's essay referred to earlier.

> The romantic writers had a profound influence upon Mead, as upon Dewey, in so far as they stressed social evolution and made the environment in some subtle sense dependent upon the acting organism But, since Mead lived after Darwin, the romantic treatment becomes in Mead's hands divested of its mysticism and is given biological and scientific twists. Most important, the role of reason again is raised in high service to human action, where rationalists and political liberals had placed it, rather than made subordinate to faith and intuition. (Gouldner, 1973, p. vii)

Strauss noted approvingly that this enabled Mead to restate problems of autonomy, freedom, and innovation in evolutionary and social rather than mechanistic and individualistic terms (Strauss, 1956, p. viii). Strauss developed these foundations, also re-orienting and revising some key aspects. For instance, as Jörg Strübing argues (2019):

> In shifting the Blumerian emphasis from *symbolic* interaction towards a more material view of sociality as situated activity, and thereby blurring the somewhat artificial separation of action from structure, Strauss both established a strictly anti-dualistic view of the social and showed the dynamic tension between doubt and belief to be the mover of human activity.[8]

In the context of GTM this foundation of Pragmatism and SI was taken up and articulated in the work of Kathy Charmaz (2000, 2006, 2008, 2014, 2017a, b), developing this rich combination initially through her pioneering of Constructivist GTM, subsequently taking this further with an unequivocal and relentlessly critical orientation to social justice. Her later writings were specially aimed at "locat[ing] the research process and product in historical, social and situational conditions," "excavating the structural contexts, power arrangements and collective ideologies" in the study focus (Charmaz, 2017a, pp. 34–35). For Charmaz, justice and injustice are "*enacted processes*" (2005, p. 508).

Emerging in part from feminism, anti-racism and related commitments to social justice, Clarke developed SA to create a more explicitly critical approach that seeks to engage, name, and address variation, heterogeneity and complexity of social life and social research methods. SA builds on Charmaz's focus on social justice by empirically rendering power relations through Strauss's concern with making the invisible visible. The maps are meant to demonstrate not only what is in the situation but also who and what are absent as an instantiation of power relations. Positional maps are particularly helpful here, allowing the analyst to specify positions that are *not* taken in the materials and to determine whether there are "implicated actors" in the situation. Tracing those who are not able to represent themselves in a situation is one of the key ways in which SA attends to power relations analytically, making invisibility empirically visible. It is in this way that SA seeks to contribute to social justice projects.

Both constructivist GTM and SA offer means for doing research for social justice in two ways. First, both are open empirically, being accessible and useable in heterogeneous research settings. Rather than preconfiguring what matters, both allow the foregrounding of elements and issues salient to the situation of inquiry as identified by researchers and participants and in extant discourse materials (Charmaz, 2017b). Both are also fiercely situated (Haraway, 1991) or, as decolonizing Indigenous researchers term it, "context-dependent" (Bainbridge et al., 2019, p. 277). Both resist "acontextual description" (Charmaz, 2006, p. 271), addressing some of the concerns that Strauss and Corbin sought to address with conditional matrices. Second, both GT coding and SA map-making and analysis are readily available for collaborative endeavors, demonstrated for many years in the "working group" format of doing GT research (Lessor, 2000; Wiener, 2007) now extended to SA.

Again, Constructivist GTM and SA, both individually and in concert, build on and enhance the Pragmatist and SI bases of GTM. Other variants encompass this, albeit not necessarily overtly or as primary features.

THE VARIETIES AND ESSENCES OF GTM

GTM now encompasses several *varieties*, a term introduced in Bryant's (2019) discussion of GTM; a stand-alone overview which also serves as an extended introduction to the Handbook of Current Developments in Grounded Theory (Bryant, 2019; Bryant & Charmaz, 2019). These varieties encompass (1) the canonical works written by Glaser and Strauss – including *Awareness, Discovery, Time*, and *Status Passage*; (2) Strauss and Corbin's work – now numbering four editions; (3) Glaser's *Classic* GT – encompassing his widely varied writings from the 1990s to 2022, also the contributions to *The Grounded Theory Review*; (4) Constructivist GT – initially articulated by Kathy Charmaz, particularly in *Constructing Grounded Theory* (2006), later developed by Charmaz and Bryant; (5) Straussian GT – emanating from the German-speaking tradition, centered on Pragmatism, that developed in the wake of Strauss's teaching in Germany in the 1980s.

There is considerable congruence across some of these, for instance the Constructivist and Straussian perspectives build upon similar foundations in a mutually supportive and enhancing manner. It is also not an exhaustive list. For example, there are those who write from a perspective of Critical GTM, and Informed GTM. There is also Situational Analysis which, as we explained earlier, is best seen as an important adjunct to GTM, among other things harnessing Strauss's non-GTM writing on social arenas and social action. In addition, the current interest in Mixed Methods has resulted in advocacy of using GTM with other approaches including Action Research and Ethnography (e.g., Friese, 2022; Johnson & Walsh, 2019).

The early divergence in GTM developed from Glaser's partially justified concern at the ways in which the Strauss-Corbin approach might result in undermining the initial motivations and innovations of GTM evinced in the early

ANTONY BRYANT AND CARRIE FRIESE

Glaser-Strauss writings. This was a key motivation in many of Glaser's writings from 1990s, unfortunately often incorporating exaggerated and misconceived arguments concerned with distancing his Classic GTM from anything else claiming to be a valid form of the method. Although this unfortunate trend continues to the extent among some GTM practitioners, in the large there is a far more open-minded view in the GTM user community. GTM researchers for the most part readily accept that there are a variety of orientations to the method, with differing stresses and primary concerns. These are most constructively seen as complementary rather than antagonistic.

Glaser himself often stressed that GTM was itself a grounded theory. As such it must satisfy the criteria that Glaser and Strauss themselves specified for a grounded theory. It must be useful – i.e., "work," have grab and fit, and be "modifiable." Strauss and Corbin also understood this, their chapter in The Handbook of Qualitative Research (1994) contains the following; ...

> no inventor has permanent possession of the invention – certainly not even its name – and furthermore we would not wish to do so. No doubt we will always prefer the later versions of grounded theory that are closest to or elaborate our own, but a child once launched is very much subject to a combination of its origins and the evolving contingencies of life. Can it be otherwise with a methodology? (Strauss & Corbin, 1994, p. 283)

We would argue that the development of constructivist GTM, Straussian-Pragmatist GTM, and SA in particular fall within this remit, exemplifying ways in which this innovative and challenging approach to social inquiry provides the basis for enhancement and rearticulation of its founding statements while adhering to the criteria and key aspects of the method. To demonstrate this, we now offer an outline of what can be termed the *essences* of GTM, illustrating the ways in which Pragmatism and SI comprise key foundations for the method.

Aristotle is credited with raising the distinction between the essential and the accidental characteristics of an entity. The SEP entry on this distinction offers the following summation:

> The distinction between essential versus accidental properties has been characterized in various ways, but it is currently most commonly understood in modal terms: an essential property of an object is a property that it must have while an accidental property of an object is one that it happens to have but that it could lack. (Robertson Ishii & Atkins, 2008)

Chapter 4 of Bryant's book on GTM explains the numerous *accidents* of GTM, aspects that were included in the earlier GTM texts, but which can be and have been dispensed with or surpassed in later years – examples include delaying the literature review, and the rationale for using GTM when "there is no existing research" (For further details see Bryant, 2017; Table 4.4).

The Senior Editor's introduction to The Handbook of Current Developments in Grounded Theory lists the essences as follows:

- Coding-cum-analysis-cum-memoing – the form and strategy for coding in GTM was and remains innovative in many ways, including its starting point,

68 *Symbolic Interaction and the Grounded Theory Method*

and its iterative aspect; also, the link to memoing, which was absent from the earliest writings, but is now a key aspect.

- Substantive and formal theory generation – this developed in part from Merton's idea that research should aim to provide theories of the middle range. In contrast to mid-twentieth-century preoccupations with hypothetical structural explanations of whole societies, Merton (1957) advocated constructing theories to explain empirical problems – both Substantive Grounded Theories and Formal Grounded Theories are examples of this. Herbert Blumer, a close colleague of Strauss in Chicago, similarly criticized "grand theory" in his essay "What is wrong with social theory?" (1954).
- Purposive/convenience sampling followed by theoretical sampling – qualitative sampling was and still is misunderstood, particularly by those whose research experience and expertise is derived largely or wholly from a quantitative background; GTM offers a basis for clarifying sampling issues for qualitative research in general.
- Theoretical saturation – often seen as a weakness of GTM, but, used correctly, it is in fact a strength of the method, since unlike many methods, it offers the rationale for claiming to have reached an interim end-point for a research endeavor.
- Use of the literature – initially to establish the basis for the research, but far more importantly, to refer to and engage with the relevant literature as an additional and critical form of data against which interim or later analyses can be positioned – this is what is referred to as theoretical coding.
- Criteria – fit, grab, work, modifiability; and also Charmaz's credibility, originality, resonance, usefulness.
- Openness to serendipity.
- Pragmatism – particularly the ways in which GTM now has to be understood as a method for "enacting abstraction and abduction."

(Bryant, 2017, p. xxvi)

To this list we would now add that GTM necessarily involves investigating "action and the social world *from the point of view of the actors themselves*," drawing on theoretical perspectives including "symbolic interactionism, phenomenology, hermeneutics, ethnomethodology" with an orientation toward "meaning, context, interpretation, understanding and reflexivity" (Knoblauch et al., quoted by Clarke, 2017, p. 5) This was present in GTM from the start, albeit unacknowledged or merely hinted at. But as we stated above, this Pragmatist-SI foundation is now far more widely recognized and has been further articulated in GTM-oriented research with the advent of Constructivist GTM and SA.

INDUCTION AND ABDUCTION

Before concluding it is important to address the issue of induction and abduction. Glaser insisted throughout his writings that GTM is inductive.

Modifiability is basic to grounded theory. Because they are generated through inductive logic, grounded theories are naturally modifiable. With induction, the analyst generalizes from a number of cases in which something is true and infers that the same thing is true of a whole class. In grounded theory, these inferences take the form of tentative hypotheses (Glaser, 1978, 2009)

GT is simply a general inductive method that conceptualizes into a generated theory, which explains the latent patterns in any type of data of a general area, whether substantive or formal. (Glaser, 2005)

In the 2005 piece from which the extract above is taken, Glaser uses the term "induction" or "inductive" 11 times in support of his argument that GTM is a method "possessed by no discipline or theoretical perspective or data type" – particularly not by SI.

It is now a commonplace for people to characterize GTM as "an inductive method" when reporting on their research, whether in a doctoral thesis or journal article. The term is mentioned in *Discovery*, but in a very specific manner. It first appears in Chapter V where Glaser and Strauss (1967, p. 104) refer to grounded theory as "the constant comparative method," and distinguish it from "analytic induction" as follows:

Analytic induction has been concerned with generating and proving an integrated, limited, precise, universally applicable theory of causes accounting for a specific behavior (e.g., drug addiction, embezzlement). ... It tests a limited number of hypotheses with all available data, consisting of numbers of clearly defined and carefully selected cases of phenomena. ... The theory is generated by the reformation of hypotheses and redefinition of the phenomena forced by constantly confronting the theory with negative cases, cases which do not confirm the current formulation.

In contrast to analytic induction, the constant comparative method is concerned with generating and plausibly suggesting (but not provisionally testing) many categories, properties, and hypotheses about general problems (e.g., the distribution of services according to the social value of clients). Some of these properties may be causes, as in analytic induction, but unlike analytic induction, others are conditions, consequences, dimensions, types, processes, etc. ... the constant comparisons required by both methods differ in breadth of purpose, extent of comparing, and what data and ideas are compared. (quoted in Bryant, 2017, p. 95, emphasis added)

Kelle (2019) offers a helpful note on analytic induction:

[T]heoretical propositions are developed, built and modified through chains of inferences. To obtain a deeper understanding of this process it is important to differentiate between different kinds of theoretical statements with regard to their scope, source, degree of explicitness and empirical content.

Hammersley (2004, 2010, 2011) has written extensively on analytic induction and its comparison with GTM. He traces the former through the work of several colleagues and mentors of Strauss, including Becker and Lindesmith, the latter with whom Strauss co-authored an enduring standard text on social psychology (2009). Hammersley argues that Glaser and Strauss were at pains to distinguish between GTM and analytic induction. GTM was a method that used "explicit coding ... [to] ... serve the function of ... generating and developing theories." In contrast, analytic induction was a method to generate theory "by the *reformulation of hypotheses and redefinition of the phenomena forced by constantly confronting the theory with negative cases*, cases which do not confirm the current formulation" (Hammersley, 2010, emphasis added).

It must be stressed that most of the discussion on induction in *Discovery* refers to something distinct from GTM itself – i.e., analytic induction, not induction per se. There is, however, one succinct and unambiguous statement that is clearly the source of the mantra-like statement found in numerous GTM writings: "Grounded Theory is an inductive method."

> In comparing incidents, the analyst learns to see his categories in terms of both their internal development and their changing relations to other categories. For example, as the nurse learns more about the patient, her calculations of social loss change; and these recalculations change her social loss stories, her loss rationales and her care of the patient. *This is an inductive method of theory development.* (Glaser & Strauss, 1967, p. 114, emphasis added)

Glaser's subsequent writing consistently reiterated this view, albeit offering little or no further explanation. Strauss on the other hand soon distanced himself from this assertion. In the chapter on GTM he and Corbin wrote for the first edition of The Handbook of Qualitative Research they noted the following:

> Thoughtful reaction against restrictive prior theories and theoretical models can be salutary, but too rigid a conception of induction can lead to sterile or boring studies. Alas, grounded theory has been used as a justification for such studies. This has occurred as a result of the initial presentation of grounded theory in The Discovery of Grounded Theory that had led to a persistent and unfortunate misunderstanding about what was being advocated. *Because of the partly rhetorical purpose of that book and the authors' emphasis on the need for grounded theory, Glaser and Strauss overplayed the inductive aspects.* (Strauss & Corbin, 1994, p. 277, emphasis added)

Yet well before this Strauss began to stress that GTM was not fundamentally an inductive method. Charmaz notes that as early as 1969 Strauss described GTM as "an abductive method" (2014, pp. 200–203), although the ramifications of this were not developed by Strauss in his later writings.[9] On the other hand, he must have developed this in his teaching in Germany since it is a striking feature of this strand of GTM. If it was not widely understood beforehand, then it certainly came to the fore in the 2007 Handbook with the contributions particularly of Reichertz and Strübing, and this aspect of GTM has been developed and widely discussed in the aftermath, evidenced for instance in the chapters by NAMES in Current Developments (Bryant & Charmaz, 2007, 2019).

Charmaz in the first edition of *Constructing* offered the following definition.

> Abduction: a type of reasoning that begins by examining data and after scrutiny of these data, *entertains all possible explanations for the observed data*, and then forms hypotheses to confirm or disconfirm until the researcher arrives at the most plausible interpretation of the observed data. (Charmaz, 2006, p. 186, emphasis added)

Abduction is indelibly associated with the writings of Peirce. It is a third mode of reasoning, additional to and distinct from induction and deduction. (See Bryant, 2017, Chapter 13) Jo Reichertz, one of Strauss's students in Germany, has written extensively on this topic in the context of GTM. He notes that the term itself was "[F]irst introduced in 1597 by Julius Pacius to translate the

ANTONY BRYANT AND CARRIE FRIESE

Aristotelian concept *apagoge*." For a further 300 years or so it "remained quite unnoticed" until it was taken up by one of the founders of Pragmatism, C. S. Peirce, who defined it as "the process of forming explanatory hypotheses." Peirce's assertion was that "[I]t is the only logical operation which introduces any new idea" (Peirce, C. S. (1931–1935). He also claimed that abduction incorporates "all the operations by which theories and conceptions are engendered" (CP 5.590). Given the stress that Glaser and Strauss placed on GTM as a process of developing new theoretical insights, and noting Strauss's background in Pragmatism it is not surprising that there is now a growing recognition that although the process of induction certainly has a limited role in GTM, it is abduction that needs to be understood as a far more important – indeed essential – aspect.

Reichertz defined abduction as follows:

> Something unintelligible is discovered in the data, and *on the basis of the mental design of a new rule the rule is discovered or invented* and, at the same time, it also becomes clear what the case is. The logical form of this operation is that of abduction. Here one has decided (with whatever degree of awareness and for whatever reasons) no longer to adhere to the conventional view of things. (Reichertz, 2007, p. 219 emphasis added)

From this assertion by Reichertz, abduction can be seen to be something of a process involving a logical "leap," as opposed to the more careful and considered processes of induction and deduction. Moreover, abduction is both a cognitive process and a logical one. The two aspects being at least equal, perhaps with the former predominating at least in the early phases.

For Peirce abduction was not a logical form of inference in the same category as induction and deduction. Abduction occurs "like lightning," rather than as a careful and considered thought process. This might seem to imply that the discovery of new ideas is something of a haphazard process, requiring luck and perhaps precisely those instances of "immaculate conceptualization" that Glaser disdains. But this is to ignore the ways in which even experienced practitioners and experts often respond to the unexpected and seemingly inexplicable. At such times, unable to resort to the rules and the received wisdom, one must allow oneself "to experience surprise, puzzlement, or confusion in a situation which [is] uncertain or unique."

Reichertz stresses that although

> ...abductions cannot be forced by a specific procedural program, one can induce situations... in which abductions fit. According to Peirce, the presence of genuine doubt or uncertainty or fear or great pressure to act is a favorable *weather situation* for abductive lightning to strike. (Reichertz, 2007, p. 221, emphasis in original)

Peirce also advised the investigator to "let his mind wander with no specific goal." A "mental game without rules he calls *musement*, a game of meditation, or daydreaming."

Although these two may seem to differ

> [I]n both cases the procedures mean that the consciously working mind, relying on logical rules, is outmanoeuvred. Peirce-the-detective allows no time for the calculating mind to busy itself with the solution of his problem, and Peirce-the-daydreamer switches off his power of logical judgment by entrusting himself to the *breath of heaven*. (Reichertz, 2007, p. 221)

72 *Symbolic Interaction and the Grounded Theory Method*

These both resonate with the GTM advice to enter the research setting with an open mind, ready to be surprised, allowing the "data" to influence the process of investigation; then moving swiftly through the data, to facilitate this "out-maneuvering" of one's prior knowledge and expectations. Abduction is a cognitive process closely related to or perhaps even subsumed by Glaser and Strauss's concept of theoretical sensitivity, emanating from the researcher(s) working closely with the data.

Reichertz explains the divergence between Glaser and Strauss in their later writings in terms oriented around the idea of abduction. Strauss takes it up and uses it to distance his idea of the method, not only from verificationist deductive methods of investigation but also from being inductive in any straightforward manner: The stress is on generating new ideas and concepts. Glaser, on the other hand, adheres to the centrality of induction and emergence.[10] To justify his view of Strauss's work, Reichertz offers an example in Strauss's writings.

> Example (a): One passage is very clear as regards "induction" as a basis of coding. It here becomes apparent that *Strauss doesn't mean the logical conclusion "induction" at all* but rather all the actions and attitudes which lead to a hypothesis, and exactly this is also addressed by Peirce with his considerations: "Induction refers to the actions that lead to discovery of a hypothesis – that is, *having a hunch or an idea, then converting it into an hypothesis* and assessing whether it might provisionally work as at least a partial condition for a type of event, act, relationship, strategy, etc." (Strauss, 1987, p. 11f; quoted in Reichertz, 2007, p. 224; emphasis added)

GTM, taking its prompt from Peirce, offers an approach to investigation that enhances the possibility of new insights arising precisely by guiding researchers to "stay close to the data," open their minds to new insights, encourage opportunities for serendipity, and generally outwit the "consciously working mind" that all-too-often results in simply confirming our existing ideas – confirmation bias – and reinforcing our "overlearning."

GTM writers now cannot ignore abduction, either needing to explain how it operates or to discount it in some manner. Ultimately, we concur with Reichertz (2019) who argues that "[T]he logic of Strauss's GT thus permits abductive reasoning, counts on it, enables it, grants it place. More is not necessary."[11]

Many texts, however, continue to claim simply that GTM is "an inductive method," a trope that has been taken up by generations of students and other researchers in a largely unexamined manner.[12]

CONCLUSION

The opening paragraph of *Discovery* contains the following statement and claim.

> Mentioning the Department of Sociology at Columbia University brings to mind Merton's middle-range theory and Lazarsfeld's quantitative methodology. On the other hand, the "Chicago tradition" (from the 1920's to the 1950's) is associated with down-to-earth qualitative research, a less than rigorous methodology, and an unintegrated presentation of theory. By an ironic conjunction of careers, the authors of this book were trained, respectively, at Columbia and Chicago. The point is noted only to emphasize our conviction that neither of

these traditions – nor any other in postwar sociology – has been successful at closing the embarrassing gap between theory and empirical research. The gap is as wide today as it was in 1941, when Blumer commented on it, and in 1949, when Merton optimistically suggested a solution.

Although our key concern here has been to stress the ways in which GTM developed ideas already present in Pragmatism and SI, in no way are we disparaging other aspects drawn on by Glaser and Strauss from their distinctive backgrounds. Each contributed to GTM, offering a profound, powerful, and challenging research strategy that has stood the test of time and is now recognized as one of, if not the most widely used research methods. A popularity that is inevitably accompanied by examples of misuse and unfounded claims by researchers, but this is more than outweighed by the many insightful and practical outcomes of GTM-based research.

In 1998, Glaser offered his account of the development of GTM in a chapter "The Roots of Grounded Theory."[13] It opens with the bizarre claim that "Grounded theory was discovered, not invented" (Glaser, 1998, p. 21). To be fair, this is somewhat tempered by what follows, namely the view that

...its discovery is rooted in what may be considered some of the best schools and methodological thought in sociology in the sixties. ... Columbia University (New York) and the University of Chicago. ... also [drawing] on the methodology work done at the Sorbonne, Michigan, Standford and Harvard. (Glaser, 1998, p. 21)

Glaser's account stresses the input particularly from the influence of Paul Lazarsfeld and Robert Merton at Columbia, "... I was learning inductive quantitative analysis from Lazarsfeld et al. ... I was studying theory construction ... from Merton. His most valuable lesson to me was theoretical coding."

Anyone looking to understand the archeology and genealogy of GTM must acknowledge Glaser's influence.[14] The chapter referred to above details many key techniques which Glaser incorporated into GTM, including "index formation and constat comparisons," "latent patterns," and the primacy of generation over verification. Glaser explains each of them, and their importance for GTM, but they are of a different order to the influence of Pragmatism and SI on the method. Glaser's techniques provide researchers with clear guidelines for what to do and how to progress when using GTM. The philosophical basis, rationale, and overarching motivation, however, all come primarily from Pragmatism and SI.

GTM is the most widely used research method, something that was already apparent in the 1990s, 30 years after its "discovery"! In the subsequent 30 years this development has continued, accompanied by further articulation and enhancement of the method itself. In effect this is testimony to the power of the method, and its *modifiability*. Strengthening the link between GTM and SI is not a case of a disciplinary takeover, with SI "institutionalizing GTM as its own," rather it is an indication of the potency of a method that offered a challenge and confidence-giving innovation to researchers in the 1960s, and which continues to provide a rich foundation and insight to researchers in all stages of their career and across all levels of experience.

NOTES

1. For further details of these two schools see Pascale, C. -M. (2010). *Cartographies of Knowledge*. Sage.

2. Glaser was certainly in contact with Gouldner. In his 1963 paper on the scientist–supervisor relationship, Glaser specifically thanks Gouldner for his help in its preparation (Glaser, 1963/2010).

3. The image of the lone researcher is discussed in Bryant (2019, Chapter 4).

4. Examples of this plethora of perspectives can be found, for instance, in the Editors' introduction and chapters in the various editions of *The Handbook of Qualitative Research* (Denzin & Lincoln, 1994–2011).

5. The problematic idea of the researcher as a tabula rasa has been a sustained aspect of critiques of GTM.

6. Charmaz noted that Blumer criticized *Discovery* and GTM in general, arguing that "the tabula rasa view is open to serious doubt"; going on to accuse Glaser and Strauss of "espousing pure induction" (Charmaz, 1990, repr, Glaser, 1994 (Ed), p. 71).

7. Glaser contended erroneously that *Mirrors and Masks* failed to sell because it was not fully *emergent* (Glaser, 2016, p. 5). The book was first published in 1959, well before Strauss met Glaser, and it is clearly the product of someone immersed in The Chicago School, rather than someone developing a Grounded Theory; forced or emergent!

8. Strauss sought to overcome the duality between action and structure. This is the core of *Continual Permutations of Action* (Strauss, 1993).

9. Kathy often related the episode of how in 1968 Strauss came dancing up to her and announced that Grounded Theory was not an inductive method but an abductive one.

10. A recent article in the Glaserian journal *The Grounded Theory Review* by its then editor, Alvita Nathaniel, seeks to incorporate abduction into Glaser's *Classic GTM*, equating the term with Glaser's *Theoretical Codes*. Although the discussion includes a reasonable if somewhat cryptic summary of abduction, the article fails to address any of the GTM-oriented or more general literature on the topic, simply referring briefly to Peirce. The noteworthy aspect of the piece, however, is the belated – albeit misunderstood – recognition of abduction among this group of GTM researchers (Nathaniel, 2023).

11. Tavory and Timmermans on the other hand have taken a different and highly specious approach, arguing that what they term "abductive analysis" is completely distinct from GTM (Tavory & Timmermans, 2019). Their position is based on a highly questionable and partial characterization of GTM, largely based on Strauss and Corbin's coding paradigm. See Bryant (2019, pp. 74–76).

12. Abduction is an important and complex topic, particularly so for GTM. This section draws on key chapters from both Handbooks, also from Bryant (2019, Chapter 13). Readers are advised to go to these sources for further explanation and suggestions for further reading.

13. This chapter also contains Glaser's claim that he "wrote 90% of the book (*Discovery*) while he (Strauss) was in Europe ... he reviewed my eight chapters, added here and there, and then wrote three more chapters himself" (p. 22). This has been seen by those following *Classic* GT as some justification for Glaser's proprietorial claim to the method, but the assertion is highly contentious. Strauss died in 1996, so there was no-one who could counter the assertion. Moreover, Glaser's writings from the late 1990s onwards, published through *The Sociology Press*, which he owned and ran, are written in a very different style to the well-argued and fluent language of *Awareness* and *Discovery*. It may well be that Glaser drafted much of the material for *Discovery*, but given the substantive content of the canonical GTM books they co-authored, to relegate Strauss to a minor contributor is highly questionable.

14. These two aspects of GTM are discussed in Bryant (2017, pp. 17–21).

REFERENCES

Bainbridge, R., McCalman, J., Redman-Maclaren, M, & Whiteside, M. (2019). Grounded theory as systems science: Working with indigenous nations for social justice. In A. Bryant & K. Charmaz (Eds.), *Sage Handbook of current developments in grounded theory.* Sage.

Baszanger, I. (1992). Les chantiers d'un interactionniste américain. In A. Strauss (Ed.), *La trame de la negociation: Sociologie qualitative et interactionnisme* (pp. 11–63) L'Harmattan.

Baszanger, I. (1998). The work sites of an American interactionist: Anselm L. Strauss, 1917–1996. *Symbolic Interaction, 21,* 353–377. https://doi.org/10.1525/si.1998.21.4.353

Becker, H. (1998). *Tricks of the trade: How to think about your research while you're doing it.* University of Chicago Press.

Becker, H., Geer, B., Hughes, E. C., & Strauss, A. L. (1961). *Boys in white.* University of Chicago Press.

Berger, P., & Luckmann, T. (1966). *The social construction of reality: A treatise in the sociology of knowledge.* Doubleday Anchor Books.

Blumer, H. (1954/1969). *Symbolic interactionism: Perspective and method.* Prentice-Hall.

Blumer, H. (1973, December). A note on symbolic interactionism. *American Sociological Review, 38*(6), 797–798.

Bryant, A. (2017). *Grounded theory and grounded theorizing: Pragmatism in research practice.* Oxford.

Bryant, A. (2019). *The varieties of grounded theory.* SAGE Swifts.

Bryant, A. & Charmaz, K. (Eds.). (2007). *The SAGE handbook of grounded theory.* Sage.

Bryant, A. & Charmaz, K. (Eds.). (2019). *The SAGE handbook of current developments in grounded theory.* Sage.

Charmaz, K. (1990/1994). Chapter 3 "Discovering" chronic illness: Using grounded theory. In B. Glaser (Ed.), *More grounded theory methodology: A reader* (pp. 65–94). Sociology Press. Originally in *Soc Sci Med, 30*(11), 1161–1172, 1990.

Charmaz, K. (2000). Grounded theory: Objectivist and constructivist methods. In N. K. Denzin & Y. S. Lincoln (Eds.), *Handbook of qualitative research* (2nd ed., pp. 509–535). Sage.

Charmaz, K. (2005). *Grounded theory methods in social justice research.* Denzin and Lincoln.

Charmaz, K. (2006). *Constructing grounded theory: A practical guide through qualitative analysis.* Sage.

Charmaz, K. (2008). Grounded theory. In J. A. Smith (Ed.), *Qualitative psychology: A practical guide to research methods* (2nd ed., pp. 81–110). Sage.

Charmaz, K. (2014). *Constructing grounded theory: A practical guide through qualitative analysis* (2nd ed.). Sage.

Charmaz, K. (2017a). The power of constructivist grounded theory for critical inquiry. *Qualitative Inquiry, 23*(1), 34–45.

Charmaz, K. (2017b). Continuities, contradictions, and critical inquiry in grounded theory. *International Journal of Qualitative Methods, 16,* 1–8. https://doi.org/10.1177/1609406 917719350

Charmaz, K. (2020). 'With Constructivist Grounded Theory You Can't Hide': Social justice research and critical inquiry in the public sphere. *Qualitative Inquiry, 26*(2), 165–176.

Clarke, A. (2005). *Situational analysis.* Sage.

Clarke, C. (2017). Situating grounded theory and situational analysis in interpretive qualitative inquiry. In A. Bryant & K. Charmaz (Eds.), *The Sage handbook of current developments in grounded theory.* Sage.

Corbin, J. M., & Strauss, A. L. (2008). *Basics of qualitative research: Techniques and procedures for developing grounded theory* (3rd ed.). Sage.

Corbin, J. M., & Strauss, A. L. (2015). *Basics of qualitative research: Techniques and procedures for developing grounded theory* (4th ed.). Sage.

Denzin, N. K., & Lincoln, Y. S. (Eds.). (2011 [1994, 2000, 2005]), *The SAGE handbook of qualitative research* (1st–4th ed.). SAGE.

Dewey, J. (1927). *The public and its problems.* Henry Holt.

Dewey, J., (1931). The development of American pragmatism. In J. Dewey (Ed.), *Philosophy and civilization* (pp. 13–35). Minton, Balch.

Ferrell, B. (2012, June). Tribute to Jeanne Quint Benoliel, DNSc, RN, FAAN. *Journal of Hospice & Palliative Nursing, 14*(4), 245–246.

Friese, C. (2022). Reflections on using SA in a large, mixed-methods project. In A. Clarke, R. Washburn, & C. Friese (Eds.), *Situational analysis in practice: Mapping relationalities across disciplines.* Routledge.

Giddens, A. (1984). *The constitution of society.* Polity Press.

Glaser, B. G. (1963/2010). Attraction, autonomy, and reciprocity in the scientist – Supervisor relationship. repr *The Grounded Theory Review, 9*(1). Originally published in Administrative Science Quarterly, *8*(3), 1963, 379–398.

Glaser, B. G. (1978). *Theoretical sensitivity.* Sociology Press.

Glaser, B. G. (1992). *Basics of grounded theory: Emergence vs. forcing.* Sociology Press.

Glaser, B. G. (1994). *Ed More grounded theory methodology: A reader.* Sociology Press.

Glaser, B. G. (1998). *Doing grounded theory: Issues and discussions.* Sociology Press.

Glaser, B. G. (2005, March). The impact of symbolic interaction on grounded theory. *Grounded Theory Review, 4*(2). See also (Chapter 10), *Grounded theory perspective III: Theoretical coding.* Sociology Press. http://ground-edtheoryreview.com/2005/03/30/1575/

Glaser, B. G. (2004, May). Remodeling grounded theory. *Forum Qualitative Sozialforschung [Forum: Qualitative Social Research (FQS)], 5*(2). 4. [Barney G. Glaser with the assistance of Judith Holton]. http://www.qualitative-research.net/index.php/fqs/article/view/607/1315

Glaser, B. G. (2008). *Jargonizing: Using the grounded theory vocabulary.* Sociology Press.

Glaser, B. G. (2009). *Doing quantitative grounded theory.* Sociology Press.

Glaser, B. G. (2016). *The grounded theory perspective: Its origins and growth.* Sociology Press.

Glaser, B. G., & Strauss, A. L. (1965). *Awareness of dying.* Aldine.

Glaser, B. G., & Strauss, A. L. (1967). *The discovery of grounded theory: Strategies for qualitative research.* Aldine.

Glaser, B. G., & Strauss, A. L. (1968). *Time for dying.* Aldine.

Glaser, B. G., & Strauss, A. L. (1971). *Status passage.* Aldine Atherton.

Goffman, E. (1959). *The presentation of self in everyday life.* Doubleday Anchor Books.

Gouldner, A. (1973). Romanticism and classicism: Deep structures in social science. In A. Gouldner (Ed.), *For sociology: Renewal and critique in sociology today.* Basic Books. www. autodidactproject.org/other/ gouldner5.html

Hammersley, M. (2004). Analytic induction. In M. S. Lewis-Beck, A. Bryman, & T. F. Liao (Eds.), *The Sage encyclopedia of social science research methods* (pp. 16–18). Sage.

Hammersley, M. (2010). A historical and comparative note on the relationship between analytic induction and grounded theorising. *Forum Qualitative Sozialforschung [Forum: Qualitative Social Research], 11*(2). https://doi.org/10.17169/fqs-11.2.1400

Hammersley, M. (2011). On Becker's studies of marijuana use as an example of analytic induction. *Philosophy of the Social Sciences, 41*(4), 535–566.

Haraway, D. (1991). Situated knowledges: The science question in feminism and the privilege of partial perspective. In D. Haraway (Ed.), *Simians, cyborgs, and women: The reinvention of nature* (pp. 183–202). Routledge.

Hildenbrand, B. (2007). Mediating structure and interaction in grounded theory. In A. Bryant & K. Charmaz (Eds.), *Handbook of grounded theory* (pp. 539–564). Sage.

Jahoda, M., Lazarsfeld, P. F., & Zeisel, H. (1932/1971). *Marienthal: The sociography of an unemployed community.* Routledge. Originally published in German, 1932.

James, W. (1902). *The varieties of religious experience.* Longmans.

James, W. (2000). *Pragmatism and other writings.* Penguin Classics.

Joas, H. (1989). A sociological transformation of the philosophy of praxis: Anthony Giddens's theory of structuration. In Joas, H. (Ed.), *Pragmatism and social theory.* U of Chicago Press. Published in English in International Sociology Vol. 2 (1987), pp. 13–26; © 1989 by Hans Joas. (Originally published in German, in Zeitschrift für Soziologie 15, 1986.)

Johnson, R. B., & Walsh, I. (2019). Mixed grounded theory: Merging grounded theory with mixed methods and multimethod research. In A. Bryant, & K. Charmaz (Eds.), The *Sage* handbook of current developments in grounded theory. Sage.

Kelle, U. (2007). The development of categories: Different approaches in grounded theory. In A. Bryant & K. Charmaz (Eds.), *The SAGE handbook of grounded theory* (pp. 191–213). Sage.

Kelle, U. (2019). The status of theories and models in grounded theory. In A. Bryant & K. Charmaz (Eds.), *The SAGE handbook of current developments in grounded theory*. Sage.

Legewie, H., & Schervier-Legewie, B. (2004). Anselm Strauss: Research is hard work, it's always a bit suffering. Therefore, on the other side research should be fun. *Forum Qualitative Sozialforschung, [Forum: Qualitative Social Research (FQS)]. 5*(3). https://doi.org/10.17169/fqs-5.3.562

Lessor, R. (2000). Using the team approach of Anselm Strauss in action research: Consulting on a project on global education. *Sociological Perspectives, 43*(4), S133–S147.

Lindesmith, A. R., & Strauss, A. L. (1968). *Social psychology.* Holt, Rinehart & Winston.

Lofland, J. (1970). Interactionist imagery and analytic interruptus. In T. Shibutani (Ed.), *Human nature and collective behavior: Essays in honor of Herbert Blumer.* Transaction Books.

Merton, R. K. (1957). *Social theory and social structure.* Free Press.

Nathaniel, A. (2023, June). From the editor's desk: Research Publishing: The unique value of the grounded theory review. *The Grounded Theory Review, 22,* 1. https://groundedtheoryreview.com/2023/06/22/from-the-editors-desk-6/. Accessed 9 December 2024.

Nunes, E. D., & de Barros, N. F. (2014). Boys in white: A classic of qualitative research turns 50. *História, Ciências, Saúde – Manguinhos, 21*(4). http://www.scielo.br/hcsm

Peirce, C. S. (1931–1935). *The collected papers of Charles S. Peirce.* 8 Volumes. Harvard University Press.

Quint, J. (1967). *The nurse and the dying patient.* Macmillan.

Reichertz, J. (2007). Abduction: The logic of discovery in grounded theory. In A. Bryant & K. Charmaz (Eds.), *The Sage handbook of grounded theory* (pp. 214–228). Sage.

Reichertz, J. (2019). Abduction: The logic of discovery of grounded theory – An updated review. In A. Bryant & K. Charmaz (Eds.), *The SAGE handbook of current developments in grounded theory.* Sage.

Robertson Ishii, T., & Atkins, P. (2008). Essential vs. accidental properties. In E. N. Zalta & U. Nodelman (Eds.), *The Stanford encyclopedia of philosophy* (Spring 2023 Edition), https://plato.stanford.edu/archives/spr2023/entries/essential-accidental/. Accessed December 9, 2024.

Rorty, R. (1979). *Philosophy and the mirror of nature.* Princeton University Press.

Shibutani, T. (1955). Reference groups as perspectives. *American Journal of Sociology, 60,* 562–569.

Star, S. L. (1991). The sociology of the invisible: The primacy of work in the writings of Anselm Strauss. In D. R. Maines (Ed.), *Social organization and social processes: Essays in honor of Anselm Strauss* (pp. 265–283). Aldine de Gruyter.

Star, S. L. (2007). Living grounded theory: Cognitive and emotional forms of pragmatism. In A. Bryant & K. Charmaz (Eds.), *The Sage handbook of grounded theory* (pp. 75–94). Sage.

Star, S. L., & Griesemer, J. (1989). Institutional ecology, 'Translations' and boundary objects: Amateurs and professionals in Berkeley's museum of vertebrate zoology, 1907–1939. *Social Studies of Science, 19,* 387–420.

Star, S. L. (1995/2015). Introduction. In S. L. Star (Ed.), *Ecologies of knowledge: New directions in the sociology of science and technology* (pp. 1–35). State University of New York Press. Reprinted in Geof Bowker, Stefan Timmermans, Adele E. Clarke, & Ellen Balka (Eds.), *Boundary objects and beyond: Working with Susan Leigh Star* (pp. 14–46). MIT Press.

Strauss, A. (1956). Editor's introduction. In A. Strauss (Ed.), *The social psychology of George Herbert Mead.* Phoenix Books.

Strauss, A. (1959). *Mirrors and masks.* Sociology Press.

Strauss, A. L. (1987). *Qualitative analysis for social scientists.* Cambridge University Press.

Strauss, A. L. (1993). *Continual Permutations of action.* Aldine de Gruyter.

Strauss, A., Bucher, R., Ehrlich, D., Sabshin, M., & Schatzman, L. (1964). *Psychiatric ideologies and institutions.* The Free Press of Glencoe.

Strauss, A. L., & Corbin, J. (1990/1998). *The basics of qualitative analysis: Grounded theory procedures and techniques* (1st & 2nd eds.). Sage.

Strauss, A. L., & Corbin, J. (1994). Grounded theory methodology: An overview. In N. K. Denzin & Y. Lincoln (Eds.), *Handbook of qualitative research* (1st ed., pp. 273–285). Sage.

Strübing, J. (2019) The pragmatism of Anselm L. Strauss: Linking theory and method. In A. Bryant & K. Charmaz (Eds.), *The SAGE handbook of current developments in grounded theory*. Sage.

Tavory, I., & Timmermans, S. (2019) Abductive analysis and grounded theory. In A. Bryant, & K. Charmaz (Eds.), *The SAGE handbook of current developments in grounded theory*. Sage.

Wiener, C. (2007). Making teams work in conducting grounded theory. In A. Bryant & K. Charmaz (Eds.), *Handbook of grounded theory* (pp. 293–310). Sage.

QUALITATIVE MEDIA ANALYSIS

Christopher J. Schneider[a] and David L. Altheide[b]

[a]*Brandon University, Canada*
[b]*Arizona State University, USA*

ABSTRACT

Digital media and information technologies provide challenges and opportunities for social scientists to examine historical and contemporary mediated cultural products and experiences. Qualitative Media Analysis (QMA) is an application of qualitative research methodology for the study of documents. A document is broadly defined as any symbolic or textual representation that is recordable and retrievable, including aural, video, and digital recordings, print, photographs, and visual images. Distinct from quantitative approaches of "content analysis" that treats enumerations as relevant findings, QMA utilizes an investigator's ethnographic immersion in selected documents to discern meanings and thematic emphases as a feature of the mediated contexts of use and interpretation. We outline QMA research designs and selected findings on print, visual, and digital media, including various phases of internet content, X (formerly Twitter), Facebook, YouTube, and TikTok. We conclude with a brief discussion of the importance (and prospects) of QMA in symbolic interactionist research drawing attention to issues concerning how some digital documents can add additional layers of complexity to QMA research projects.

Keywords: Mass media; digital media; social media; document analysis; media logic

INTRODUCTION

Qualitative Media Analysis (QMA) was developed from research projects on print and visual media. This methodology has been used in hundreds of theses, dissertations, and publications. This chapter reports the basic rationale and impetus for this methodology by drawing on selections from our 2013 book (Altheide & Schneider, 2013) as well as updates on challenges from digital and social media.

Essential Methods in Symbolic Interaction
Studies in Symbolic Interaction, Volume 60, 79–92
Copyright © 2025 Christopher J. Schneider and David L. Altheide
Published under exclusive licence by Emerald Publishing Limited
ISSN: 0163-2396/doi:10.1108/S0163-239620250000060005

Our methodological approach to studying the mass media was closely connected to ongoing studies of the mass media themselves; we learned that a different method would be required to answer the kinds of questions that we were asking of the media data. The explosive growth in academic publications, including qualitative methods books and journals, has undoubtedly contributed to the quest for more specific guidelines for specialized approaches to qualitative research (e.g., depth interviewing, life-history reporting, auto ethnographies, and document analysis). Qualitative methods have increasingly been embraced by disciplines ranging from sociology to education to health and nursing to marketing research. Literally hundreds of citations could be mentioned, but suffice it for our purposes to simply note the immense popularity and scholarly significance of the *Handbook of Qualitative Research* (Sage), edited by Norman K. Denzin and Yvonna S. Lincoln. First published in 1994, this compendium of innovative approaches to qualitative research is now in its 6th edition (2023). Much of this shift is due to an avalanche of literature documenting and supporting the importance of understanding social meanings for actors, including social contexts, situations, and emotions. The focus on perspective and voice in a plethora of qualitative research coupled with developments in technology and culture has also supported more interest and awareness in document analysis. Computer technology and digital data bases of content, ranging from print and visual media, including video, greatly expands research opportunities to query data bases on a wide range of topics. Changes in media and communication research approaches and paradigms contributed to the expanding interest in qualitative approaches to studying mass media, and later social media. It became apparent that traditional approaches to understanding electronic media documents were inadequate in dealing with newer information and perspectives about how documents were constructed and the ways in which media were being shaped and used by claims-makers, journalists, and different audiences. This has especially become the case with the emergence and expansion of social media ushering in changes in the communicator–audience framework.

The development of ethnographic content analysis (a distinctive version of qualitative media analysis) and its use by researchers was influenced by an awareness by many researchers that simply studying the content of the mass media was not enough; it was also important to be aware of the process, meanings, and emphases reflected in the content, including discursive practices. We understood from our research that there was an underlying "media logic" that guided – but did not determine – how information technology, communication formats, and media content were defined, selected, organized, perceived, and interpreted by audiences.

Culture is more available to document analysis today partly because the electronic and information technology revolution that is the source of such research is also the single greatest contributor to cultural change. Consider the impact that the internet and digital media have had on culture and interaction. Dating, banking, entertainment, shopping, and so on take place in digitally mediated spaces – all social activities that produce documents for retrieval and analysis.

The increased technological capacity to record and retrieve information has expanded the range of potential documents. For example, the availability of

CHRISTOPHER J. SCHNEIDER AND DAVID L. ALTHEIDE

video cameras since the 1970s now makes routine interaction documentable in a way that was not readily available and affordable even with 8-mm and 16-mm film. The transition to widespread access to mobile devices (i.e., smart phones) connected to the internet has made documenting and sharing the minutia of everyday matters to a vast online audience a normative practice.

Our social world is awash in an endless array of documents such as surveys, interview schedules, official records, and statistics (e.g., the FBI Uniform Crime Report), newspaper or television news transcripts, photographs, text messages, email reports, Facebook exchanges, Instagram comments, YouTube and TikTok videos, or a researcher's field notes. These are all documents that the researcher intends to reflect some event or activity within a sphere of interest. There are numerous information bases available for researchers to use; the documents have been pulled together electronically and can be easily accessed with a computer or smart phone. The trick, however, is to know how to explore these bases to discover and select appropriate documents to help answer research questions, and then be able to systematically collect relevant information. This can be especially challenging when working with social media as the available data are boundless, akin to drinking water from a fire hose. A basic aim for researchers becomes making a case for when to begin and end data collection, and on which platform(s) (see also Schneider, 2018a). The topic or problem under investigation together with the logic of digital media platforms can contribute to the approach and methodological rationale of the researcher.

WHAT IS QUALITATIVE MEDIA ANALYSIS?

QMA was originally conceived as Ethnographic Content Analysis (ECA) to distinguish the rationale, method, and data from conventional quantitative content analysis that was driven by assumptions about well-defined indicators of variables that could be counted and analyzed statistically. In qualitative document analysis, the frequency and representativeness are not the main issues, conceptual adequacy is. The major emphasis of qualitative document analysis is to capture the meanings, emphasis, and themes of messages and to understand the organization and process of how they are presented (Glaser & Strauss, 1967).

QMA seeks to "surround" a topic presented in documents. This requires that we include the widest range of relevant messages in our sample. It is difficult, however, to know what this range and variety is at the start of the research. It will often emerge as the researcher inspects and reflects on some initial materials. Initial inspection will produce some types or recurring terminology, phrases, or characterizations. This preliminary inspection may reveal a few patterns, but the next illuminating step is to look in additional documents for examples that don't fit the initial grouping. The search for different or deviant cases is a form of theoretical sampling, where a pattern or hunch directs further investigation. For example, upon initial inspection of documents a researcher might observe actions by men, but are there also documents showing relevant actions by others, like women, children, or persons who do not identify within the gender binary? This kind of critical comparison helps shape and clarify the topic or problem under investigation. To illustrate the point, consider a QMA thesis project that proposed exploring non-binary identity in feminist zines by utilizing a "third space" approach to assist with data collection and analysis to explore media representations that exist outside of binary identification (Mahr, 2018).

QMA is similar to but distinctive from wide-ranging approaches to qualitative analysis, notably grounded theory (Glaser & Strauss, 1967). QMA stresses identifying and capturing the relevant data that covers the range of, say, news coverage of a topic, while grounded theory focuses on what one does with the data after it is collected. Grounded theory is more oriented to theory development. Whereas the basic assumption behind QMA is that the general process of data collection, reflection, and protocol refinement is more significant for a study and that details involving coding procedures, practices, and categories do emerge from the research process. QMA is not primarily oriented to theory development, but rather with clear descriptions and definitions compatible with the data materials, which can help generate concepts appropriate for theoretical testing with other types of documents. Nevertheless, QMA provides rich data compatible with an extensive array of sociological concepts with theoretical relevance.

Once the key elements are identified and demonstrated and the data gathering protocol and relevant codes are refined, then the sample can be extended to focus mainly on the entire time period under consideration. This can be illustrated with research on the Iranian hostage crisis in 1979, investigations about the widespread use of the word "fear" in popular culture, and research investigating riots on social media, among numerous research projects utilizing QMA.

Regarding the Iranian hostage crisis, whereas the initial study involved 15 to 20 reports, the unfolding event lasted for months and received hundreds of reports. Additional reports were added to the sample to cover the relevant time frame. Ultimately, Altheide's (1982) study of the Iranian hostage crisis covered more than 900 reports over 444 days. These many reports, however, would not be necessary now because several conceptual points about sampling were demonstrated and clarified in this and other work. Another example is Schneider's (2016a) study of the 2011 Vancouver riot that was documented on a Facebook group page devoted to posting pictures of rioters. While the prosecution of rioters took nearly five years, due in large part to the massive volume of user-generated documentation on social media, user activity on the Facebook group page diminished quite significantly just two weeks following the riot. This time frame was determined as best suited for data collection and analysis.

THE PROCESS OF QUALITATIVE MEDIA ANALYSIS

QMA can be outlined in 12 specific steps, these steps are as follows:

(1) pursue an original idea on a specific topic;
(2) become familiar with the information source and review any existent literature on the topic;

(3) become familiar with about a half a dozen examples of relevant documents, note the format of these documents, and identify the unit of analysis (Facebook posts, TikTok videos, news reports, etc.);
(4) list several categories (i.e., variables) on a data collection sheet or protocol;
(5) test the protocol by gathering data from various documents;
(6) update and revise the protocol to reflect additional cases;
(7) employ sampling rationale and strategy (e.g., theoretical sampling);
(8) collect descriptive examples (i.e., data) using preset codes, add additional categories to protocol if necessary and complete data collection;
(9) conduct data analysis;
(10) compare and contrast extremes and significant difference in each category and write summaries;
(11) combine summaries with typical examples of the key differences (i.e., extremes);
(12) integrate these materials with your findings and interpretations in another draft in what will become your manuscript.

These considerations inform an approach to documents. Documents are approached with an open mind to identify relevant meanings and emphases. Some guidelines for understanding the context of discovery in documents, the process or life cycle of a document, and the use and meaning of that document emerge over the 12 steps of QMA. The general flow moves from an original idea about a topic to some ethnographic materials about a relevant or related setting, context, or culture. The initial first two steps of QMA are intended to help clarify what the problem to be investigated is, or what the "research question" is, as well as what is the appropriate unit of analysis from which to collect data. By unit of analysis, we simply mean how large a chunk of a document matters. For example, are we focusing on individual news reports, or on certain scenarios and themes presented in the report? If the former, we would look for specific news articles, but if the latter, we might focus on fewer articles that have several scenarios or themes within them. We can approach social media documents much the same way.

Depending on the study, one might ask questions such as: Is the topic a social media post and an investigation of replies or comments made about the post? Is the research concern with reviewing a selection of posts made to a single social media feed of an individual? Or perhaps an account (or accounts) associated with a brand or members of an organization? The approach concerning which materials to include and exclude depends upon the research question. Consider Schneider's investigations of police use of social media.

In one study, Schneider's (2016b) research question sought to understand what police activity in Toronto on X (formerly Twitter) could add to our awareness of police communication on social media as a presentational strategy. In looking to help clarify what police accounts he might investigate on X, he first located a listing of 119 official social media accounts on the Toronto Police Service web-page. He discovered that police accounts ranged from individual officers to accounts representing corporate strategy and divisional policing. A preliminary review of these materials suggested that a sampling across these police accounts was best suited for answering his research question. A later study (Schneider, 2024) sought to further investigate the expansion of police presentational strategies to TikTok. Schneider quickly discovered, that unlike X, which is very popular among police in Toronto (and elsewhere), that official Toronto police presence on TikTok was comparatively, rather limited. As such, Schneider's later study instead focused on a select few Toronto officers using TikTok in their official capacity as police.

Step 3 entails actually examining a few relevant documents with an awareness of relevant themes in mind and then, following steps 4 through 12, drafting a protocol for data collection, coding, and analysis and drafting the report. Police professionalism and community policing, dominant themes from Schneider's (2016b) study, provided a direction and analytical framework from which to later investigate police use of TikTok. Schneider watched hundreds of police TikTok videos and read thousands of user-generated comments posted in response to videos on TikTok in developing a research protocol from which to collect TikTok data.

A protocol or data collection instrument helps query the unit of analysis in an appropriate document. The challenge is to be able to ask the "right" questions that will provide the data necessary to help answer our research question. This is a very inductive process, meaning that we read a few sample articles, look at TikTok videos and comments (or whatever the documents are), and derive some questions on the protocol that will help us get that information. Then we have to check the data collection sheet with a few more examples of data to see how it works.

We have emphasized to this point some of the key steps, links, feedback, and emergence as a qualitative project unfolds. After the research question or interest is defined, we construct a data collection sheet or protocol to guide our inquiry; then, based on our understanding of the unit of analysis, we determine the best sampling strategy, or which documents we want to select, and how. Hannem and Schneider's (2022) investigation of the emerge and impact of the #MeToo social movement helps to clarify a few of these points.

The #MeToo movement rose to prominence in 2017 initially on X (formerly Twitter) when "Me Too" was joined with the hashtag (#). Use of the hashtag provided a space for public discussions about sexual misconduct to organize and spread online. Tens of millions of individual #MeToo posts appeared on sites like X, Instagram, and Facebook, and across other platforms. Hannem and Schneider's research interest sought to explore individual definitional boundaries of what constituted sexual misconduct. In drafting a research protocol, Hannem and Schneider first had to choose which platform(s) to investigate, determine a basic unit of analysis (i.e., individual posts with the hashtag), which social media documents to select, and a suitable data collection timeframe. The #MeToo movement was sparked on the X platform by Hollywood actor Alyssa Milano on October 15, 2017, so X was selected for investigation.

Following a preliminary review of an assortment of #MeToo posts on X emerged additional protocol categories, including #MeToo first-person accounts (i.e., disclosures of sexual harms, the primary research area), statements supportive of the movement that made use of the hashtag, and an "other" category to also include tangentially related data such as third-person posts not directly associated with individuals (e.g., posts with news reports featuring #MeToo). These protocol categories ensured that a wide range of potential #MeToo posts were included.

The researcher then not only collects the data on the protocol (data collection sheet) but also keeps the original data (e.g., a complete newspaper article, text, a social media post, or video) in a file that can be accessed later. In their study of #MeToo, for instance, Hannem and Schneider collected a selection of X posts generated by the site's top post algorithm returning a batch of user posts over a one-year period following the emergence of the #MeToo hashtag. A sample of the top 20 tweets from each day were collected, a total of 7,300 user posts over the year period. While not intended as a representative sample, the algorithm did return a range of user messages relevant for analysis. These posts were saved into a single Adobe portable document (PDF), a file (data set) consisting of a 1,682-page PDF document. These data were continuously reviewed while Hannem and Schneider developed and refined their data collection instrument, or protocol.

Several projects that collected documents from YouTube followed a similar trajectory. The topic of investigation can direct the researcher to narrow focus to a certain social media site, e.g., #MeToo on Twitter. Each platform is also oriented to a different format, which may contribute to the research topic. For instance, posts mostly limited to 280-characters are posted on X, images on Instagram, and videos on TikTok and YouTube. While videos, images, and texts can be shared to each of these platforms, user *orientation* to each platform differs.

For instance, in one study that investigated user judgments of police conduct depicted in body-worn camera footage, Schneider (2018b) focused on YouTube primarily because of its video-focused format. Preliminary searches of YouTube for "police body camera" yielded millions of returned results, far too many for a qualitative research project. To narrow the search parameters, Schneider sorted the results by most viewed, and then discovered that many of the most viewed videos were uploaded to YouTube on a single account. Search terms were refined to this account for videos with at least one million views and "bodycam" in the title of the video. Eight videos met these criteria. After watching each video on YouTube, Schneider scrolled to open and view user comments in response to each video and saved them as PDF files. Gathering data in this manner, while time intensive, allowed Schneider to immerse himself in the comments during data collection. Prolonged immersion in these data aided with initial protocol development. Continued careful reading and sorting through the PDF files informed his data sampling and analysis.

After several protocols have been completed, the researcher then reviews the materials, especially the data collection sheets (which will probably also be in a computer file), to be certain that the kind of information necessary to answer key questions is being collected. This might entail revising, adding, or dropping items to our protocol. The final step in answering the research question is to code, or organize the data that have been collected, summarize and group these in appropriate ways. Simply using a word-processor works well, or qualitative software including an expanding array of web-scraping tools available to extract online data can come in handy. However, using a basic word-processor to sort through files is most usually sufficient since this processing of data allows for immersion and is also often advantageous for nuanced qualitative discoveries. Aggregated searches of the above noted #MeToo PDF data set, as one concrete example, were helpful for Hannem and Schneider in their investigation of Twitter posts (units of analysis), to delineate what was emphasized by individual users, allowing for their discovery of key themes. Now the researcher can begin to make some descriptive statements about specific segments of data. These statements will then be the basis for a more elaborate writing of the research report.

Documents, then, enable us to (a) place symbolic meanings in context, (b) track the process of its creation and influence on social definitions, (c) let our understanding emerge through detailed investigation, and (d) if we desire, use our understanding from the study of documents to change some social activities, including the production of certain documents. The research process of investigating the context of symbolic meanings can be illustrated with Altheide's (2002) study of news coverage of terrorism.

A discourse of fear set the stage for how the mass media, leaders and citizens would define the 9/11 attacks. Previous work on the nature and extent of fear construction and use in the mass media guided subsequent research into how terrorism would be covered. That research examined how fear was presented during the 1980s and 1990s, with particular interest in how fear was associated with different problems and issues over a period. The studies of fear pointed to the importance of repeated, persistent, and pervasive uses of fear with a wide range of topics. For example, the data revealed that over time, fear "traveled" from one topic to another (e.g., from crime to AIDS to immigrants to children).

The discourse of fear emerged during this study. Fear becomes a matter of discourse when it "expands" beyond a specific referent to use as a more general orientation (Ericson et al., 1989; van Dijk, 1985). Entertainment formats contribute to the emphasis on "fear" rather than, say, "danger," which is more specific and more easily incorporated within an everyday life perspective. When fear is repeatedly used with children and the spaces they occupy, e.g., schools, a meaningful association emerges. Over time, with repeated usage, nuances blend, connotations become denotations, fringes mix with kernels, and we have a different perspective on the world. This is why the distinctions between meaningful borders like children, school, and community are so important. When they are joined with fear, more than a visit is in the works; there is an incursion. We traced the development of a discourse of fear surrounding "children" over time in order to demonstrate how fear has come to be associated with certain topics and issues as part of a problem frame, or a clearly formatted way of linking problems to the following elements of "story telling:"

- Narrative structure
- Universal moral meanings

- Specific time and place
- Unambiguous
- Focus is on disorder
- Culturally resonant

The problem frame combines the universal and non-situational logic and moral meanings of a morality play (Unsworth, 1995) with the temporal and spatial parameters of a news report – something happened involving an actual person in an actual location (e.g., street address). A comparison was made with a morality play in which the characters are abstractions facing death and damnation. News reports focus on "actual" people and events to package the entire narrative as "realistic." Complex and often ambiguous events and concerns are symbolically mined for moral truths and understandings presumed to be held by the audience, while the repeated presentations of similar scenarios "teaches" the audience about the nature and causes of "disorder" (Ericson et al., 1989).

Consider again the problem of sexual misconduct. Hannem and Schneider's study followed a similar tracking discourse approach to Altheide's investigation of terrorism and fear when they examined nearly four decades of news media coverage of sexual misconduct. Throughout the 1980s and 1990s, the term "sexual misconduct" appeared with increased duration and frequency across media reports. An investigation of news coverage of sexual misconduct was discovered to have involved a wide array of sex-related topics, ranging from consensual sexual relationships such as infidelity that was associated with political scandals, group sex, sexual encounters between teenagers, to illegal sexual behaviors (e.g., rape, pedophilia). Hannem and Schneider found that repeated coverage that joined together narratives of untoward, unconventional, and otherwise criminal sex acts allowed contemporary conversations around sexual misconduct to materialize into a common public discourse. The discourse of sexual misconduct set the stage for the #MeToo movement and related movements drawing widespread awareness to sexual harms.

THE CONCEPTUAL SIGNIFICANCE OF QMA IN SYMBOLIC INTERACTIONISM

The QMA approach to document analysis is derived from a theoretical and methodological position set forth by George Herbert Mead and Herbert Blumer as well as by Alfred Schutz (1967; see also Berger & Luckmann, 1967) and others. There are three general points. First, social life consists of a process of communication and interpretation regarding the definition of the situation. The symbolic order we join as infants infuses our own view of ourselves, others, and our future.

Second, it is this communicative process that breaks the distinction between subject and object, between internal and external, and joins them in the situation that we experience and take for granted. Third, the notion of process is key because everything is under construction, even our most firmly held beliefs, values, and personal commitments. What we consciously believe and do is tied to many aspects of "reality maintenance," of which we are less aware, that we have made part of our routine "stock of knowledge." The general methodological stance is called Analytic Realism, as Altheide and Johnson (1994, p. 489) explain:

> "Analytic Realism" is based on the view that the social world is an interpreted world, not a literal world, always under symbolic construction (even everyday life is informed by social contexts and uses of evidence). As originally formulated, these five dimensions of qualitative research include problematic issues pertaining to validity. Indeed, we argued that the "ethnographic ethic" calls for ethnographers to substantiate their interpretations and findings with a reflexive account of themselves and the process(es) of their research.

(1) the relationship between what is observed (behaviors, rituals, meanings) and the larger cultural, historical, and organizational contexts within which the observations are made (the substance);

(2) the relationship between the observer, the observed, and the setting (the observer);

(3) the issue of perspective (or point of view), whether the observer's or the member(s)', used to render an interpretation of the ethnographic data (the interpretation);

(4) the role of the reader in the final product (the audience); and

(5) the issue of representational, rhetorical, or authorial style used by the author(s) to render the description and/or interpretation (the style).

> Each of these areas include questions or issues, which must be addressed and pragmatically resolved by any particular observer in the course of his or her research.

In broad terms, these assumptions are consistent with the symbolic interactionists' perspective, which includes a focus on the meaning of activity.

CONCLUDING THOUGHTS: THE IMPORTANCE (AND PROSPECTS) OF QMA IN SYMBOLIC INTERACTIONIST RESEARCH

The corpus of symbolic interactionist research and theorizing has taught us that reality is symbolically constituted. Media – conventional and social media – are an essential part of the symbolic process through which individuals construct meanings. Media formats play a consequential role in influencing how people define situations, and how individuals understand, and then act upon situations. Consider, for instance, the role of media on various understandings of war and conflict (Israel's war on Gaza as genocide or self-defense and Russian's impetus for its invasion of Ukraine, as contemporary examples). Or media's influence on election outcomes or determining responses to global pandemics and vaccine uptake (e.g., COVID-19), and so on.

For interactionists thinkers, the interaction order framework provides a foundational basis for social order, where many spend time in the "immediate presence of others" (Goffman, 1983). While Goffman and numerous interactionist inspired scholars have studied and written about social activities that occur before an audience, more contemporary shifts in the communicator–audience framework contribute to changes in how social order is accomplished, for instance with how messages are tailored to audience's expectations. Altheide's (2023) study of the media dynamic surrounding former president Donald Trump's electoral strategies illustrates some key points.

In exploiting a new media environment, Trump, speaking to his legions of followers through Twitter, publicly said things about government, the rule of law, and minorities, destroying the traditional political party structure. Opinions now mattered more than facts. In channeling fear, anger, and unbridled resentment to his Twitter followers, Trump stood for and validated claims about the corruption of major institutions, including government, election, education, science, and the justice system. Trump, in a matter of speaking, was them. This is gonzo governance. Trump had become a meme, a recognizable symbol spread electronically from person to person. The use of digital media in advancing partisan goals had become personal, instantaneous, and visual. The point to stress is that the manner in how people communicate is more consequential for what is conveyed to audiences. Users of digital technologies are complicit in modifying and altering grammar, discourse, institutional norms, rules, guidelines, and even laws. Users of digital information technologies now participate in their own enlightenment and deception. Gonzo governance is more than attracting voters, rather, voters are recruited to both participate and be complicit in altering foundational institutional structures like politics and government.

Shifts in social order that include gonzo governance signal the importance for QMA in symbolic interactionist research projects investigating the digital media communication environment. A good example is Monahan and Maratea's (2021) QMA study of nearly 4,000 of Donald Trump's tweets promoting his gonzo story telling that he was the savior of a failed nation. Using a protocol developed along the lines discussed above, data were collected on the context, process, and emergence of meaning. The codes that emerged for analyzing how Trump told his gonzo story were threat-culprit, perceived failings, substitute approach, self-adulation, popular appeal, and delegitimation. Their analysis suggests that a gonzo storytelling framework evinces a coherent narrative structure that both aligns with supporters biases and needs as well as media formats.

Advancements in digital media in our mediated communication order, including user interactions across numerous social media platforms, rivals the physical world in terms of its relative cultural significance (see Schneider, 2019). To be social is to be mediated, a digital process that produces a near infinite supply of documents as data for possible collection and analysis. On the one hand, document analysis of digital media formats provides opportunities for researchers to peer into the minutiae of daily interactions offering empirical insights into a range of symbolic meanings and social activities. While on the other hand, studying documents as products of institutional actors offers some important clarity around changes to institutional structures, like politics or policing. However, attention to issues over how digital documents are produced and shaped through their respective media formats adds additional layers of complexity to researcher's conducting QMA. Consider the role of algorithms, which not only feed and build audiences but also directly influence the kinds of documents made available to researchers, for review, collection, and analysis.

The logic of each individual social media platform, whether X, TikTok, Instagram, or another platform, is governed by secret algorithms in unseeable coded environments (Van Dijck & Poell, 2013). Algorithms, which are subject to manipulation by site owners at any time without notice, present unique obstacles for researchers, challenges unforeseen and evolving. While social media companies "say their algorithms are scientific and neutral tools, it is very difficult to verify those claims" (Pasquale, 2016, p. 14). Social media algorithms sort which messages and accounts an investigator sees, like the kind of content that appears in a researcher's social media feed. Given that the data and empirical findings for most QMA projects are not intended for generalization, the undue influence of algorithms is not necessarily an urgent concern, conceptual adequacy is. That said, QMA provides flexibly to reflexively adapt during the research process. One strategy to circumvent some issues posed by algorithms is to develop research questions around hashtags.

The hashtag (#) is culturally ubiquitous. Hashtags can make algorithms "cultural meaningful" in ways that users organize around the use of a particular hashtag (Gillespie, 2016). As noted by journalism professor Jeff Jarvis, "more than Twitter itself, more than social media itself, the hashtag is a platform. *No one owns it. No one controls it.* Those who use it imbue it with meaning and power" (New York Times, 2023; *emphasis added*). Hashtags like #MeToo, or the discovery of a hashtag that emerges during the research process, can help make aspects of digital culture more meaningful and available to document analysis as the source of research and as a contributor to social change. Beyond issues like content concerns driven by secret algorithms, companies like X have monetized access to their data which can also complicate data collection.

Consider when Schneider began studying police use of Twitter in 2013. At the time, Twitter allowed access to the most recent 3,200 tweets of public accounts which could be saved with relative ease as a digital file (a searchable PDF document). However, the ability to save tweets as PDF files during later research projects that investigated hashtags like #MeToo and #PublicCriminology (see Schneider, 2023) was somewhat more challenging due to changes to the site, in particular what the platform allowed for data capture. Adapting to changes on the X platform, Schneider was able to save some tweets as PDFs and had to capture other posts both as screenshots and copied and pasted as text files. It is important to save posts whenever feasible, as posts might later become relevant for analysis, since user content can be deleted or modified, and certain materials could later be determined as theoretically relevant as the research process develops. Then there are evolving concerns about research ethics.

The sampling of digital documents from social media is never entirely free of potential ethical concerns like considerations over privacy or anonymity (Mills, 2019). There might be guidelines in place by university research ethics boards concerning collection of social media data that the researcher should be aware of, but there is also the additional matter of the terms of conditions of each social media site that govern the use of each platform by its users, and possible use by researchers (see Townsend & Wallace, 2016 for a discussion). The terms and conditions of each site are also subject to change at any time without notice. As the cultural and media landscape evolves, these changes are of course impossible to predict with any certainty, but it is certain that the importance of QMA in symbolic interactionist research will continue to remain relevant.

REFERENCES

Altheide, D. L. (1982). Three-in-one news: Network coverage of Iran. *Journalism Quarterly, 59,* 482–486.

Altheide, D. L. (2002). *Creating fear: News and the construction of crisis.* Aldine de Gruyter.

Altheide, D. L. (2023). *Gonzo governance: The media logic of Donald Trump.* Routledge.

Altheide, D. L., & Johnson, J. M. (1994). Criteria for assessing interpretative validity in qualitative research. In N. K. Denzin & Y. S. Lincoln (Eds.), *Handbook of qualitative methodology* (pp. 485–499). Sage.

Altheide, D. L., & Schneider, C. J. (2013). *Qualitative media analysis* (2nd ed.). SAGE Publications.

Berger, P. L., & Luckmann, T. (1967). *The social construction of reality: A treatise in the sociology of knowledge.* Doubleday.

Denzin, N. K., & Lincoln, Y. S. (Eds.). (2023) *The SAGE Handbook of qualitative research* (6th ed.). Sage.

Ericson, R. V., Baranek, P. M., & Chan, J. B. L. (1989). *Negotiating control: A study of news sources.* University of Toronto Press.

Gillespie, T. (2016). #trendingistrending: When algorithms become culture. In R. Seyfert & J. Roberge (Eds.), *Algorithmic cultures: Essays on meaning, performance and new technologies* (pp. 52–75). Routledge.

Glaser, B. G., & Strauss, A. L. (1967). *Discovery of grounded theory: Strategies for qualitative research.* Aldine de Gruyter.

Goffman, E. (1983). The interaction order. *American Sociological Review, 48,* 1–17.

Hannem, S., & Schneider, C. J. (2022). *Defining sexual misconduct: Power, media, and #MeToo.* University Regina Press.

Mahr, J. A. (2018). *Non-binary identity in feminist zines: Media spaces and oppositional consciousness.* http://hdl.handle.net/10230/36071

Mills, K. A. (2019). *Big data for qualitative research.* Routledge.

Monahan, B., & Maratea, R. J. (2021). The art of the spiel: Analyzing Donald Trump's tweets as gonzo storytelling. *Symbolic Interaction, 44*(4), 699–727.

New York Times. (February 10, 2023). *Opinion: How twitter changed the world, in 25 tweets.* www.nytimes.com/interactive/2023/02/10/opinion/twitter-alltime-tweets.html

Pasquale, F. (2016). *The black box society: The secret algorithms that control money and information.* Harvard University Press.

Schneider, C. J. (2016a). Police presentational strategies on Twitter in Canada, *Policing & Society: An International Journal of Research and Policy, 26* (2) 129–147.

Schneider, C. J. (2016b). *Policing and social media: Social control in an era of new media,* Lexington Books.

Schneider, C. J. (2018a). Making the case: A qualitative approach to studying social media documents. In A. Bryman & D. A. Buchanan (Eds.), *Unconventional methodology in organization and management research* (pp. 105–124). Oxford University Press.

Schneider, C. J. (2018b). An exploratory study of public perceptions of police conduct depicted in body worn camera footage on YouTube. *Annual Review of Interdisciplinary Justice Research, 7,* 118–148.

Schneider, C. J. (2019). 2017 Couch-Stone symposium keynote address: The interaction order in the twenty-first century and the case of police legitimacy, *Studies in Symbolic Interaction, 50,* 97–115.

Schneider, C. J. (2023). #Publiccriminology on twitter. In D. Jones, M. Jones, K. Strudwick, & A. Charles (Eds.), *Public criminology: Reimagining public education and research practice* (pp. 283–305). Palgrave.

Schneider, C. J. (2024). *Policing and social media: Social control in an era of digital media* (2nd ed.). Lexington Books.

Schutz, A. (1967). *The phenomenology of the social world.* Northwestern University Press.

Townsend, L., & Wallace, C. (2016). *Social media research: A guide to ethics.* The University of Aberdeen.

Unsworth, B. (1995). *Morality play.* Hamish Hamilton.

Van Dijck, J., & Poell, T. (2013) Understanding social media logic. *Media and Communication 1*(1): 2–14.

van Dijk, T. A. (1985). *Discourse and communication: New approaches to the analysis of mass media discourse and communication.* Walter de Gruyter.

SYMBOLIC INTERACTIONIST METHODS FOR STUDYING MUSIC

Joseph A. Kotarba

Texas State University, USA

ABSTRACT

Symbolic interactionist methods for studying music are important for two reasons. First, these methods allow us to investigate numerous facets of the everyday life world of music, one of the more accessible areas of culture. Second, these methods can be applied to and translated for use in examining other realms of culture in the arts, communications, and language. In this chapter, I organize and evaluate symbolic interactionist-inspired research on music in terms of the concepts used to drive this research. These concepts include *subculture, self, identity, community, scene, idioculture, interaction,* and authenticity. *This line of research highlights the value of team-oriented studies; true participant-observation; applied projects; and the application of findings from music research to interactionist theory.*

Keywords: Symbolic interactionism; music; concepts; research methods; qualitative methods

INTRODUCTION

Music is honey: we really love the music we study and share in its romance, wonder, imagination, and possibilities. Good concepts are analytical filters that let the magic of music through but allow us to catch our breath long enough to think and write about what we just witnessed firsthand. I do not think I could write much about Van Halen's "Jump" until I could *see* it as an example of children's music enjoyed by teenagers who were not quite ready to give up the joys of play. (Kotarba, 2010, 2023)

The application of symbolic interactionist (SI) ideas to the study of music has evolved as a rich area to explore the place culture holds in everyday life. Although modern SI can be traced at least as far back as the turn of the 20th century, interest in music is relatively recent and began as a topic in of study in

---

Essential Methods in Symbolic Interaction
Studies in Symbolic Interaction, Volume 60, 93–104
Copyright © 2025 Joseph A. Kotarba
Published under exclusive licence by Emerald Publishing Limited
ISSN: 0163-2396/doi:10.1108/S0163-239620250000060006

the serious and policy-intensive field of deviant behavior instead of the bit more gentile field of culture studies. One might easily argue that SI and music was born in the work of Howard Becker and his now iconic analysis of the jazz musician and marijuana use in the beat era of the 1950s (Becker, 1951). Since then, SIers have investigated a constantly widening range of topics including the music, the musician, the audience, and the social settings where it all takes place.

As is the case with all sociological projects, research in music has two distinct features. The first is the payoff for symbolic interactionist literature. The major contributions in this light come to the formation, modification, and actualization of relevant *concepts* that can ultimately and ideally be applied theoretically to a range of phenomena in everyday life. The heart of SI's perspective on social life lies in the realm of concepts. Concepts are focused, summary, instructive, and illuminating portraits of significant aspects or components of social life. One of the major thinkers establishing the foundations of SI was Herbert Blumer (1969), who felt that concepts provide a practical mechanism for ordering and inspiring research on more complicated and broader features of social life. He argued through his notion of *sensitizing concepts* that concepts should be modest in scope and should serve most importantly as directions for further and more in-depth research into a topic. In a recent essay, I presented an inventory of the concepts most visible in the literature in the sociology of music including, for example, *subculture, self, identity, community, scene, idioculture, interaction,* and *authenticity*.

In this essay, I will explore the second distinct feature of SI research in music: research methods. There is a close relationship among a researcher's scholarly questions, the methods they choose for exploring those questions and the concepts that connects the study to the more general SI literature and, ultimately and ideally, the SI canon.

Subculture

We can define *subculture* as "a culture that differs from the 'mainstream' through marginality or opposition" (Williams, 2011). The members of a subculture, by definition, do not totally oppose the meanings and values of the dominant culture, but simply carve out a cognitive, and sometimes physical, space to address their wants and needs. Music subcultures can be assembled from any number of characteristics, ranging from ethnicity and gender to age and music style.

Howard Becker (1951) conducted one of the foundational SI studies of music subcultures in examining the world of the professional dance musician and their audience. A regular practicing jazz pianist in the clubs of Chicago, himself, he conducted a participant-observation study of the scene. Participant-observation refers to the method by which the researcher becomes an active member of the group they are studying. The researcher is then able to observe their own activities, behaviors, thoughts, and emotions as sources of data as well as analytical insight. Becker played piano with several jazz bands while graduate student at the University of Chicago in the 1950s. Becker's participation in the jazz scene provided him with certain experiences not readily to a researcher simply observing from a distance, perhaps as a member of the audience. For example, Becker practiced the insider terminology that served to indicate that one was truly a jazz musician, talk that established boundaries between the musicians and those not able, fit, or sufficiently talented to share the musicians' world. These terms included "square," "be cool," "daddio," and "hip." The insider use of and appreciation for marijuana also served as a demarcation from outsiders such as audience members.

Participant observation of subcultural activities in music are no longer relegated to face-to-face interaction. The widespread availability of social media has allowed qualitative researchers to directly engage subcultural interaction. J. Patrick Williams (2011), for example, studied an internet forum dedicated to the straight-edge subculture, which is defined by its opposition to drug use. Williams has long established his reputation as a major expert on music and subcultures, within an interactionist framework, by focusing on rapidly changing media forms. The internet communicates meanings that can either supplant or extend the music's meanings (e.g., lyrics) per se (Williams, 2013).

In similar fashion, I applied my *interactionist optic*, as Fred Davis (1991) once put it so elegantly, to a contrasting subcultural scene: music as a feature of the online discussion of illegal club drugs. Members of the world of popular music have developed many rich, functional, and complex discursive traditions through which they talk, disseminate information, and share experiences about drugs and music. The nature of this discourse has taken different forms over the years as styles of illegal drug use, the objectives of drug talk, and the media by which this talk takes place have all evolved. I conceptualized this activity as *drugmusictalk*. A contemporary style of *drugmusictalk* is the communication taking place in the world of rave parties, techno dance clubs, and designer drugs – the focus of this study (Kotarba, 2007). Thus, the *drugmusictalk* that takes place in clubs provides us with a glimpse into the world of club or designer drugs, rave parties, dance, and high technology at the same level and style of communication as the participants experience. I should note that that larger team study of which *drugmusictalk* was a component (Murguia et al., 2007) abided by fairly traditional rules of human subjects protection/informed consent. We sought and achieved permission from *drugmusictalk* participants whenever we contacted them directly and personally. Otherwise, their identities were hidden by the consistent use of pseudonyms and the avoidance of photographs online, given the illegal nature of many of the activities described.

Thus, gaining access to online subcultural interaction is considerably easier than acquiring situational, face-to-face access in traditional subcultural scenes. As a general rule, the identities of researchers in subcultural scenes should approximate the identities of regular participants as much as possible. A recognizable identity portrays the researcher as someone who might have empathy for respondents if not shared values and commitment. My best example is a project I conducted for the State of Texas' Attorney General's office in 1993 (Kotarba, 1993). While I was teaching at the University of Houston, I received a telephone call from a staff member. They said that, since I studied teenagers and their music, they would like for me to look into the emerging rave music scene making headlines in the local newspapers. They told me they received several telephone calls from irate parents who wanted to know more about the strange dance music parties, conducted in obscure and hidden locations like abandoned buildings, where their 14-year-old daughters and sons snuck out to attend at two in the morning. Drugs, of course, were a constant worry.

A modest grant from the AG's office allowed me to assemble a team of graduate students to investigate rave parties. Team structures for qualitative field studies fit the spirit of symbolic interactionist research. Jack Douglas (1976) referred to this as the *multi-perspectival approach.* SI argues that social situations are complex insofar as each participant is likely *to* perceive, interpret, and respond to features of the situation differently (Melnikov & Johnson, 2021). Various participants experience a rave party differently and are there for different purposes. Various team members can help unpack this complexity by talking with different participants, expressing their gender and lifestyles individually, etc. In this particular study, however, the primary value of the team was to let participants know who they are not! They are likely to not be undercover police, members of the media, or parents looking for their child. During my first visit to a rave party, I had difficulty attracting participants to talk with me. After additional inquiry, we learned that participants did not feel I was an undercover cop; the belief is that they are usually much younger than me, in their 30s, wearing a short black leather jacket, chewing gum and casing out the scene visually from side to side. Worse, especially among teenage and early adult male ravers, I could be an angry father looking for my absent young daughter and the punks with whom she is hanging around.

Data collection in subcultural settings should be informal, conversational and colloquial. It goes without saying, field research must not be judgmental.

The Self and Identity

The *self* may be the most important concept in symbolic interactionism. The self is a reflexive object. George Herbert Mead (1934) reminds us that the self is a constant process, a way of "self-ing" ourselves into being as a result of our actions as a subject (the "I"), and as an object of our actions (the "*me*") (Kotarba, 2018, p. 67).

The *self* has been the most important suggestive concept in all my work as a symbolic interactionist. In my dissertation research at UCSD on the chronic pain experience, I forged the concept of the *impaired self* to display the many ways constant discomfort if not suffering affect the ways people experience who they are physically, cognitively, morally, and affectively (Kotarba, 1983). How did I study the self under these conditions? By spending time in situations in which pain people find themselves trying to manage if not cure their pain: physicians' offices, chiropractic offices, acupuncturist offices, meditation services, church, miraculous locations, etc. My "in" for most of these encounters was the fact that I in fact experienced chronic pain at that time in my life.

The value of sharing in the phenomenon in question, of conducting true participant-observation, is not only a valuable tool for entrée regarding music phenomena but a sign of productive membership. Music is pervasive in everyday life.

Everyone loves and enjoys music, at least at certain time in their lives. Music is perhaps the most common if not most powerful source of meaning for everyday life.

Song lyrics provide a useful avenue by which to see the Meadian view of the self in action. The self in the SI view is both simultaneously subject and object and thus the lyricist and the lyric, respectively. Songwriters may write about the self both as the I and as the generalized other, melding biography and assumptions about the perceptions of others.

Symbolic interactionists generally do not assume music is a somewhat unique experience in everyday life that emerges in certain groups under specific circumstances. Music is not simply the purview of subcultures. Music is a ubiquitous feature of everyday life. Often the sociological study of music has focused on the most intense and oppositional deviant music subcultures (e.g., heavy-metal, punk, and hip-hop fans), but music is central not only to the intense interests of these subcultures but to people in all settings and at all times. Music is important to study because it is such a widespread, yet often taken-for-granted, source of meaning for self and situations. In this regard, symbolic interactionists take seriously a profound claim made by an earlier, honored scholar who was somewhat of a predecessor to the perspective: William James. James wrote about the idea – or concept – of *music-at-once*. This idea points to the complexity of the world that itself is packed with ideas, feelings, histories, events, and everything else scholars in the humanities and social sciences would ponder. As a recent scholar and skilled intellectual biographer of James, Bruce W. Wilshire (2016), put it: "The moreness of the world pummels, pokes, provokes, and pricks and feeds us from all directions." In interactionist terms, *moreness* is more or less synonymous with culture, and music is a great example of *moreness* (Kotarba, 2023).

The pervasiveness of music in everyday life provides the opportunity to conduct a study of music as a feature of or appendage to other phenomena under inquiry. One of my most fruitful sources of insight into the place music has in the world of work has been my work as qualitative researcher at the Institute for Translational Sciences at the University of Texas Medical Branch in Galveston (Kotarba, 2013, 2019). The more general research project study has been the impact of the translational science movement on the work and self-identity of the contemporary bio-medical scientist (who scientists are to themselves and how they appear to and are defined by others). I learned that scientists should integrate the arts into their self-identity, but also that they in fact do so. Music not only provides a charming accompaniment to thought, as Pesic put it, but also serves as a particular sort of buffer between the scientist's self and the outside world. The concept of the *existential self* is a very useful framework for exploring the dynamics of this buffer. All paradigms in sociology posit essential relationships between the individual and society. In symbolic interaction, this relationship is conceptualized in terms of the self and society, the self being the person's sense of and experience of individuality (Blumer, 1969). A variation of the symbolic interactionist model of the self is the existential model, which posits a *confrontational* relationship between the self and society (Kotarba, 1984). The existential self-concept regards the individual as an active agent in seeking meaning for problematic situations in everyday life (Melnikov & Kotarba, 2017).

The point is that scientists already meld science and the arts into their self-identities to help manage everyday life problems. More specifically, a common strategy among translational scientists is to use music as a *buffer* against the stressors that the translational science movement both locally and in general places upon the security of their sense of self (Douglas, 1970).

For example, translational scientists use music to help achieve a sense of a *balanced self*, to reinforce the self-definition of intellectual, to serve as an escape from the over-rationalized culture of science, to provide another outlet for creativity, and to facilitate a rhythm for exploration Younger, laboratory-based researchers often play rock music while working at the bench. They will play their music through noise-limiting headphones or buds for two purposes: to keep from disturbing other scientists in the lab, and also as an act of resistance, so to speak, to the seemingly endless meetings and discussions that accompany the growing team-science movement in every day biomedical research. In interviews, some foreign-born scientists take great pride in celebrating the music of their homeland, especially by contrasting the elegant "classical" styles they recall with the more common populist styles of popular music in the United States (Kotarba, 2023).

The question now is how to interject questions about music and the arts in an otherwise formal interview about biomedical science and careers? My strategy here is one I use in other research settings: I simply ask "What kinds of music do you like?" Most respondents are taken back a bit, but quickly start listing their favorite singers, bands, songs, and concerts. For me, this line of inquiry helps rejuvenate an otherwise stagnant interview while generating data of pleasure and great interest for most respondents.

A final word on the search for the concept of *identity* in everyday life. *Identity* refers to the (cognitive, evaluative, and affective) appearance of oneself to others as well as one's efforts to control or manage that appearance (Charmaz et al., 2020). From a symbolic Interactionist perspective, the study of identity is very much an observational endeavor, followed by inquiries into the social construction of identities through interviews.

Community

Music is a shared activity that occurs in the presence of others. The self that is constructed through music, discussed in the previous section, is a social reality constructed in the presence of others: in *communities*. Communities provide a source of meaning and a sense of belonging to their participants (Ferris & Stein, 2012). The concept of *community* orients us to attend to the ways that people come together, physically or virtually, around shared ideas, goals, and/ or histories. Within interactionism there are particular aspects of community that fit our focus on music in everyday life. These are *scene*, *sense of place*, and *idioculture*. These aspects of community each call for different research strategies.

The Music Scene

The social scene is a useful concept for organizing thinking about culture in a community setting. John Irwin (1977) wrote about the scene as an inclusive concept that involves everyone related to a cultural phenomenon (e.g., artists, audiences, management, vendors, and critics); the ecological location of the phenomenon (e.g., districts, clubs, recording studios, and rehearsal rooms); and the products of this interaction (e.g., advertisements, concerts, recordings, and critical reviews). Scenes generally evolve around entertainment-oriented phenomena, such as music, theater, and dance. People typically enter or join a scene for its expressive and direct gratification, not future gratification. Participation is voluntary, and access is generally available to the public, occasionally for the simple price of admission. Irwin's original formulation of the scene used illustrations from 1960s and 1970s California lifestyles, but we will generalize his concept to include a wide range of music communities.

Barry Shank (1994) applied his notion of scene to the production of live music in Austin, Texas. He describes the "6th Street" phenomenon, near to and nurtured by the University of Texas, in terms of its history, cultural roots, and economic context. His focus is on the effects the production of music scenes has on the identities of their participants, an area of interest in this study as well. Pete Peterson and Andy Bennett (2004) extended these ideas in formulating the following definition of a music scene as the geosocial location that provides a stage on which all of the esthetic, political, social, and cultural features of local music are played out. Of particular relevance to our research is Peterson and Bennett's focus on the way participants use local music scenes to differentiate themselves from others.

It should be clear, based on these general definitions, that there can be many kinds of music scenes. Peterson and Bennett (2004) discuss the following music scenes in their book: jazz, blues, rave, karaoke, Britney Spears, salsa, riot grrrls, goth, skatepunk, anarcho-punk, alternative country, and others. We will now discuss a study of the Latino Music Scenes in Houston, Texas. I conducted this study with the help of a group of graduate students at the University of Houston (Kotarba et al., 2009; Nowotny et al., 2010). Each student was responsible for a particular Latino music scene. These scenes included: rock en Espanol, salsa, Tejano, Norteno, gay Latino dance, mariachi, and professional soccer supporters. We designed the study to be an *ethnography* that involved spending considerable time in the field examining the everyday activities of participants in the scene.

Mapping a range of music scenes in a broader community like a major American city like Houston is quite a task, requiring more planning and engagement than the typical "Lone Ranger" ethnography for which symbolic interactionist notorious. The first step is to understand that an inductive and exploratory strategy should be the basis of research design. A grounded theory approach can fit the bill here (Psaroudakis et al., 2021). Grounded theory is the methodological strategy that can systematically organize an otherwise exploratory study. The unknowns encountered are issues such as number (e.g., how

100   *Symbolic Interactionist Methods for Studying Music*

many members, groups, or styles); variety (i.e., what are the different sorts of phenomena to be discovered); and breadth (i.e., how widespread is the community geographically and culturally).

A second step is to assemble the team. The Latino Music Scenes study contained several features from the beginning to be dealt with. We would need team members who were bilingual. More specifically, we would need the capacity to communicate not only in English and Spanish but also in various sub-dialects in Spanish. The team members not only had to be graduate students, in order to ensure research talent and skill levels, but also students interested in converting their team work into viable and publishable thesis project. We also needed students who were mobile and able to get around a large and sprawling city like Houston. Finally, we also required students who were very interested – no, excited – about music and learning about the great variety of Latino music performed sand enjoyed in Houston.

Over the course of the semester we functioned as a team, we met weekly to compare notes, share ideas, and in general support each other in order to complete the project successfully. We had a total of eight grad students onboard, four of whom completed masters theses from the project. We all contributed to and shared authorship on two very sophisticated published papers.

I have also conducted studies of all-ages heavy metal music clubs; large music festivals (e.g., South by Southwest and Austin City Limits); and church choirs, among others. In all cases, team research was the best sway to cover complex and ever-changing music scenes.

Idioculture

The second concept under community I will discuss is *idioculture*. Gary Fine (1979 p. 733) developed the interactionist concept of idioculture to stress the importance of studying culture of any kind – including music – in terms of the small groups in which it is lived. For rock en Espanol, the small groups include the bands, promoters, producer, publicists, fans, and performance venues. Within these groups, fundamental features of rock en Espanol are worked, out, for example, the integration of English and Spanish in composing and performing music favored by all possible audiences. One of the most important and common ways that people use the scene and the idioculture that pervades it is the experience of the *becoming of self*. As Joe notes from an existentialist perspective (Kotarba, 1984), the self is continuously evolving, changing, and adapting in a continually changing, contemporary social life. The resources for assessing and shaping a sense of self ultimately come from cultural experiences. The becoming of self is analytically noteworthy in our study of Latino music scenes many of our respondents are faced with rapidly changing social, political, and cultural environments in which they experience the self. These changes include high mobility (which leaves them with a problematic sense of place), navigation of multiple language communities, and unusual sets of life circumstances that include an ongoing quest for survival among the working class and the development of multiple identities. In light of this, the scene – and the music central to it – becomes an important medium for the "becoming of self" because music is an important cultural resource in Latino communities in general.

Conducting idiocultural research almost begs for personal, participant-observational involvement. My work with Susanna's Kitchen in Wimberley, Texas, is a good example. The SK is a monthly program presented at the First Baptist Church of Wimberley, TX. An Americana (singer-songwriter) artist or band performs for three hours in the side chapel of the church. My volunteer job has been to sell tickets ($25 each) and greet fans as they arrive. The audience of about 100–125 is comprised largely of middle aged and older local residents. There are numerous retired engineers and businesspeople present who really enjoy SK because they can drive to it in about 5 minutes without driving 35 miles all the way to Austin for live adult music.

I have made the point (Kotarba, 2023) that the audience exemplify the process of the continuing *becoming of self* as people age. Their sense of who they are continues to change if not grow as they adapt to aging, extra leisure-time and all the other aspects of retirement. Baby boomers in general have not "graduated" – grown up–to serious styles of music like Jazz or classical music as the critics in the 1950s and 60s claimed. The music miracle that takes place is the typical 60-year-old former professional whose taste in music was rock and roll, pop, and perhaps a little church music thrown in. They may not have been country music fans growing up in Houston or Chicago, but they sure enjoy belonging to a music scene otherwise known as Americana music... without having to give up their rock and roll roots.

Now, how to study a scene like this? Becoming a fixture in the scene like I have is relatively easy and a portal to everyday talk about everything, including music. Americana music is simple, easy to enjoy, and lyric intensive. Local, idiographic scenes like this are easy to dissolve into, especially in a small town like Wimberley where everyone volunteers for something – sometimes too many things. The best data come from regular conversations. I donated one of my recent new books, *Music in the Course of Life,* to be raffled off at the next concert. Everyone was grateful to me, thought it was very generous of me, and hoped they would win. Now, that's an easy scene to explore...

Interaction

Another idiographic community interactionists have begun to explore is the world of social media and games. The key feature here is interaction. Simon Gottschalk (2018) examined a very contemporary form of interaction involving music: music as a feature of video games. His analysis of improvisation in *Guitar Hero* points to the technological limitations placed upon the player's attempts to improvize – an action that we commonsensically assume is quite individualistic. For example, Guitar Hero has five uniform keys, strum bar, and whammy bar, in contrast to the six strings on a real guitar. These technological limitations mirror the social limitations prohibiting unrestrained improvisations in everyday-life interaction. Put simply, improvisation is always collaborative in music ensembles. Research design? Plug it in and turn it on.

Authenticity

Authenticity is a very popular and powerful concept in symbolic interaction today. Whereas mainstream, structural sociology posits a social world where issues and data are either true or false, empirically supported or anecdotal, the presence of an idea like authenticity gives support to our claim that social life – as well as our interpretations of it – are problematic, subjective, slippery, questionable, and debatable. Authenticity, in sum, is an *idea* that the meaning of which, like art, is very much in the mind of the beholder. In their excellent collection of interactionist-inspired essays on authenticity, J. Patrick Williams and Phillip Vannini (2009) locate authenticity in several arenas: culture, self, and society. In one of the chapters, I take a more in-depth, phenomenological approach by framing authenticity claims as tools by which the individual affects, modifies, justifies, excuses, or modifies the self, all of which takes place *in* particular concrete situations. Individuals will claim their expertise in discerning authentic popular music (e.g., in terms of artists' styles or talent) as a positive feature of their self-identity, whether or not the artist or performance in question is in any objective sense "authentic." William Force (2009, p. 296) studied the punk music scene and found that authenticity among punks involves more than just music styles. Authenticity is also gauged by participants' consumption styles: "it was clear that rare or limited-edition vinyl is more highly regarded than regular (black, nonnumbered, not limited) vinyl. Any color record has greater symbolic value than the CD format."

Authenticity issues thus seem to fit best with research methods that focus on audience perceptions, typically measured by marketing criteria. Put differently, authenticity is very much a concern of the consumer fan, who uses authenticity as a criterion for purchasing music. The fan may see authenticity as a real feature of music, whereas authenticity to the symbolic interactionist is a moral or ethical perception not specifically or necessarily based on facts.

CONCLUSION

Symbolic interaction provides a multitude of strategies for studying music in everyday life. This mandate has resulted in music studies taking the lead in the evolution of SI approaches to culture and specific art forms. I will close with a mention of two very creative essays in which the authors use music to help build symbolic interaction as a paradigm.

Philip Vannini and Dennis Waskul (2006) argue that symbolic interaction functions very much as music does: both deal with esthetics, whereas interactionism discloses meaning and self in society much like music does. Analytical frameworks in SI such as dramaturgy and narrative analysis are grounded in metaphors that see life as theater and life as a story. In related fashion, Vannini and Waskul argue for the creation of another metaphor: life as music. Viewing selfhood and symbolic interaction as music sensitizes us to observe and understand an important but much too neglected dimension of social life: the esthetic. Drawing from the pragmatist philosophy of John Dewey, they say that the realm of the esthetic, of beauty, should not be confined to museums and art galleries. The perception of beauty constitutes the very foundation of individuals' embodied experiences of their life worlds. They argue that the metaphor of life as music can make us aware of the diverse rhythms, melodies, and harmonies that make social life alive and vibrant. Like Goffman's concept of seeing life as theater, or narrative analysts seeing life as story, seeing life metaphorically as music allows us to conceive of the social world as a patterned world with its changing tempos and varying esthetics.

And, symbolic interaction has had a significant influence on artists who were also concerned with music and the self. As Serena Yang (2017, p. 354) notes, John Cage wrote in his book A Year from Monday (1967) that the "current use for art [is] giving instances of society suitable for social imitation – suitable because they show ways... people can do things without being told or telling others what to do." Cage's ideal anarchic music emphasizes not only renouncing compositional control but also the process of self-discovery happening to everyone, a process that leads participants to discover their creative abilities. Yang argues that Cage's penchant for self-discovery came from his understanding of George Herbert Mead's theories of the process of individuation (the "me" and the "I"). Cage discovered Mead through reading Zen and American Thought by his friend Van Meter Ames (1962), a professor of philosophy at the University of Cincinnati who saw the compatibility between Zen and Mead's concept of self in the capacity of the "I," a phase of self whose unpredictable steps contribute to human innovation. As Yang (2017, p. 354) summarizes,

> Cage found the possibility of overthrowing the thought of the world through triggering a self-discovery of the "I" in everyone. He realized this idea in his happenings, such as 0'00", by requiring performers to respond to the simple descriptions without specifying sound or duration.

REFERENCES

Ames, V. M. (1962). *Zen and American thought*. University of Hawaii Press.

Becker, H. S. (1951). The professional dance musician and his audience. *American Journal of Sociology*, *57*(2), 136–144.

Blumer, H. (1969). *Symbolic interactionism: Perspective and method*. Prentice Hall.

Cage, J. (1967). *A year from Monday*. Wesleyan University Press.

Charmaz, K., Harris, S. R., & Irvine, L. (2020). *The social self and everyday life*. Wiley.

Davis, F. (1991). *Fashion, culture, and identity*. University of Chicago Press.

Douglas, J. D. (1970). *Understanding everyday life*. Aldine.

Douglas, J. D. (1976). *Investigative social research*. Sage Publications.

Murguia, E., Tackett-Gibson, M., & Lessem, A. (Eds.). (2007). *Real drugs in a virtual world: Drug discourse and community online*. Lexington Press.

Ferris, K., & Stein, J. (2012). *The real world: An introduction to sociology* (3rd ed.). Norton.

Fine, G. (1979). Idioculture: Small groups and culture creation. *American Sociological Review*, *4*(5), 733–745.

Force, W. (2009). Consumption styles and the fluid complexity of punk authenticity. *Symbolic Interaction*, *32*(4), 289–309.

Gottschalk, S. (2018). *The terminal self: Everyday life in hypermodern times*. Routledge.

Irwin, J. (1977). *Scenes*. Sage.

Kotarba, J. A. (1983). *Chronic pain: Its social dimensions*. Sage.

Kotarba, J. A. (1984). The existential self in society: A synthesis. In J. A. Kotarba & A. Fontana (Eds.) *The existential self in society* (pp. 222–234). University of Chicago Press.

Kotarba, J. A. (1993). *The rave scene in Houston Texas: An ethnographic analysis.* Submitted to the Texas Commission on Alcohol and Drug Abuse: Research Briefs.

Kotarba, J. A. (2007). Drugmusictalk on-line: An ethnographic analysis. In E. Murguia (Ed.), *Real drugs in a virtual world: Drug discourse and community online* (pp. 161–179). Routledge.

Kotarba, J. A. (2010). The impact of popular music on symbolic interaction: An introduction. *Studies in Symbolic Interaction, 35,* 3–4.

Kotarba, J. A. (2013). *Baby boomer rock 'n' roll fans: The music never ends.* Rowman and Littlefield.

Kotarba, J. A. (2018). *Understanding society through popular music* (3rd ed.). Routledge.

Kotarba, J. A. (2019). The everyday life intersection of translational science and music. *Qualitative Sociology Review, 15*(2), 44–55.

Kotarba, J. A. (2023). Symbolic interaction and music. In W. H. Brekhus, T. Degloma, & W. R. Force (Eds.), *The oxford handbook of symbolic interaction* (pp. 258–274). Oxford University Press.

Kotarba, J. A., Fackler, J. L., & Nowotny, K. M. (2009). An ethnography of emerging latino music scenes. *Symbolic Interaction, 32*(4), 310–333.

Mead, G. H. (1934). *Mind, self, and society.* University of Chicago Press.

Melnikov, A., & Johnson, J. M. (2021). Situational analysis: Existential and interpretive perspectives. *Studies in Symbolic Interaction, 53,* 135–149.

Melnikov, A., & Kotarba, J. (2017). Jack Douglas and the vision of existential sociology. In M. H. Jacobsen (Ed.), *The interactionist imagination-studying meaning, situation, and micro-social order.* Palgrave Macmillan.

Nowotny, K. M., Fackler, J. L., Muschi, G., Vargas, C., Wilson, L., & Kotarba, J. A. (2010). Established Latino music scenes: Sense of place and the challenge of authenticity. In N. K. Denzin (Ed.), *Studies in symbolic interaction* (Vol. 35, pp. 29–50). Emerald Publishing Limited.

Peterson, R. A., & Bennett, A. (2004). *Music scenes.* Vanderbilt University Press.

Psaroudakis, I., Muller, T., & Salvini, A. (Eds.). (2021) *Dealing with grounded theory.* University Press.

Shank, B. (1994). *Dissonant identities: The rock 'n' roll scene in Austin.* Wesleyan University Press.

Vannini, P., & Waskul, D. (2006). Symbolic interaction as music: The esthetic constitution of meaning, self, and society. *Symbolic Interaction, 29*(1), 5–18.

Williams, J. P. (2011). *Subcultural theory: Traditions and methods.* Polity Press.

Williams, J. P. (2013). Music, the internet and deviant subcultures. In J. A. Kotarba et al. (Eds.), *Understanding society through popular music* (pp. 96–100). Routledge.

Williams, J. P. & Vannini, P. (Eds.). (2009). *Authenticity in everyday life.* Ashgate.

Wilshire, B. W. (2016). *The much at once: Music, science, ecstasy, the body.* Fordham University Press.

Yang, S. (2017). John Cage and George Herbert Mead: The unknown influence of Van Meter Ames. *Journal of the Society for American Music, 11*(3), 354–369. https://doi.org/10.1017/S1752196317000244

STATISTICAL METHODS AND SYMBOLIC INTERACTIONIST THEORIZING

Jeffery T. Ulmer

Penn State University, USA

ABSTRACT

This chapter expands on Herbert Blumer's and others' position that quantitative data and statistical methods are useful for studying outcomes *of social interaction processes. If we define sociology as a scientific enterprise, and if symbolic interactionism is to be a general sociological framework, then an anti-quantitative stance would be as limiting and unworkable as shunning qualitative data and methods. Statistical analysis is popularly associated with positivism in sociology, but there is no need for contemporary sociologists to yoke themselves to this epistemology to use quantitative data and statistics. To that end, I demonstrate the value of quantitative data and statistical analysis for foci that have long been central to symbolic interactionism: (1) probability, (2) variation, (3) contingency, (4) social context, and (5) causality. I then describe the under-recognized value of statistical data for Charles Peirce's analytical strategy of abduction, popularized and extended recently by Timmermans and Tavory. Statistical analyses can identify surprising or unexplained patterns that call for closer qualitative inquiry into social processes. Indeed, this may be the most valuable use of quantitative research.*

Keywords: Research methods; pragmatism; statistical analysis; causality; abduction

INTRODUCTION

David Maines (2001), a prolific interactionist scholar, often made the point that symbolic interactionism does not have an inherent research method. Yet symbolic interactionism has often been characterized, mostly externally but also internally,

---

Essential Methods in Symbolic Interaction
Studies in Symbolic Interaction, Volume 60, 105–118
Copyright © 2025 Jeffery T. Ulmer
Published under exclusive licence by Emerald Publishing Limited
ISSN: 0163-2396/doi:10.1108/S0163-239620250000060007

as a perspective that rejects quantitative data and statistical analysis (Esposito & Murphy, 1999, 2001; Huber, 1973, 1995). In my view, such a standpoint would be profoundly limiting of interactionism's scope and value for research. Thankfully, I think this characterization has never been accurate.

This chapter expands on Herbert Blumer's and others' position that quantitative data and statistical methods are useful for studying *outcomes* of social interaction processes (Maines, 1988; Ulmer, 2001; Ulmer & Wilson, 2003). In fact, Blumer saw statistical data and analyses as valuable for studying what he called the products of social processes (Blumer, 1969, p. 25). Blumer and many other interactionists have advocated a principled catholicity of methods. That is, the data and research methods must be appropriate to the research problem at hand. If we define sociology as a scientific enterprise (I recognize that this is not universally agreed upon), and if symbolic interactionism is to be a general sociological framework, then an anti-quantitative stance would be as limiting and unworkable as shunning qualitative data and methods (see Ulmer & Wilson, 2003). A scientific sociology simply must sometimes address quantitative questions concerning the distributions, aggregate patterns, probabilities, and correlations.

Statistical analysis is popularly associated with positivism in sociology, but there is no need for contemporary sociologists to yoke themselves to this dated positivism in order to use quantitative data and statistical analytic tools. In fact, most contemporary sociologists probably do not agree with traditional positivist epistemological positions. To that end, I demonstrate the value of quantitative data and statistical analysis for foci that have long been central to symbolic interactionism: (1) probability, (2) variation, (3) contingency, (4) social context, and (5) causality. This chapter closes by describing the under-recognized value of statistical data for Charles Peirce's (1934) analytical strategy of *abduction*, popularized and extended recently by Timmermans and Tavory (2012). Statistical analyses can identify surprising or unexplained patterns that call for closer qualitative inquiry into social processes. Indeed, this may be the most valuable use of quantitative research.

SYMBOLIC INTERACTIONISM: EMPIRICISM, NOT POSITIVISM

First, a brief (and quite oversimplified) sketch of the contrast between positivism and pragmatism is necessary. These distinctions have been explained extensively elsewhere (e.g., Joas, 1993; Perinbanayagam, 1986; Shalin, 1986, 1991). Logical positivism and neo-positivism (hereafter, positivism) are quite complex, but it is safe to say that these perspectives have several distinctive characteristics (Westby, 1991). First, positivism assumes an objectively true natural reality, which exists apart from human observation, that can be discovered by independent observers (Shalin, 1991). Second, these independent observers – scientists – can, in principle, discover this objective natural reality with fidelity. This observation is only distorted through measurement error. Third, universal causal laws exist, and scientists can in principle discover them through independent observation. In principle, with the purest and most ideal measurement techniques, there would be no measurement error and we could capture objective reality. The quest of any science becomes one of striving to obtain the most valid and reliable measurements and minimizing measurement error.

However, empiricism is not the exclusive property of positivism. Pragmatism, upon which symbolic interactionism is based, similarly seeks a grounding for science (particularly for studying human mind, behavior, and group life) but differs from positivism. They seek to go in similar directions, but come from quite different philosophical foundations. Whereas positivism derives from philosophical realism, pragmatism stands between realism and idealism (Maines, 2001; Shalin, 1991). Pragmatists such as Peirce, James, and Mead recognized, in Mead's words, a "world that is there:" an external reality that is obdurate and independent of any particular observation. Crucially, however, we can only know that reality through perception. Thus, we inhabit a world that is mediated by our perceptions, and constructed by us as objects, to be interpreted and acted upon. Pragmatism/interactionism recognizes that: (a) the act of observation constitutes what is observed, that is, creates it as a social object, and (b) observation does not occur in neutral language, but is instead structured by the language of the observer (Shalin, 1991). Therefore, if there is an obdurate reality, we can only know it pragmatically, through the processes in (a) and (b). These two points also mean that universal causal laws are not possible. We can make generalizations, and test probabilistic causal propositions, and try to develop concepts from sensitizing to more definitive (Blumer, 1969), but these are always tentative, subject to further perception and reconstruction, and bounded by conventions of language and meaning. Furthermore, this all takes place within particular intersubjective arenas of discourse, with their particular narrative structures (Maines, 2001). In its recognition of these points, pragmatism, and symbolic interactionism, can be seen as more empirical than positivism and sociological approaches based on it, because pragmatism/interactionism is less naïve about the act of observation.

Quantitative data and statistical analysis are not inherently incompatible with these pragmatist epistemological positions. The major danger to guard against is the misplacing of agency, and forgetting that quantitative data are symbolic representations just as much as textual data are (Maines, 1993). When one codes and analyzes data statistically, one must treat them for what they are: numerical stand-ins for individual and joint actors and their interactional products. This was the thrust of Blumer's (1956) critique of "variable analysis." It is not that coding data with numbers and defining them as variables is inherently problematic, it is the misplacement of causal agency onto those variables. That is, variables do not think or do things, people do, and we create variables to *represent* those things. To take an example from criminological theory, Robert Merton's (1938) theory of anomie and social structure proposes that the group condition of anomie leads to higher rates of crime within that group. If one were to commit the "variable analysis" fallacy critiqued by Blumer, one would treat the variable anomie as an external force that pushes or causes rates of behaviors that break the law. Seen through interactionist lenses, anomie is a concept that describes a set of group-level experiences of alienation from and cynicism toward dominant societal goals and norms. In the face of these experiences, individuals adapt in various ways. Some of those adaptations entail breaking societal laws. In the first rendering of this conceptual relationship, the agency and action are attributed to the variables. In the second, they are attributed to the social actors as they confront their social structural contexts. The crucial point is to keep the focus on agency and causality not as a property of variables or statistical relationships but of individual and group social actors, acting with situations.

The analytical act of coding, whether quantitative or qualitative, is the process of deciding how to represent empirical observations, which are themselves interpretations (Maines, 1993). Quantification is simply useful for abstracting and representing empirical observations of outcomes in numerical ways to manipulate them statistically. Quantitative data and statistical analysis are thus valuable for understanding the most basic features of the social world. These include probability, variation, contingency, context, and causality.

PROBABILITY

Applied statistics is, of course, based on the mathematics of probability. Probabilistic, not hard, determinism is central to contemporary statistical methods (Agresti & Finlay, 1986). In positivistic treatments of statistical methodology, the sources of indeterminacy, or imperfect prediction, are measurement error, lack of adequate data (including "omitted variable bias"), or other biases. But indeterminacy has another, more pragmatist interpretation. Interactionists since Mead and Blumer see indeterminacy as inherent in human activity and agency, not merely measurement error. Indeterminacy, rather than strict determinism, is built into statistical methods. For example, ordinary least squares and similar regression methods assess strength of the ability of explanatory variables to predict the *mean* of the dependent variable at given values of the explanatory variables, not the specific value of particular observations. Regression in fact assumes a degree of indeterminacy (the error term) in the very structure of the equation. Statistical analysis provides the tools for not only examining probabilistic determinism but also simultaneously indeterminism (Ulmer & Wilson, 2003). In other words, analyses such as these give researchers not only information on the likelihood of an event, behavior, or condition, but also a quantitative sense of the amount of room for indeterminacy and what Mead called "emergence" (see Agnew, 1995).

VARIATION

The study of human variation is central to all of social science. In fact, Charles Darwin showed us that variation is inherent in all life. Describing and explaining variation is the essence of theory and science. Note that I did not say "variance" in the statistical sense, but variation in the sense of variety, diversity, and difference. Pragmatism, from which symbolic interactionism derives, incorporated Darwin's emphasis on variation, and variation was central to the work of Mead, Park, Blumer, Strauss, and others. Glaser and Strauss (1967) articulated the crucial importance of the constant comparative method in the development of grounded theory, and Strauss (1993) emphasized the importance of variation and comparison for symbolic interaction in general. Statistical analysis allows the researcher to make very complex comparisons of relationships, properties, events, and actors – more complex and refined than are probably possible with qualitative analytic methods alone. In fact, the purpose of multivariate regression-style statistical models is to make complex comparisons between relationships of covariation across numbers of observations or cases.

CONTINGENCY

Maines (2003) interpreted the term "variables" as indexing dimensions of situations, how they vary, and how these dimensions affect acts or interpretations. Variables often represent situational conditions such as statuses and identity markers (e.g., gender, age, occupation, race/ethnicity), constraints (e.g., residential segregation, poverty), events (e.g., life course transitions, turning points, migration), relationships (e.g., marriage, children, cohabitation), and other important features of social circumstances. Viewed this way, statistical analysis can enable a researcher to engage in analysis of how outcomes vary according to the contingencies and conditions of situations. For example, multivariate regression models depict the likelihood of an outcome occurring in relation to the situational contingencies indexed by predictor variables. Statistical interaction effects, where the effect of a predictor variable on an outcome depends on the presence, absence, or levels of another factor predictors, are extremely valuable in depicting situational contingencies. In other words, examining statistical interaction effects is a way of answering "it depends" kinds of questions. That is, statistical interaction effects indicate that the association between one phenomenon and another *depends on* the presence, absence, or role of a third factor. Thus, statistical interactions indicate the operation of contingencies. For example, consider the important issue of whether the criminal sentencing decisions of judges are racially biased, the subject of a massive amount of research (see reviews by King & Light, 2019; Spohn, 2000). Research commonly finds that this question does not have a straightforward, single answer, as demonstrated by several commonly found statistical interaction effects. First, the extent to which Black and Hispanic defendants receive more severe criminal punishments than White defendants with equal criminal charges, criminal histories, and other legally relevant factors are contingent upon defendants' gender and age (Spohn & Holleran, 2000; Steffensmeier et al., 1998; see reviews by Lynch, 2019; Ulmer, 2012). Second, racial and ethnic disparities in criminal punishment vary geographically; they depend on the local social contexts surrounding courts (Ulmer, 2012; Ulmer & Johnson, 2004). Discovering this kind of contingency, when statistical relationships between outcomes and what predicts them depend

SOCIAL CONTEXT

The unit of analysis for symbolic interactionists is the social act, and acts occur in contexts. Police officers work within different cities and counties, judges oversee proceedings in different jurisdictions, children attend different schools, etc. These social contexts (counties, jurisdictions, schools, organizations, etc.) can shape individual perceptions, attitudes, and behavior as people adapt to and act toward their social surroundings. Hall's (1997) interactionist framework for analyzing social organization at the meso- and macro-levels emphasizes *conditions and conditioning*. Conditioning is the process by which larger-scale structures, culture, or organization set the conditions, constraints, and opportunities for situations, which are in turn confronted by individual and joint actors. Interactionists have long recognized that larger-scale contexts condition situations, and situations (and their definition) set conditions for action and interaction, which in turn recursively maintain or modify situations and even larger scale contexts (Strauss, 1993).

Maines and Thomas's (1990) recovering of Herbert Blumer's theory of industrialization provides an excellent example of the concepts of *conditions and conditioning*. Blumer (1990, p. 32) stated that three group-level interaction processes characterize industrialization: a nucleus of mechanical production, an attached network of procurement and distribution, and an attendant service structure. Crucially, he argued that industrialization has *indeterminate* effects on societies that adopt it. Industrialization certainly alters industrializing societies, but exactly how depends on how industrialization interfaces with "nine points of entry into group life." These are: (1) the structure of positions and occupations, (2) the apparatus for filling positions, (3) new ecological arrangements, (4) the regimen of industrial work, (5) new structures of social relations, (6) new interests and interest groups, (7) monetary and contractual relations, (8) goods produced by manufacturing, and (9) patterns of income. In other words, Blumer's nine points of entry into group life *condition and contextualize* industrialization's impact in developing societies. One can see how applying this theoretical framework would necessitate quantitative, cross-national and historical data collection and analysis.

Statistical analysis, especially tools such as multilevel regression models, is a valuable asset in understanding how different layers of social contexts condition situations and action (Ulmer & Wilson, 2003). To extend the earlier example of how racial bias in criminal courts is situationally contingent on the gender and age statuses of defendants, racial and ethnic inequalities in sentencing severity also are conditioned by the organizational and sociopolitical contexts surrounding courtrooms. Extensive research has shown that the extent to which Black and Hispanic defendants, particularly young men, get more severe punishments (e.g., imprisonment rather than probation, longer prison terms) varies by the racial and ethnic composition of the communities surrounding courts

JEFFERY T. ULMER

(Feldmeyer & Cochran, 2019; Ulmer & Johnson, 2004), recent immigration patterns where courts are located (Feldmeyer et al., 2015; Ulmer & Parker, 2020), local racial segregation (Beckman & Wang, 2022; Zvonkovich & Ulmer, 2024), and even the historical legacy of lynching (Rigby & Charles, 2021).

Furthermore, knowing that statistical relationships between phenomena are different in differing social contexts can be useful for sensitizing further qualitative data collection. Such knowledge can guide the theoretical sampling (Glaser & Strauss, 1967) of different contextual settings in which to collect ethnographic data for comparisons. Differences in how social contexts condition outcomes also sensitizes qualitative research aimed at illuminating situated interaction processes that lie behind the statistical relationships and their variation across localities, organizations, or other settings. In other words, understanding contextual variation in a statistical sense can help researchers understand where to collect and compare data on the interactional and interpretive processes where social causality lies.

CAUSALITY

As discussed earlier, Blumer (1956) scolded sociologists who treated variables as if they had agency, rather than locating such agency in people and their actions. This is a crucial difference in interactionist versus positivistic conceptions of causality, even when the latter recognize that causality is probabilistic rather than deterministic. For interactionists, variables do not cause other variables, or exert action. Rather, variables are merely markers or stand-ins for people's interpretations, decisions, and interaction processes. However, Mead, James, Blumer, and others from the beginnings of the interactionist tradition did not reject the notion of causality in social behavior and group life (Maines, 1989, 2001). Causality exists in the social world, but it exists in situated human agency, interpretation, and action.

Mead explicated a distinction between "how" and "why" conceptions of causation (Maines, 2001). "How" perspectives on causality see causality in terms of conditioning processes such as those discussed earlier in this chapter. This conditioning occurs in the specious present, as actors define and act toward social objects and situational conditions. "Why" perspectives view causality as due to the action of antecedent variables, and emphasize the predictive value of modeling those variables. Mead, says Maines (2001, pp. 48–49) preferred the "how" model of causation:

> Unlike other causal frameworks, Mead temporally and situationally locates causation in the present. But more precisely, he regards its essential character as that of a process rather than as antecedent object acting upon other objects...These conditioning relationships (i.e., causes) provide for the determination of conduct with reference to the future. Therefore, they are exactly what Mead meant by causation...

The contrast between Mead's two conceptions of causality is unwittingly being played out in contemporary debates in statistical methods regarding "counterfactual causality" and "mechanistic" or theoretical causality (Sampson et al., 2013). Mechanism-based cause focuses on theorizing and then observing causal processes that lead to outcomes under specified conditions, while counterfactual causality views causation as marked by actions or events that would or would not happen *but for* the influence of an antecedent causal variable (Sampson et al., 2013). This model of causality strives to adhere as close as possible to the logic of *experimental design*, which is considered by advocates of counterfactual causality as the gold standard of research methodology. If randomized experiments are not feasible or ethical, then counterfactual causal analysis of quantitative data relies on statistical techniques and multivariate model specification to mimic the experimental logic of independent variables, dependent variables, and the ruling out of spurious effects through controls. Counterfactual approaches to causal analysis dominate contemporary econometrics and statistical design, having diffused from methodological trends in economics (Apel & Sweeten, 2010). The statistical methodology literature is now centrally focused on what it known as causal inference or identification, which emphasizes isolating the action of causal antecedent variables via randomized controlled experiments, or, if those are not feasible, using statistical techniques such as fixed-effects models, propensity scoring, instrumental variables, or difference-in-difference models (Sampson et al., 2013).

Similar to Mead, Nobel Prize–winning economist James Heckman (2005) distinguishes between statistical causality, which focuses on statistically identifying quantified causal effects, and scientific causality, which requires theory about agency and choice, conditions, and feedback. The former encompasses counterfactual causality, whereas the latter more resembles the interactionist version. Counterfactual causality also takes a "black box" approach to observing causal mechanisms/processes; whereas mechanism or scientific causality seeks to look inside the black box and observe the processes by which outcomes occur (Heckman, 2005; Sampson et al., 2013).

Interactionist theorizing, of course, is not satisfied with mere counterfactual causality. From the perspective of Mead's "how" causality and Heckman's scientific causality, no matter how sophisticated, statistical methods aimed at counterfactual causality can only produce very refined and specified *correlations*. That is, even a counterfactual causal model assessing a predictor's effect on an outcome, with numerous control variables held constant through experimental design or model specification, can only demonstrate that a correlation/ co-variation between predictor and outcome holds (is robust, in statistical parlance) after accounting for confounding variables and alternative model specifications or analytical methods. Such analyses cannot demonstrate causal mechanisms, which for Mead are *processes* occurring in the specious present of interpretation, social acts, and the situations that condition them (Maines, 2001).

However, that does not mean that statistical analysis techniques aimed at counterfactual causal inference are not useful. Far from it – these can be important tools to point toward where to look for Mead's "how" interpretive and processual mechanisms, or what Heckman would today call mechanism-based or scientific causality. In fact, these two different causal logics, together with the position that quantitative data and analysis are useful for studying *outcomes* while qualitative data are vital for understanding processes (Perinbanayagam, 1986), suggest an underappreciated way that statistical and qualitative research can mutually augment each other.

JEFFERY T. ULMER

THE VALUE OF STATISTICAL DATA FOR ABDUCTION: SENSITIZING QUALITATIVE RESEARCH

The notion that quantitative and qualitative data are complementary is not at all novel. Carl Taylor, in his 1947 ASA Presidential Address (p. 7) articulated this:

> [Qualitative] Field studies...place flesh, blood, and nervous system on the skeleton of statistical information. Everything they reveal adds to and none of it subtracts from the quantitative information. Furthermore...the quantitative analyses reveal certain contours of behavior which help to focus qualitative observations.

It is common in contemporary sociology to find calls for multi-method research. Indeed, such research is now quite common. Typically, research methods texts describe how qualitative research is useful for the development and pretesting of surveys, or the suggestion of research propositions to be deductively tested by statistical analysis (Brandt & Timmermans, 2021).

However, it is less commonly recognized that quantitative data and analyses of outcomes can sensitize qualitative data collection aimed at interactional and interpretive processes. In fact, given the distinction between counterfactual and scientific/theoretical causality discussed above, the most valuable approach might be to "work backwards" from statistical analyses to qualitative research that captures interpretive and interaction processes, and their situational conditioning, that comprise the actual causal mechanisms of social life, as emphasized by scientific or theoretical causality.

This strategy of using statistical analyses (perhaps even counterfactual causal methods) to guide and inspire qualitative data collection to uncover causal mechanisms links well conceptually with Charles Peirce's (1934) analytical method of *abduction*. Tavory and Timmermans (2014) and Timmermans and Tavory (2012) have rediscovered Charles Peirces' logic of abduction, and extended it to formulate an approach to qualitative research that provides an alternative to Glaser and Strauss' (1967) analytical induction–based method of grounded theory (for a description of how abduction and grounded theory differ, see Timmermans & Tavory, 2012). According to Timmermans and Tavory (2012, p. 170) "abduction refers to an inferential creative process of producing new hypotheses and theories based on surprising research evidence." As described by Peirce (1934, p. 117) himself, the logic of abduction proceeds as follows: "The surprising fact C is observed. But if A were true, C would be a matter of course. Hence, there is a reason to suspect that A is true."

Thus, abduction seeks surprising or anomalous empirical findings and used them as a roadmap to search for explanations, in a recursive dialog with theory and method (Timmermans & Tavory, 2012). "Abductive analysis emphasizes that rather than setting all preconceived theoretical ideas aside during the research project, researchers should enter the field with the deepest and broadest theoretical base possible and develop their theoretical repertoires throughout the research process" (Timmermans & Tavory, 2012, p. 180). Anomalous findings from theoretically guided statistical analyses, or even deductive hypothesis

114   *Statistical Methods, Symbolic Interactionist Theorizing*

testing, can be a valuable challenge to existing theory that call out for further qualitative inquiry into what lies behind those anomalous findings.

While Brandt and Timmermans (2021) have recognized the value of computational "big data" mining for abductive analysis, I am unaware of any attempts to connect more traditional statistical analysis to abduction. However, it may be that the most powerful use of statistical analyses in connection with qualitative research is the former's capacity to uncover surprising or unexplained patterns. These patterns then call out for further theoretically informed qualitative inquiry and abductive logic. Note that the use of statistical analysis to guide abduction would *not* consist of merely "data mining" or "regression fishing," where researchers would simply run a great number of analyses on quantitative datasets to see what turns up. This might be a viable strategy for inductively conceptualizing patterns in "big data" (Brandt & Timmermans, 2021), but it would violate abduction's tenet of juxtaposing theoretical expectations and actual empirical findings. After all, findings are only anomalous or surprising from some theoretical standpoint. Instead, an interplay of statistical analysis and qualitative research would use findings from the former which contradict extant theoretical expectations to direct qualitative research procedures such as theoretical sampling, selecting comparative cases, the search for negative cases, and coding. The result would be new theoretical understandings that illuminated previously unaccounted for causal mechanisms.

From my own research specialization of criminology, here are three examples of research that discovered anomalous findings from quantitative research, and followed these to direct qualitative inquiry that uncovered new explanations, developed conceptual modifications to existing theory, or led to the development of new theory. None of these examples explicitly refer to abductive analysis, but each provides a, perhaps unwitting, exemplar of it. Hester (2017) conducted an extensive study of judicial sentencing patterns in South Caroline. His statistical analyses of quantitative data from South Carolina courts uncovered the surprising fact that there was far less variation in sentencing severity in South Carolina than was typical in research on other states. That is, extant theory and literature suggested that judges in different counties' criminal courts would diverge widely in the severity of sentences they gave criminal defendants, even those convicted of the same types of crimes. The comparative uniformity he found in sentencing patterns across county courts was even more puzzling because South Carolina did not have sentencing guidelines, which foster more uniformity and less disparity in criminal sentences for similarly situated cases and defendants (Kramer & Ulmer, 2009). Hester's qualitative research sought explanations. Interviews with trial judges pointed to the importance of a unique policy of judge rotation between South Carolina counties. Judges would travel in a circuit between counties, hearing and sentencing cases across the circuit. This judge rotation provided more opportunities for interaction between judges across counties and courts than was typical elsewhere, and fostered "cross pollination" of informal sentencing norms. Judicial rotation led to "norm spreading" and "trading ideas" (Hester, 2017, p. 227). However, some differences among the rotating judges remained evident. These remaining between-judge differences

JEFFERY T. ULMER

then enabled extensive "judge shopping," even as judicial rotation blunted between-county differences in sentences.

Kramer and Ulmer (2002) analyzed quantitative data from Pennsylvania court sentencing and found that there was an unexpectedly high rate of lenient sentences that departed below the state's sentencing guidelines for serious violent crimes. In fact, the likelihood of a more lenient sentence than called for by sentencing guidelines increased with the severity of crimes – the more severe violent crimes were most likely to see these "downward departures" below the sentencing guidelines. Kramer and Ulmer (2002) then selected a theoretical sample of serious violent crime cases that received such guideline departures, from a variety of county courts, and interviewed the sentencing judges. The researchers asked judges about the features of the cases, and how they contrasted from other cases that did not receive these kinds of lenient sentences. Kramer and Ulmer's (2002) qualitative analysis found that several complex reasons lay behind these deviations below sentencing guidelines for certain serious violent crimes. First, prosecutors often agreed to more lenient sentences as a part of plea bargains, and judges were simply following these plea agreements. Such plea bargains often occurred when prosecutors had comparatively weaker evidence for a serious crime that might not withstand the scrutiny of a jury trial, and the prosecutors were willing to trade a less severe sentence in order to gain a conviction. Second, in certain cases, judges felt that the sentencing guidelines offense severity and prior record scores overstated the severity of either the crime or the defendant's criminal history. In these cases, judges would "correct" the sentencing guidelines by departing below them and giving a more lenient sentence than guidelines recommended. This research, in turn, helped to further extend theoretical understandings of judicial sentencing and courts organizational culture, and would eventually contribute to conceiving of criminal courts as "inhabited institutions" (Hallett, 2010; Ulmer, 2019).

A final, very impactful example of using quantitative data to sensitize and guide qualitative research is Giordano et al.'s (2002) study of gender and desistance from criminal careers. Giordano et al. (2002) collected longitudinal self-report survey data from men and women who had been arrested for criminal activity when they were juveniles. They then conducted in-depth life history interviews with these same men and women. However, the statistical analyses revealed that the quantitative measures were not as strongly predictive of criminal desistance as expected, and several theoretically expected relationships did not even appear. These lackluster statistical findings structured their coding of the qualitative data. Their analysis of the life history interviews uncovered several explanations for why the quantitative data looked the way they did, and uncovered new dimensions of variation and unsuspected relationships between factors that the quantitative analysis did not and could not show. For example, their life history analysis showed that: (1) desistance from crime was a strongly gendered process; that is, it qualitatively differed for men and women, (2) that adult social bonds operated differently between men and women in terms of their connection to criminal activity, (3) that many of the women who did not desist from crime in adulthood faced such severe socioeconomic disadvantage that opportunities to build conventional adult social bonds were all but foreclosed, and (4) a process of identity renegotiation and self-redefinition was a necessary, but not sufficient, cause of desistance from crime for both men and women. Giordano et al. (2002) went on to develop what they call a "symbolic interactionist theory of desistance from crime," and argued that the dialog between their quantitative and qualitative data were necessary for the theory's development.

CONCLUSION

I attended graduate school in sociology during the late 1980s and early 1990s in a very positivistic-oriented department with a strong sense of methodological and theoretical orthodoxy, and at best, an indifference toward symbolic interactionism. This graduate program provided me with excellent training in quantitative methods, and despite my mediocrity at math, I did very well in statistics, and came to find quantitative research enjoyable and even exciting. But my theoretical leanings were always with symbolic interactionism, and I gravitated toward the one major interactionist scholar in the department, along with the handful of interactionist-friendly faculty. Thankfully, the mentorship I received from David Maines and my exposure to his work elucidating Blumer's and others' positions on research methods and causality became a foundation from which I approached all my research, both quantitative and qualitative (see Ulmer, 2023).

Three decades later, I perceive that the dualistic debates about quantitative versus qualitative research, and the quasi-ideological adherence to one or the other, has greatly dissipated. If this is true, I am very gratified. In this chapter, I have elaborated on some directions for continued integration of statistical analysis and qualitative inquiry, perhaps leading to a more methodologically complete interactionism.

REFERENCES

Agnew, R. (1995). Determinism, indeterminism, and crime: An empirical exploration. *Criminology*, *33*(1), 83–110.

Agresti, A., & Finlay, B. (1986). *Statistical methods for social scientists*. Dellen.

Apel, R. J., & Sweeten, G. (2010). Propensity score matching in criminology and criminal justice. In A. Piquero & D. Weisburd (Eds.), *Handbook of quantitative criminology* (pp. 543–562). Springer.

Beckman, L., & Wang, X. (2022). Revisiting the minority threat perspective: Examining the main and interactive effects of segregation on sentencing severity. *Justice Quarterly*, *39*(4), 745–771.

Blumer, H. (1956). Sociological analysis and the 'Variable'. *American Sociological Review*, *21*, 683–690.

Blumer, H. (1969). *Symbolic interactionism: Perspective and method*. Prentice-Hall.

Blumer, H. (1990). *Industrialization as an agent of social change* Ed. D. Maines & T. Morrione. Aldine de Gruyter.

Brandt, P., & Timmermans, S. (2021). Abductive logic of inquiry for quantitative research in the digital age. *Sociological Science*, *8*, 191–210.

Esposito, L., & Murphy, J. (1999). Desensitizing Herbert Blumer's work on race relations: Recent applications of his group position theory to the study of contemporary race prejudice. *The Sociological Quarterly*, *40*, 397–410.

Esposito, L., & Murphy, J. (2001). Reply to Ulmer: Symbolic interactionism or a structural alternative? *The Sociological Quarterly, 42*(2), 297–302.

Feldmeyer, B., & Cochran, J. C. (2019). Racial threat and social control: A review and conceptual framework for advancing racial threat theory. In J. D. Unnever, S. L. Gabbidon, & C. Chouhy (Eds.), *Building a black criminology: Race, theory, and crime, advances in criminological theory* (pp. 283–316). Routledge.

Feldmeyer, B., Warren, P. Y., Siennick, S. E., & Neptune, M. (2015). Racial, ethnic, and immigrant threat: Is there a new criminal threat on state sentencing? *Journal of Research in Crime and Delinquency, 52*(1), 62–92.

Giordano, P., Cernkovich, S., & Rudolph, J. (2002). Gender, crime, and desistance: Toward a theory of cognitive transformation. *American Journal of Sociology, 107*(4), 990–1064.

Glaser, B., & Strauss, A. (1967). *The discovery of grounded theory.* Aldine.

Hall, P. (1997). Meta-power, social organization, and the shaping of social action. *Symbolic Interaction, 20*, 397–418.

Hallett, T. (2010). The myth incarnate: Recoupling processes, turmoil, and inhabited institutions in an urban elementary school. *American Sociological Review, 75*(1), 52–74.

Heckman, J. J. (2005). The scientific model of causality. *Sociological Methodology, 35*, 1–97.

Hester, R. (2017). Judicial rotation as centripetal force: Sentencing in the court communities of South Carolina. *Criminology, 55*(1), 205–235.

Huber, J. (1973). Symbolic interaction as a pragmatic perspective: The bias of emergent theory. *American Sociological Review, 38*(2), 274–283.

Huber, J. (1995). Institutional perspectives on sociology. *American Journal of Sociology, 101*(1), 194–217.

Joas, H. (1993). *Pragmatism and social theory.* University of Chicago Press.

King, R. D., & Light, M. T. (2019). Have racial and ethnic disparities in sentencing declined? *Crime and Justice, 48*, 365–437.

Kramer, J., & Ulmer, J. T. (2002). Downward departures for serious violent offenders: Local court 'Corrections' to Pennsylvania's sentencing guidelines. *Criminology, 40*(4), 897–931.

Kramer, J. H., & Ulmer, J. T. (2009). *Sentencing guidelines: Lessons from Pennsylvania.* Lynne Rienner Publishers.

Lynch, M. (2019). Focally concerned about focal concerns: A conceptual and methodological critique of sentencing disparities research. *Justice Quarterly, 36*(7), 1148–1175.

Maines, D. R. (1988). Myth, text, and interactionist complicity in the neglect of Blumer's macrosociology. *Symbolic Interaction, 11*, 43–57.

Maines, D. R. (1989). Herbert Blumer on the possibility of science in the practice of sociology. *Journal of Contemporary Ethnography, 18*, 160–177.

Maines, D. R. (1993). Narrative's moment and sociology's phenomena: Toward a narrative sociology. *The Sociological Quarterly, 34*, 17–38.

Maines, D. R. (2001). *The faultline of consciousness: A view of interactionism in sociology.* Aldine de Gruyter.

Maines, D. R. (2003). Interactionism's place. *Symbolic Interaction, 26*(1), 5–18.

Maines, D. R., & Thomas, M. (1990). On the breadth and relevance of Blumer's perspective: Introduction to his analysis of industrialization. In D. Maines & T. Morrione (Eds.), *Industrialization as an agent of social change* (pp. xi–xxiv). Aldine de Gruyter.

Merton, R. K. (1938). Social structure and anomie. *American Sociological Review, 3*(5), 672–682.

Peirce, C. S. (1934). *Collected papers of Charles Sanders Peirce. Vol. 5, Pragmatism and pragmaticism.* Harvard University Press.

Perinbanayagam, R. S. (1986). The meaning of uncertainty and the uncertainty of meaning. *Symbolic Interaction, 9*(1), 105–128.

Rigby, D., & Charles, S. (2021). Capital punishment and the legacies of slavery and lynching in the United States. *Annals of the American Academy of Political and Social Science, 694*(1), 205–219.

Sampson, R. J., Winship, C., & Knight, C. (2013). Translating causal claims: Principles and strategies for policy relevant criminology. *Criminology and Public Policy, 12*, 1–30.

Shalin, D. N. (1986). Pragmatism and social interactionism. *American Sociological Review, 51*(1), 9–29.

Shalin, D. N. (1991). The pragmatic origins of symbolic interactionism and the crisis of classical science. *Studies in Symbolic Interaction, 12*(1), 223–251.

Spohn, C. C. (2000). Thirty years of sentencing reform: The quest for a racially neutral sentencing process In J. Horney (Ed.), *Criminal justice 2000: Volume 3. Policies, processes, and decisions of the criminal justice system* (Vol. 3, pp. 427–501). Indiana University.

Spohn, C., & Holleran, D. (2000). The imprisonment penalty paid by young unemployed Black and Hispanic male offenders. *Criminology, 38*, 281–306.

Steffensmeier, D., Ulmer, J. T., & Kramer, J. (1998). The interaction of race, gender, and age in criminal sentencing: The punishment cost of being young, Black, and male. *Criminology, 36*, 763–798.

Strauss, A. (1993). *Continual permutations of action.* Aldine de Gruyter.

Tavory, I., & Timmermans, S. (2014). *Abductive analysis: Theorizing qualitative research.* University of Chicago Press.

Taylor, C. C. (1947). Sociology and common sense. *American Sociological Review, 12*, 1–12.

Timmermans, S., & Tavory, I. (2012). Theory construction in qualitative research: From grounded theory to abductive analysis. *Sociological Theory, 30*(3), 167–186.

Ulmer, J. T. (2001). Mythic facts and Herbert Blumer's work on race relations. *The Sociological Quarterly, 42*(2), 289–296.

Ulmer, J. T. (2012). Recent developments and new directions in sentencing research. *Justice Quarterly, 29*(1), 1–40.

Ulmer, J. (2019). Courts as inhabited institutions: Making sense of difference and similarity in sentencing. *Crime and Justice: A Review of Research, 48*, 483–522.

Ulmer, J. (2023). David R. Maines: Embedding symbolic interactionism at the heart of sociology. *Symbolic Interaction, 46*(1), 3–25.

Ulmer, J. T., & Johnson, B. D. (2004). Sentencing in context: A multilevel analysis. *Criminology, 42*(1), 132–172.

Ulmer, J., & Parker, B. (2020). Federal sentencing of Hispanic defendants in changing immigrant destinations. *Justice Quarterly, 37*(3), 541–570.

Ulmer, J. T., & Wilson, M. S. (2003). The potential contributions of quantitative research to symbolic interactionism. *Symbolic Interaction, 26*(4), 531–552.

Westby, D. L. (1991). *The growth of sociological theory: Human nature, knowledge, and social change.* Prentice-Hall.

Zvonkovich, J., & Ulmer, J. (2024). Segregation and group threat: Specifying Hispanic-White punishment disparity. *Social Problems.* https://doi.org/10.1093/socpro/spad032

PART B

NEW INTERACTIONIST RESEARCH

COLONIAL VIOLENCE AND THE CHICAGO SCHOOL: THE IMPACT OF ELLSWORTH FARIS'S MISSIONARY EXPERIENCES IN THE CONGO

Daniel R. Huebner

University of North Carolina Greensboro, USA

ABSTRACT

Building on a growing body of literature showing how colonialism has shaped the content and production of social scientific knowledge, this project traces an unacknowledged, but influential, case in which colonial violence witnessed by a Christian missionary became a basis for sociological theorizing. Ellsworth Faris, one of the earliest American missionaries in the Belgian Congo, witnessed violence and exploitation of native people at the hands of colonial authorities, and contributed evidence to the infamous 1904 "Casement Report" that exposed atrocities. This paper argues that, while never turning away from his religious inspiration, Faris came to see Mead's and others' social psychological ideas as key to understanding his experiences, and this task remained the central preoccupation throughout his professional scholarship, even in seemingly unexpected contexts. These ideas led to his path-breaking critique of theories of instincts, emphasis on the socio-cultural relativity of human nature, study of social structures and impulses of punishment and hostility, and public stances against pseudo-scientific racism. Uncovering the ways secular Chicago School social science engaged with the ethics of colonial knowledge and with religiously motivated pursuits helps to recontextualize their work and raise new questions in light of contemporary scholarship. This project includes the first comprehensive bibliography of Ellsworth Faris's published work.

Keywords: Colonialism; missions; Ellsworth Faris; Belgian Congo; Chicago School of Sociology

---

Essential Methods in Symbolic Interaction
Studies in Symbolic Interaction, Volume 60, 121–168
Copyright © 2025 Daniel R. Huebner
Published under exclusive licence by Emerald Publishing Limited
ISSN: 0163-2396/doi:10.1108/S0163-239620250000060008

INTRODUCTION

What if it could be shown that the chairman of the University of Chicago Sociology Department during its classic "Chicago School" heyday of the 1920s and 1930s, the editor of the *American Journal of Sociology*, the co-editor of the classic "University of Chicago Sociological Series" of monographs, and one of the people most responsible for mentoring Herbert Blumer's "Symbolic Interactionism" and constructing the canon of American sociological theory – that this person's sociological theorizing and influence in the discipline were thoroughly entangled with his experiences as a religious missionary in the Congo during the period of its most infamous Belgian colonial atrocities? This study seeks to document these claims and makes the argument that recognizing the context of colonial violence helps us understand Ellsworth Faris's turn toward sociology and social theory and to reinterpret his sociological insights. In this way, focusing on Faris also helps us rediscover unique comparative-historical contexts relevant to the professionalization of American sociology and emergence of Symbolic Interactionism.

In order to make this argument, the introduction lays out the emerging decolonial perspective in the historiography of social science that shapes the present study. The study is then divided into two major sections that (1) lay out the historical documentation of Faris's experiences in the Congo and (2) examine the impact of these experiences on his published sociological work. The conclusion returns to a discussion of how such an analysis contributes to the contemporary literature in the history of sociology and begins to recontextualize foundational concepts of Symbolic Interactionism.

DECOLONIAL SOCIOLOGY

Some of the most productive developments in the historical study of sociology in the 21st century have come from efforts to "decolonize" sociology (e.g., Barkawi & George, 2017; Bhambra & Holmwood, 2021, 2022; Connell, 1997; Go, 2013; Go & Lawson 2017; Gutiérrez Rodríguez et al. 2010; Steinmetz, 2013). This growing literature combines a focus on reconstructing historical contexts, recovering forgotten and alternative authors to the canon, and examining how the discipline's epistemic structures are rooted in the historical and ongoing practices of imperial domination. Bhambra (2014, pp. 117, 142) has argued that such a decolonizing critique requires a thoroughgoing "reconstruction 'backward' of our historical accounts of modernity" in the service of constructing a forward-looking sociology adequate to the "'always-already' global age." Modernity, in this view, does not *produce* a connected world from previously separate, independent entities that then interact, but rather is itself a product of interconnections, often taking the asymmetric forms of domination, appropriation, dispossession, colonialism, and enslavement. She advocates "connected sociologies" that examine the intertwined histories, overlapping territories, and contrapuntal analyses (Bhambra, 2014, pp. 155–156), not in order to dismiss modern social theory but rather to reconstruct and renew it (Bhambra & Holmwood, 2021, pp. viii–ix; see also Go & Lawson, 2017). Bhambra and Holmwood (2021, pp. 23–24, 209–210) challenge researchers to "engag[e] with the past from the point of view of the present" by bringing present-day concerns and scholarship about the influences of colonial contexts on ideas to their reading and analysis of the past, with the goal of understanding both the historical context and the present differently.

Although much of this revisionist literature focuses especially on canonical European social theorists and the rediscovery of alternative non-Eurocentric social theories (e.g., Alatas, 2006, 2021; Alatas & Sinha, 2017; Connell, 2007), there has also been an increasing emphasis on classical American social theory. This literature has begun to interrogate how the sociological discourse on "race relations" in the "Chicago School," and especially in the work of its acknowledged leader, Robert E. Park, has been key to the claims to scientific legitimacy for American sociology (Ferguson, 2004; Go, 2013; Magubane, 2013; Stanfield, 1985). Park and Ellsworth Faris joined the University of Chicago Department of Sociology in 1914 and 1919, respectively, and Faris served as Park's department chair from 1925 until 1936, during the years of Park's greatest influence on the discipline. For whatever progressive work they and the other Chicago School figures understood themselves to be engaged in, reconstructive scholarship has sought to examine the racialized, gendered presuppositions that shaped the knowledge they made of the social world (see discussion in Balon & Holmwood, 2022).

In engagement with this literature, the present study builds in two important ways on the work of Zine Magubane (2013; 2014), who examines the historically situated and power-laden relations between early American social scientists, philanthropic and educational organizations, European colonial administrations in Africa, and peoples subject to these colonial practices. First, Magubane builds on Connell's (1997) and Zimmerman's (2010) contributions to show how Park's work with the Congo Reform Association and Tuskegee Institute helps us understand the shift from a pre-disciplinary sociology explicitly focused on "global difference" and empire to a post-World War I disciplinary sociology studying the problems "internal" to the metropole. In Magubane's (2013) view, this shift toward a "parochial" perspective displaces the ways sociology had been, itself, implicated in colonial rule (see also Bhambra & Holmwood, 2021; Connell, 1997; Go, 2013).

Second, Magubane (2013, p. 89) argues that a key starting point for post-colonial reconstruction of sociology is by providing an alternative institutional history, noting that "knowledge often circulates along imperial pathways." This cue helps us explain the persistence of explicit sociological theorizing based on colonial difference in this early American sociological context. Magubane (along with Blasi, 2017; Yu, 2002, Zimmerman, 2013) discusses the historical relations of Robert Park's social science and a number of religious missionaries, which have otherwise been ignored in reconstructive scholarship. Recovering these entanglements helps us to understand the body of "classical" social scientific claims that we inherit, and provides us with the materials through which to take

124   *Colonial Violence and the Chicago School*

another step in critically reconstructing the foundations of our discipline (Bhambra & Holmwood, 2021; Go, 2013).

The present article seeks to attend to Faris's ideas with the same level of scrutiny that Park's ideas have been given, and to recover some of the ways that the supposedly universalistic concepts of classical American social theory (e.g., primary group, social attitude, symbolic language, personality or self) were elaborated in an attempt to wrestle with the nature of colonial violence and difference. I show how Faris's colonial entanglements – moving from a missionary in the colonial Congo to a leading American social theorist – can enrich our understanding of how sociology transformed in this period. Faris never became "parochial" in the same sense that the discipline did, because he formulated concepts that contemporary sociologists read as being about the metropole (e.g., Cooley's "primary group") in a way premised on the recognition of colonial difference, and his connections with international missionary and religious associations outside of the contemporary discipline's taken-for-granted institutions (e.g., departments, universities, professional associations) remained central to his sociology. I attempt to show how, if we approach Faris in a way informed by decolonial scholarship, we can see the explicit ways his sociological work developed out of his colonial encounter, which further challenges the contemporary discipline to rearticulate how colonial difference remains an undercurrent in the post-World War I sociological scholarship even as it gets forgotten.

PART I: ELLSWORTH FARIS AND COLONIAL CONGO

The first empirical task of the paper is to detail the circumstances of Faris's experiences as a missionary and his subsequent professional career as an academic. The section briefly traces Faris's background and initiation into missionary endeavors, and reconstructs the extant documentation on his period as a missionary in the Congo. The paper then identifies his efforts, while still a missionary, to contribute to ethnological and linguistic scholarship and his relations to the international campaign against colonial atrocities. The section closes by outlining Faris's professional trajectory after returning from being a missionary into an academic career as a sociologist.

Ellsworth Faris as a Missionary

Ellsworth Eugene Faris was born on September 30, 1874 in Franklin County, Tennessee to Sophie Jane (*née* Yarbrough) and George Alexander Faris. Faris's father was a leader in the emerging Disciples of Christ denomination that traced its origins to the so-called "Stone-Campbell Restoration Movement" in the Second Great Awakening of 19th century America. George Faris moved the family to rural Texas early in Ellsworth's life, where George became an evangelist and later editor of the Disciples of Christ-affiliated newspaper *The Christian Courier* from 1901 to 1913 (Williams, 2006b, p. 57). He lectured intermittently at

Texas Christian University (TCU), was a member of the university's Board of Trustees, and interacted with high-level members of the church.[1]

Ellsworth Faris earned his Bachelor of Science degree from Add-Ran College (which would become TCU) in 1894, with a reported interest in becoming a civil engineer, but he was also inspired by evangelical calls for foreign missionaries (Cain, 2005, p. 32; Faris, 1970, p. 158; Odum, 1951). While teaching as Principal of Add-Ran's Preparatory Department, he was appointed as a missionary by the Foreign Christian Mission Society (FCMS), the official missionary organization of the Disciples of Christ, and he went to Cincinnati, Ohio in the expectation that he would likely be sent to China (Browning, 1952, p. 13; Williams, 2006b, p. 57). The FCMS was eager to open a missionary station in Africa, however, and saw the Belgian-administered Congo Free State as an opportunity. Faris was willing, but was not immediately dispatched, because church officials also wanted a medical doctor to accompany him.[2]

The Congo had been opened up to modern European colonization in the 1870s, most notably by the voyage of Welsh-American journalist Henry Morton Stanley up the Congo River in 1876–1877, sponsored by King Leopold II of Belgium, which was followed by establishment of colonial and commercial enterprises centered on the rubber and ivory trades (Williams, 2006a, p. 5). The 1884–1885 Berlin Conference among the European "Great Powers" legitimated and spurred the so-called "Scramble for Africa," and during that conference it was agreed by the gathered governments that Leopold II would be personal sovereign and steward over the Congo, in charge of ensuring the freedom of commerce, protection of natives, and freedom of religion in the region (Williams, 2006a, p. 6). Leopold's administration proceeded to carve out "domains" for "concessionary companies" that would have monopolies over the commerce and administration of large tracts of land and designated the remainder as "crown lands" under Leopold's personal control.

Missionaries became increasingly aware by the 1890s of systematic abuses of the native people including forced labor, excessive taxation, summary executions, mutilation of hands, forced relocations of villages, and kidnappings of women and children to compel cooperation of men. Some began to report these abuses in their published missionary journals and to protest to colonial officials (Williams, 2006a, pp. 6–8). By 1904, a broad coalition of missionaries, human rights activists, and politicians raised concerns in the international press, as well as in the British Parliament and the American Congress, about the conditions in the Congo. The controversy was ultimately enough to lead the Belgian parliament to compel Leopold II to give up direct control of the territory, and to establish a parliamentary-controlled, formal Belgian colony in the Congo in 1908, lasting until political independence in 1960 (Williams, 2006a, p. 8).

Faris met his new missionary companion, Dr Harry N. Biddle, in Ohio in 1897, after which they traveled to Boston, London, Paris, and Antwerp, before departing for the Congo. While on this voyage, Faris and Biddle met with officials of the FCMS, American Baptist Missionary Union, the London-based Institute for Home and Foreign Missions, and others – to learn about their enterprise from other missionaries, to negotiate possible missionary station locations, to purchase supplies and equipment, to arrange bank credit and purchasing agents, and to proselytize for their enterprise (Browning, 1952, p. 14).

They arrived on the central African coast on May 28, 1897 and immediately started visiting a variety of mission stations of the American and English Baptists, Adventists, Roman Catholics, Swedish Free Church, and others, in the Belgian- and French-colonized Congo as well as the Portuguese-colonized Angola, largely by boat, train, and on foot accompanied by groups of native porters. They reported traveling thousands of miles on these journeys and went far into the interior of the country along the upper Congo River and its various tributaries. They waited over a year before being able to establish a mission station, because the Belgian colonial officials repeatedly delayed and denied their requests. The colonial administrators were seeking to clamp down on the establishment of new Protestant missions, because the missionaries had already been vocal critics of colonial practices. Faris was aware of this "widespread criticism of the treatment of the natives by the government in those days" and the opposition of the government to expansion of missionary work because "the missionaries were regarded as unwelcome," according to his own recollections (Browning, 1952, p. 14; Williams, 2006a, p. 9).

Finally, Faris and Biddle found a work-around when the American Baptists agreed to sell an existing mission station at Bolenge to the Disciples of Christ.[3] During this first itinerant year, both Faris and Biddle had gotten dangerously ill on several occasions, and Biddle contracted such a severe illness that he never got to help establish the mission at Bolenge (Browning, 1952, p. 15). He was taken away by steamship to the Canary Islands where he ultimately died in a hospital. Meanwhile Faris arrived in February 1899 at Bolenge, which is almost directly on the spot that the Congo River crosses the equator, where he started studying the local language, Lonkundo, learning about the people and geography, and helping the departing Baptist missionaries.[4] He awaited the replacements for Biddle, Dr Royal Dye and Eva Dye, for over three months.

During his first 1897–1901 period as a missionary at Bolenge, Faris dedicated much of his time to language learning, opening and teaching in a school, and taking many "itinerating" trips throughout the region to proselytize, while other missionaries also focused on providing medical treatment and the construction of buildings (Browning, 1952). Prior to returning to the US in 1901 for a furlough, he was also directed to consult with missionaries in Portuguese Angola about consolidating their work, which took him on another long journey through the interior of central West Africa (Browning, 1952, p. 15; Williams, 2006a, p. 62). After Faris became a professional sociologist in 1918–1919, he would come to rely heavily on observations from his time in the Congo and his knowledge of the language in his published articles, as discussed in subsequent sections of this study.

While on furlough back in the United States, Faris spoke in a variety of settings about his missionary work, including at the national convention of the Disciples of Christ in Minneapolis. He married Elizabeth (Bessie) Homan, a daughter of a Disciples preacher, during this period as well. They spent two quarters in 1901 studying at the University of Chicago Divinity School, where

DANIEL R. HUEBNER 127

Ellsworth focused on Greek and Hebrew (Browning, 1952, p. 15). At some point during this early coursework (or his subsequent summer quarter at the University of Chicago in 1906), he must also have been drawn in the direction of the social sciences and philosophy, which would ultimately lead to his later PhD coursework in psychology at the university (discussed further below).

Ellsworth and Bessie Faris arrived back at Bolenge in 1902. Bessie Faris began learning Lonkundo and working especially with the local women and girls (Browning, 1952, p. 15). Ellsworth Faris held nightly religious gatherings with local people, and he performed the first baptisms for the mission in 1902 (Williams, 2006b, p. 65). Although it was not until Faris's second period that the first native converts were baptized by the Disciples of Christ missionaries, there were dozens of congregants at their native church by the time Faris departed only two years later in 1904 (Browning, 1952, p. 15). Later historians have emphasized the important role of these early native converts and evangelists in developing the church into an established mainline Protestant denomination in the contemporary Congo with approximately a million adherents (Sundkler, 2000, pp. 771–780; Williams, 2006b). Despite the initial delays and denials of local officials, and their ongoing suspicions about Protestant missionaries, Faris reportedly maintained cordial relations with the local colonial officials during this period (Lagergren, 1970; Vinck, 1992, pp. 77–78, 84; Williams, 2006a, pp. 4–5). He and his colleagues also participated in early ecumenical conferences among the various denominations of missionaries in the Congo in which discussions of colonial conditions, native languages, educational efforts, and other topics were discussed (Yates, 1987).[5]

The Farises were "invalided" home in 1904 for reasons of ill health (Faris, 1970, p. 30; Kivisto, 1999, p. 713; Odum, 1951). Throughout the voyage home, Ellsworth Faris was apparently bedridden and was hospitalized for weeks upon his return. The illness left him so weak that he could do almost no work for a year afterward (Browning, 1952, p. 15). In his recollections, he claimed that he had been ill over 50 times during his seven years in the Congo and could still recall the illness-related deaths or departures of almost every missionary who had arrived during his time. In an extended, autobiographical statement written by Ellsworth Faris and compiled by Louise Browning in 1952 at the end of his life, Faris noted that the seven-year period in the Congo was "the most valuable and most fruitful" of his career, and that he wanted his epitaph to read simply "Ellsworth Faris—He founded the Bolenge Mission" (Browning, 1952, p. 13). Note that this is after a 22-year professional career as a sociologist, in addition to another 12 years as a philosophy and psychology professor and 14 years as emeritus and visiting professor of sociology. As a result, we cannot easily dismiss his missionary experiences as defining a single period or passing concern prior to a separate, secular professional career.

Ethnologist and Witness to Atrocities

In order to see the changes and continuities across Faris's life, it is important to focus, first, on Faris's efforts during and immediately after his period as a missionary, before shifting to consider his publications as a professional socio-logist and social psychologist beginning in 1914. Faris's published letters and reports while in the Congo include scattered remarks on what he would later professionally call the "folkways" and "culture" of the people, but most of what he published about the native cultures that he observed appears much later. His major scholarly accomplishments prior to his 1914 dissertation include compiling and publishing a list of 313 stories, adages, and proverbs in Lonkundo, and translating the biblical Gospel of Mark into that language, both with the help of fellow missionary Royal Dye (Faris & Dye, 1904; Faris & Dye, 1905).[6] Faris's 1904 departure from the Congo was even reportedly delayed long enough for him to finish his translations (Browning, 1952, p. 15). Many of the proverbs Faris collected were later translated into English by Frederick Starr, a professor of anthropology at the University of Chicago and Faris's later senior colleague (1909, pp. 177–196).[7] Faris also contributed to W. H. Stapleton's (1903, pp. 234, 237–238) *Comparative Handbook of Congo Languages*, which has been called the "beginning of comparative linguistic work among the Protestant missionaries" in the Congo (Samarin, 1986, p. 148), for which Faris contributed a specimen translation of the "Parable of the Prodigal Son" translated into Lunkundo.

The missionaries functioned as "knowledge brokers" in that they maintained an effective monopoly on printing facilities and literacy instruction in the Congo of this period, thus they had considerable control over the spread of "knowledge beyond that learned through practical experience" (Samarin, 1986; Yates, 1987, p. 311). No major language of the Congo had been systematized in a written form prior to the modern establishment of Christian missions with the exception of Swahili, which had spread along the Muslim trading routes in the east of the region; but from 1879 to 1908, 19 Congolese languages were put into written form by missionaries (Yates, 1987). Protestant missionaries in the Congo emphasized literacy education, the transcription of spoken languages into written form, and working in people's vernacular languages (not European languages or regional trading languages), as important to evangelizing and teaching a personal knowledge of the bible (Samarin, 1986; Yates, 1987, pp. 319, 322). Among these efforts, the Foreign Christian Missionary Society to which Faris belonged was especially active, with only the much larger American and British Baptist Mis-sionary Societies contributing more substantively. As might be expected, the vast majority of the printed material in this period concerned religious themes, and only about five percent of the publications could seriously be considered "secular" (Yates, 1987, p. 326). Thus, Faris is unique in contributing both to the religious and, through his recording of local proverbs, the relatively rare secular publications. Yet, despite how constitutive "colonial sociology" would become to early Belgian social science, Faris seems to have departed just prior to the first formal sociological inquiries in the Congo by the Belgian Sociological Society in 1905 (Steinmetz, 2023, pp. 190–193).

Protestant missionaries were "almost daily witnesses of the exploitation of land and people" in the colonial Congo Free State and brought scandals to the knowledge of the outside world, providing vital material for the emergence of the Congo Reform Association's campaign against atrocities (Sundkler, 2000, p. 285).[8]

So, a 100 years after Faris inaugurated the Disciples of Christ Congo Mission, missionary officials and denominational publications of the Disciples of Christ held contentious debates about whether Faris and his colleagues could be considered "culture-destroying collaborators of a ruthless colonial regime" (Williams, 2006a, pp. 3–4). Professional historiographical contributions to these discussions argued that Faris, in particular, had to have known about the large numbers of killings at the hands of colonial officers and corporate soldiers, and that the relative absence of documented public protest on his part suggested a deliberate silence on the matter (thereby perhaps also setting a precedent that made church officials reluctant to engage politically with later abuses). The literature acknowledges the "friendly relations" between the colonial state and the Bolenge mission station after the Disciples of Christ took over operation, but church historian Paul A. Williams (2006a, pp. 4–5) also points out that there is substantial published and private evidence that the missionaries participated in the movement to oppose the abusive practices of the state. Among other considerations that may help us understand their position, Williams (2006a, pp. 14–15) notes that the Disciples of Christ were relatively recent arrivals to an area already fraught with tensions between missions and colonial officials; that they had extraordinary difficulties in getting established and dealing with the sheer amount of daily work involved in renovating a mission and acquiring a familiarity with local culture and language; that there were pervasive and often debilitating health problems among the missionaries; and that they espoused a sense of religious vocation that may have discouraged political activism.

Studies of missionaries in colonial Africa have demonstrated the interstitial status of missionaries who were, on the one hand, certainly part of the "colonial ordering process," but who, on the other hand, had motives and agendas independent of the political and military authorities and frequently came from cultures different from the colonial administrators (Comaroff & Comaroff, 1986; Williams, 2006a, p. 8). For the Disciples of Christ Congo missionaries, this ambiguity can be examined in terms of different "phases" of the relationship between the missionaries and the colonial state, according to Williams (2006a). In the early "itinerant years" of 1897–1899, Faris and Biddle encountered the resistance of the colonial state to new Protestant missions, and they noted concerns in their correspondence regarding state-sponsored policies of "plunder[ing] the natives" and villages that had been "driven away by the state" and forced to settle elsewhere. Extracts of these letters were published in the Disciples of Christ journal *Missionary Intelligencer* (Williams, 2006a, pp. 9–10). In this period, Faris and Biddle were in the "awkward" or "delicate" position of petitioning the administration for permission to establish a mission while already observing concerning practices of that state, which may help account for their more "tentative" remarks in this period (Williams, 2006a, p. 9).

In the 1899–1903 period, after Faris negotiated the purchase of the Bolenge station and began to establish a permanent mission, he and his colleagues attempted to cooperate with the state officials while Faris's reports of the mission published back home also contained remarks about native people having "fled from the state soldiers," "compelled to hunt rubber," "murdered by the soldiers,"

130   *Colonial Violence and the Chicago School*

and who regarded the state's actions as "oppression" but were not able to "offer any resistance" (Williams, 2006a, p. 10). Faris also complained to a government official about the abusive treatment of natives on at least one documented occasion in 1899, as recorded in his diary (later published as part of the Casement Report, discussed below). Still, Williams (2006a, p. 11) points out that Faris remained somewhat guarded about his own opinions of these practices in his published reports and only somewhat accidently became an important public source of documentation of abuses. In the period after Faris's departure from the Congo, his colleagues Edwin A. Layton and R. Ray Eldred assumed a more public and activist stance in criticizing abuses by helping to draft statements and testimony for the US Senate Foreign Relations Committee, publishing statements in a variety of religious journals, and presenting reports at religious conventions (Williams, 2006a, pp. 12–13). Notably, their testimony formed the centerpiece of Robert E. Park's (1904) first published article on the Congo in his work on behalf of the American Congo Reform Association, before he became a secretary for Booker T. Washington and, subsequently, a professional sociologist.

The Casement Report and Aftermath

The focal document that, more than any other, exposed the international public to the atrocities in the Congo and led to the creation of the Congo Reform Association was the so-called "Casement Report" of 1904. In response to growing concerns, the British Consul to the Congo, Roger Casement, was instructed by resolution of the House of Commons to investigate. Casement toured around the colony for weeks by boat and on foot, interviewing current and former government officials, missionaries, and native people, and keeping detailed diaries and notes. Casement visited Bolenge in August 1903 during these investigations, and Faris served as his guide in the area for two days, according to Casement's diary (Ó Síocháin & O'Sullivan, 2003, pp. 256–257). During this visit, Faris allowed Casement to copy down an account written into his own diary from August 23, 1899 in which Faris recorded his attempt to draw attention to an alarming situation: he had a discussion with an official who revealed that the soldiers sent out to patrol rubber collections were expected to bring back a severed hand for each rifle cartridge discharged during their patrols (Ó Síocháin & O'Sullivan, 2003, pp. 76, 88–89). Casement noted that Faris reported his concern about this conversation to the Governor-General of the Congo (the highest-ranking colonial official) in October 1900 on his way back to the US and that, as a result, the Governor-General issued a circular that month limiting the private concessionary companies' "right of police" to employ armed militias with unlicensed rifles. Prior to that circular, the companies "appear to have engaged in military operations on a somewhat extensive scale, and to have made war upon the natives on their own account," but Casement's own subsequent observations of unlicensed sentries and guards led him to further remark that the new regulations "do not seem to be strictly observed," and that the continued extensive use of armed militias "as a means to

DANIEL R. HUEBNER 131

enforce the compliance with demands for india-rubber... is not denied by anyone I met on the Upper Congo" (Ó Síocháin & O'Sullivan, 2003, pp. 87–89).

Although Casement sought to downplay the extent to which his findings were derived from the work of Protestant missionaries (Jacobsen & Daniel, 2014, p. 11), Faris's diary entry was included with the 20 pages of supplementary evidence submitted by Casement along with his forty-page report. Casement gave his first public report to Parliament in September 1903, which was published in the House of Commons Parliamentary Papers of 1904, and his findings were excerpted in a large number of subsequent newspaper articles, pamphlets, and books. Faris's diary entry was even copied verbatim (although attributed to "one of my [i.e., King Leopold II's] government officers") in Mark Twain's (1905, p. 18) *King Leopold's Soliloquy*, which sought to bring public awareness to the atrocities through his signature satire, and from which Twain donated all the proceeds to relief efforts.[9] In effect, Faris's diary entry "served as one of the sources for the three most prominent writers in the Congo reform movement, Roger Casement, E. D. Morel [founder of the international Congo Reform Association], and Mark Twain" (Williams, 2006a, p. 11).

Faris was also involuntarily involved in the most well-publicized attempt by the colonial administration to discredit the Casement Report, and by extension, the reform movement more generally. One of the instances Casement singled out in his report was a case of a boy named Epondo, who testified in Casement's presence, and whose testimony was confirmed by his village, that his hand had been cut off by a company sentry for not paying his rubber tax (Ó Síocháin & O'Sullivan, 2003, pp. 36–37). In response to Casement's direct involvement, the local colonial authorities established an inquiry into the case, during the course of which Epondo retracted his story. After Casement had left, Faris was called in by the authorities to witness and officially record this retraction in a letter that was later widely quoted by critics of Casement.

The founder of the Congo Reform Association, the British journalist E. D. Morel, pointed out the very "disingenuous" manner in which the colonial authorities had involved Faris to seek to provide "outside backing" to their "rather weak" defense (Morel, 1904, pp. 368–369). In a widely circulated exposé, Morel (1904, 369–370) quoted extensively from Faris's letters which, he showed, the authorities had dubiously quoted extracts from. Read in their totality, Faris's letters asserted that the officials had lied about their story, that the request for him to witness the retraction was at best unexplained since he was not initially involved in the case, that Epondo may well have been threatened in order to get this retraction, and that he was all too aware of the trick the colonial officials were attempting to play. Faris openly speculated that the officials may have taken this disingenuous and roundabout line of defense precisely "because they think they are surer to win" by "deny[ing] the fact" and by attempting to discredit Casement as "too hasty, and therefore mistaken." Morel (1904, p. 370) mocked the attempt of the state to make Faris their "pet witness," who in reality "does not seem to have a very high idea of those who sought, under the falsest of pretenes, to use him for their questionable ends."[10]

132   *Colonial Violence and the Chicago School*

Faris's role in the Epondo case is likewise mentioned in the most widely distributed English-language apologia for the colonial Congo in this period, Henry W. Wack's (1905) *The Story of the Congo Free State*. Indeed, this work and its reaction reveal something of Faris's position in these peculiar debates. Wack (1905, pp. 271–272, 303–304) quoted repeatedly from University of Chicago anthropologist Frederick Starr (who would later become Faris's senior departmental colleague) as an "independent" "scientific" witness, in order to argue that the Congo is "not so bad," and to question the "bitter attacks upon Leopold and the Free State" and the motives of the missionaries reporting abuses. Starr, for his part, first undertook ethnographic investigations of the Congo in 1905–1906, in part to examine reports of atrocities. His findings, first popularized in the *Chicago Tribune*, appeared at times to flippantly dismiss atrocities as sensationalized or no-longer-prevalent. Ironically, his ulterior motives were to criticize American and British meddling in the Congo when the US was itself engaged in imperialistic practices in the Philippines and its treatment of African Americans and when Britain was perhaps attempting to grab the Congo for its own empire (Starr, 1907). Wack and Starr were, in turn, heavily criticized by Robert E. Park (later Faris's and Starr's colleague, but then working as publicist for the American Congo Reform Association, making him perhaps the most important critic of Belgian colonial atrocities in the American press at the time) as part of the deliberate and persistent propaganda effort being made to minimize the disclosures of atrocities (Lyman, 1992, p. 237).

This discussion reveals something of the contours of authoritative claims-making about the Congo in the late 19th century and early 20th century, ranging from practical attempts to document language and customs, to explications of racial types and rankings, to anti-imperialist rhetoric. Missionaries could use their personal experiences to write with authority, while others with a claim to scientific authority could refute them on the same basis. Moral frameworks of racial "uplift" are found among both religious and secular writers, and among both defenders and critics of colonial practice. Likewise, anti-imperialist and anti-racist commitments could take on apparently strange forms when used to interpret this context: where criticisms of colonial brutalities could come from advocates of more (not less) colonialism and where critics of one polity's imperialism could dismiss evidence of imperialism elsewhere.

Still, although there has been some attention, especially by Disciples of Christ historians, to Faris's relation to the colonial-era atrocities in the Congo, two important items have been entirely missed in these discussions: (1) he co-authored a statement on behalf of his fellow missionaries directly to King Leopold II that protested against the treatment of Congo natives, and (2) he circulated a statement to the press immediately after he returned in 1904 attempting to expose atrocities to the public.

First, in January 1904, Ellsworth Faris was present at the "Second Conference of Missionaries of the Protestant Societies Working in Congoland," held at Leopoldville (now Kinshasa), which included 42 representatives from seven missionary societies based in England, the United States, and Sweden (Report of the Second Conference, 1904). As the conference went on, it became increasingly

DANIEL R. HUEBNER   133

clear that the conditions of native people were on the minds of the missionaries: one paper talked of the colonial state's monopoly on food supplies; another respondent talked of the "oppression of the natives and great cruelties practised on them"; letters from two others were read which told of the terrible conditions of "excessive taxation." By the end of the third day, the assembled missionaries voted unanimously to prepare a "memorial" that would be submitted to King Leopold II "on the questions of the cruelties and oppressive taxation," and a committee was appointed consisting of the conference chairman C. H. Harvey, along with J. H. Morgan, Joseph Clark, W. H. Stapleton, and Ellsworth Faris (Report of the Second Conference, 1904, p. 41). The committee's statement, unanimously approved by the whole conference (apparently after some alteration and discussion), read:

> To His Majesty Leopold II., Sovereign of the Congo Independent State.
>
> SIRE,—We, the members of Protestant Missionary Societies carrying on work in the Congo Independent State, and at present gathered in conference at Leopoldville on the 30th day of January 1904, while thankfully recognising the benefits which have accrued to the natives of the country in several districts, from the government of your Majesty, beg respectfully to draw your Majesty's attention to certain recent matters which have been brought under our notice by members of this Conference concerning the terrible treatment of the natives, chiefly in the districts of Bangala and Equator. The points to which reference has principally been made are the oppressive taxation and the barbarous methods of collecting india-rubber.
>
> Solely on behalf of the natives in whom we are deeply interested, and in view of the alarming death rate in these districts, we sincerely pray that your Majesty may order such changes to be effected as will result in the amelioration of the unhappy condition of these your Majesty's subjects. (Report of the Second Conference, 1904, 42; reprinted in "Congo Missionaries", 1904; "Second General", 1904)

The memorial was signed by the chairman and secretaries of the conference on behalf of all those present and was presented in both English and French to the Governor-General of the Congo Free State in March 1904, who reportedly received the statement "cordially" and sent it to the King (Report of the Second Conference, 1904, p. 44). The missionaries were assured that an official "with full powers to investigate such matters" and "to take what steps were necessary to get things on a better footing as regards the future" was being dispatched from Brussels, to whom the missionaries were "free to take any cases" for further inquiry and to make any suggestions on "the amelioration of the conditions of the natives" that they wanted.

Second, Faris circulated an extended statement on the atrocities to American newspapers, apparently without much success, after he returned from the Congo in the autumn of 1904. Faris's remarks were ultimately quoted in German on the front page of the November 2, 1904 issue of the long-standing Zürich, Switzerland newspaper *Neue Zürcher Zeitung* under the title "Atrocities in the Congo Free State" ("Grausamkeiten" 1904). This article was a contribution from a New York-based special correspondent (only credited as "R."), who was skeptical of American claims ever since the 1898 Spanish-American War to be "destined by Providence to defend weaker peoples against the tyranny and capriciousness of the stronger." Nevertheless, Faris's statement, to which the correspondent referred at length, confirmed all the most horrible conditions in the Congo: the concession of vast lands for ivory hunting and exploitative extraction of resources by private companies; the training of large native armies to brutally police rubber and ivory collections, including instances in which hundreds of people were slaughtered and whole villages burned down in a single raid; lashings by hippopotamus whip of people whose rubber collections were underweight; and meeting people everywhere throughout the Congo Free State who had hands mutilated by these patrols. Faris was quoted as writing that "not since the days of Cortez and Pizarro has anything like the horrible, systematized villainy in the Congo Free State been seen."[11] Taken together, Faris's co-authored missionary statement to King Leopold and his attempts to publish an exposé in the American press document Faris as taking a much more critical, activist approach to atrocities than existing literature has asserted.

PART II: IMPACTS OF COLONIAL EXPERIENCE ON FARIS'S ACADEMIC CAREER

Academic Career After the Congo

After Faris returned to the United States in 1904, he took a year of recuperation while he gave sporadic but well-liked talks about missions; he served as an associate editor of the *Christian Courier* that his father edited; and he became a graduate student at Texas Christian University (TCU), earning his masters degree in 1906 (Cain, 2005, p. 32). During the summer semester of 1906, Faris was also a graduate student again at the University of Chicago (Cain, 2005, p. 32). He was hired as a Professor of Sacred History and Missions at TCU's College of the Bible, and as Professor of Philosophy in TCU's philosophy department (Cain, 2005, p. 32). Faris taught at TCU from 1906 to 1911, at which time he was either given a leave of absence to complete his PhD or was fired for his unorthodox religious views, depending on different recollections of the events (Cain, 2005, p. 34).[12] It is difficult to reconstruct his views in this period in detail, but his apparent advocacy of historical criticism of the bible suggests that he was already moving in a more social scientific direction. After his initial 1904–1905 push to publicly condemn colonial practices, Faris does not appear to have had any further substantial involvement with the Congo Reform Association or related organizations, as far as I can reconstruct from available records. It is tempting to speculate about a conspicuous silence on Faris's part, perhaps related to the trauma of his experiences or a fear of speaking out in a local environment dominated by intense religious scrutiny, but direct evidence is lacking to confirm or deny this view.

What is clear is that, throughout this period, and indeed throughout his life, Faris maintained a sincere religious faith, so that his post-missionary secular career cannot be understood as a disavowal of his earlier convictions. Perhaps the clearest indication of that faith in this period is a letter Faris published in response to the pointed questions he received from pastors skeptical of his

DANIEL R. HUEBNER   135

teaching. TCU's Board of Trustees had been receiving complaints and rumors about Faris's teachings from fundamentalist pastors and financial donors from as early as 1907 (Cain, 2005, pp. 34–41, 47). They were concerned that his teaching and writing was too "radical" and "modern" on theological issues, especially in engaging with new historical criticism of the bible that they viewed as destructive or unsettling to the faith of students. In a published response to one of these critics, Faris wrote:

> At an early age I consecrated my life to the gospel of Christ. . . . I risked my life for the sake of the gospel of Christ and that I might preach where He was not named. . . . I have ministered to the sick by the hundreds and seen scores of people die. . . . Within a period of eight years I was sick fifty-seven times and often my life was despaired of. My colleague and friend died. . . . For days I have lain tossing with fever in a lonely village. . . I have been sick with fever on the open veldt, too weak to march, with only two black attendants and the lions howling nightly around our little campfire. And the only motive in all of it was to preach Jesus Christ. . . . At one time we were weeks without bread. At another time I lived for days on shelled corn and had no other food. . . . Grasshoppers and hippopotamus meat have been my diet. Do the good brethren who love the truth think that I should have been willing to preach in this way if I did not heartily believe in the Christ of God and the record of His life and teachings that we have in the Bible? (quoted in Cain, 2005, p. 38)

And yet, Faris made the decision in 1911 to go back to school again, in the discipline of psychology, at the age of 36 – moving hundreds of miles from Fort Worth, Texas to Chicago, Illinois "at considerable effort. . .taking along his wife and four children" (Faris, 1970, p. 30).

In 1911–1912, after leaving his professorship at TCU, Faris took graduate-level coursework in philosophy, psychology, education, and sociology at the University of Chicago and became minister of a Disciples of Christ Church in Waukegan, Illinois north of Chicago. His son, R. E. L. Faris (1970, pp. 35, 131), later suggested that it was during his 1911–1914 period as a graduate student that Faris shifted away from his "preacher-missionary background" and "absorbed the spirit of science" and objectivity as defining commitments of his sociology career. He completed a dissertation in the Department of Psychology under the supervision of James R. Angell and philosopher George H. Mead on "The Psychology of Punishment" (discussed in the following section), and the next year he stayed on as a teaching "fellow" in philosophy. Both Angell and Mead had followed John Dewey from the University of Michigan to the University of Chicago and formed part of the pragmatist Chicago School of Philosophy there (as did other people Faris studied with, including James H. Tufts, Addison W. Moore, and Edward S. Ames). Faris was especially influenced by Mead in this period, taking four of Mead's classes including his "social psychology" and attending informal discussion groups dedicated to discussing Mead's ideas on "social consciousness" (Huebner, 2014, pp. 99–100).

The pre-World War I University of Chicago is a context where the religious and secular coexisted more comfortably than in the post-war consolidation of secular disciplines. Certainly, Faris did not evince a sense that these necessarily conflict, and a number of the influences on Faris's scholarship (including Angell, Ames, and sociologist Charles R. Henderson) understood their scientific work to be in the service of morally or religiously motivated reforms in one form or another. Still, the post-war Chicago School of Sociology has been uniformly considered a center for secularizing the social sciences, especially through the methodological appeals to make sociology a science of human nature, to distinguish sociology from social reform and reformist social work, and to treat the city as a scientific laboratory. As the following section details, Faris worked in this period to turn his colonial observations away from an ethical context demanding direct action and practical change toward a detached, descriptive and interpretive social science orientation.

After a period from 1913 to 1918 as instructor at the University of Chicago and professor at the University of Iowa, Faris was invited to assume a tenured professorship in sociology in 1919 at the University of Sociology as a replacement for W. I. Thomas, who had been summarily fired, a position which Faris occupied continuously until his retirement in 1939. It was reportedly Faris's "interest in the ethnological material which his African experience had intensified and made concrete" that got him the invitation to the Chicago professorship, along with Angell's idea that he could be a sort of liaison between the psychology and sociology departments, given his "training in the Dewey-Mead tradition" (Faris, 1970, p. 31; Odum, 1951, p. 182).[13]

In addition to teaching Thomas's perennial "Social Origins" and "Social Attitudes" classes, one of Faris's first curricular innovations was to create a new "Introduction to Social Psychology" course that served as an informal prerequisite by which sociology students were introduced in detail to Mead's ideas and tracked into Mead's "Advanced Social Psychology" courses (which were offered in the philosophy department and later made famous through transcripts and notes published as *Mind, Self, and Society*) (Huebner, 2014, pp. 184–185). Many of Faris's students, including Blumer, recall how he was responsible for introducing them to the ideas of Mead, Dewey, Cooley, Thomas, and others and advocating for them as a coherent alternative perspective to then-mainstream social psychology (Huebner, 2014, pp. 159–160, 312). Faris's efforts in his classes and publications were important in laying out theoretical principles on the critique of psychological explanations and emphasizing the social nature of personality that he worked out in engagement with Mead (discussed further below), and Blumer later drew heavily from these efforts in articulating his "Symbolic Interactionism" (Huebner, 2014, chap. 7). Indeed, Faris wrote in a condolence letter to Mead's family, "I have for years regarded it as one of my chief aims to interpret and, if possible, extend the ideas which his great mind originated... in an academic sense I call myself his son" (quoted in Huebner, 2014, p. 310).

From 1925 until his 1939 retirement, Faris was chairman of the University of Chicago Sociology Department; from 1926 to 1936 he was editor of the flagship *American Journal of Sociology* (where he was also a frequent reviewer); and in 1937 he was President of the American Sociological Society. Faris was Blumer's dissertation chair in 1928 (with Mead and Park as the other committee members) and, as department chair, Faris hired Blumer as a sociology instructor and then as an assistant professor (Huebner, 2014, pp. 158–160). Outside the University of

DANIEL R. HUEBNER 137

Chicago, Faris served as a visiting professor at the University of Washington, Tulane University, the University of Hawaii, the Women's College of the University of North Carolina (now UNC Greensboro), and the University of Michigan prior to his retirement. After his retirement, he remained active, accepting invitations to lecture as a distinguished scholar at Texas Christian University and the University of Utah, and continuing his world travels (Browning, 1952, p. 16). Faris died December 13, 1953 at the age of 79.

The Constitutive Role of Colonial Experience in Faris's Sociology

The vast majority of the publications and professional speeches Faris wrote as a social scientist from 1914 on discuss issues that are clearly tied to his missionary work, and he continually returned to issues from his experiences including the nature and origins of punishment, the socio-cultural nature of racial difference, and related issues.

No previous study has prepared a comprehensive bibliography of Faris's work. Indeed, even in career summaries and obituaries for Faris, there has been a persistent myth that he was not a very productive scholar and wrote little (Kivisto, 1999; Odum, 1951; Suttles, 1976). And in the otherwise-revealing accounts of Odum (1951) and others, there appears to be a marked silence or disinterest in Faris's pre-sociological career. But my research demonstrates that he published well over 200 pieces in a remarkably wide range of venues across 60 years (see the appendix to this study). By the time that reprints of Faris's essays appeared in the 1970s, Symbolic Interactionism was becoming a self-consciously organized group and research approach in sociology. In that context, Faris had already been largely "obliterated by incorporation," to borrow Merton's (1968, pp. 27–28) phrase, because of the influence of his students (especially Herbert Blumer) on the discipline (see Murray, 2013, p. 173).

Faris prepared a curated collection of what he considered his most significant sociological work from 1914 to 1936, published as *The Nature of Human Nature* (Faris, 1937a) and dedicated to George H. Mead. This work can be a starting point for focusing analysis. Faris chose 31 pieces out of at least 145 that he had prepared during this 1914–1936 period to include in the volume (this collection does not include any of his pre-sociological publications in missionary and church-affiliated publications, nor any of the dozens of articles, chapters, reviews, and professional talks he completed after that date). In analyzing these works, with a focus on how they mobilize evidence in support of claims, I find that all but four of the pieces make either explicit reference to factual claims from Faris's time in the Congo or more general reference to comparative ethnological evidence. The comparative ethnological evidence ranges widely across many cultures but indicates somewhat more indirectly the importance of cultural comparisons in formulating conceptual problems and in directing his reading. However, if we focus only on counts of articles, this may suggest that his previous experience serves as mere instances, periodical references to factual claims, and

138

Colonial Violence and the Chicago School

may not give a full sense of the ways in which his colonial experiences become a "constitutive" aspect of his thought. To make this clear, a more qualitative examination of his work is necessary. In this way we can see how Faris continually returned to these problems of colonial difference in order to formulate his problematics and to develop his concepts about the relation between culture and personality.

Faris's *The Nature of Human Nature* has been republished twice, and the editors of those efforts indicated some of the outstanding themes of Faris's work. For Ralph H. Turner (1972), Faris's collected work stressed the priority of "group determination" of individual behavior and attitudes; the dynamic, volatile "process and change" character of society and of human nature; the distinctive and crucial nature of the "primary group" in forming human nature and maintaining social control; clarification and modification of the concept of "social attitudes"; and the importance of "written language" in bringing about transformations in social organization. And for Gerald D. Suttles (1976), Faris's emphases included a conception of social psychology in which personality develops through social interaction and comes to include the capacity for self-regulation; a thoroughgoing critique of "elementalism" in psychology that attempt to find irreducible elements of personality (e.g., instincts, conditioned reflexes); an analysis of the processes and mechanisms by which the individual becomes an effective social actor in a world they did not create themselves; and a stress on the importance of the "primary group" in explaining "social control" and personality. Suttles (1976, p. xii) was particularly direct in asserting that starting from the social psychology of George H. Mead and W. I. Thomas allowed Faris to treat "his own observations of the Forest Bantu of the Belgian Congo" as a prompt to interrogate the "correspondence between individual and social conceptions of self" and point to the "social conditions which were consequential for both the individual and the society." Faris's essays "exercised widespread influence on the emerging field of sociology," in Suttles's (1976, p. vii) view, and were important in "sharpening the focus of sociological study" and "linking persistent philosophical debates with the new empirical investigations going on at the University of Chicago."

For the purpose of this paper, it is useful to zoom in on two different periods of Faris's sociological publications: an early period beginning with his 1914 dissertation and encompassing his career through the early 1930s, and a later period that begins with his return expedition to the Congo in 1932 until the end of his career. In what follows, I single out two of Faris's early publications – his 1914 dissertation and his 1918 first *American Journal of Sociology* article to illustrate this early period in which Faris attempted to conceptualize his earlier experiences in proto-Symbolic Interactionist sociological terms. I then discuss Faris's work theorizing and carrying out a return expedition in 1932, which represents his efforts to more deliberately observe comparative social change and to take a leading role in directing sociological theorizing. Beyond these individual pieces there are literally dozens of contributions Faris published that develop related claims (see the Appendix).

DANIEL R. HUEBNER   139

Faris's Earliest Sociological Publications

Faris's dissertation, "The Psychology of Punishment," sought to consider punishment as a social institution and to critically scrutinize the rationales given for punitive practices in light of a pragmatic-functionalist theory of the social psychological processes drawn from Mead and Angell. The evidentiary centerpiece of the dissertation is a chapter addressing the "origin of punishment," which was also published as Faris's first article in a non-religious-affiliated journal, appearing in the 1914 *International Journal of Ethics*.[14] The chapter argues that punishment is not a primordial "instinct," but rather a social institution with an identifiable history corresponding to social psychological tendencies. He used as his primary evidence of this argument the complete absence of punishment that he observed among the Bantu tribes while living in the Congo for seven years, positing that there was absolutely no punishment of children (a point that would recur over and over in Faris's published work and become a kind of mantra in his advocacy of progressive parenting) and that violence among the native people was carried out only against people outside of the social group (Faris, 1914a, pp. 36–37). It is the close-knit, totalizing nature of the social group – a "primary group," in Cooley's terms that Faris would continue to draw upon throughout his career – that explains both phenomena. For those whose self is defined by the social group, non-conformity can be corrected through informal social controls rather than formal punishment.

Another chapter considers the social psychological effects of punishment on the person punished, positing that the popular dread that convicts face is "founded on facts," not because convicts are somehow bad by nature but rather because they have been treated with "an emphasis on the power of the stronger group to control, absolutely and arbitrarily" in a way that conceives of them as enemies, which is almost "calculated" to produce a "morbid self on the part of the prisoner" (Faris, 1914a, p. 93). Punishment, in its formal sense of inflicting pain or negative consequences on an enemy of the group by force, is likely in practice only to lead to negative outcomes, either crushing convicts or making them more savage enemies, but never restoring them to the group.

To illustrate his analysis, Faris used examples from his field observations in the Congo. At one pole, a person subject to crushing force with no remaining group support becomes a "psychological slave, no longer in opposition to the main body of society but in no true sense a member of it" (Faris, 1914a, p. 91). He had "personally witnessed" this, he wrote, in examples of "the excessive flogging of Congo natives by the Belgian authorities":

> A native who receives a hundred lashes on his bare body while stretched on the ground and held down by four soldiers during the application of the hippopotamus-hide "chicotte" [whip] will frequently exhibit a permanent loss of self-assertiveness. The larger group has succeeded in conquering him by force, but it has not made him a member of it. It has rather reduced him to the ranks of a servile inferior, where he will remain permanently. (Faris, 1914a, p. 91)

At the other pole, criminals treated with hatred tend to acquire a self that is "chiefly one of hatred" in turn, and those treated with suspicion tend to lead to "an attitude in which I am sure no one trusts me and I am[,] therefore, the enemy of all."

140   *Colonial Violence and the Chicago School*

This he again illustrated with a relevant account related to the Congo: the explorer Henry Morton Stanley attended a workhouse school in which the teacher was excessively brutal, often beating the pupils unmercifully for slight offenses, as he related in his autobiography. So when Stanley and the other boys went "out into the world," they carried "permanent remains of the brutality in their characters," and Stanley's "most cruel and hard-hearted" self exhibited in his colonizing expeditions could, Faris (1914a, p. 92) posited, be causally connected with the treatment he received in school. Examples like these, used in many of his works, demonstrate Faris's view of the social nature and genesis of personality.

Virtually all the other factual evidence that appears throughout the dissertation (for example, he also referred to the acts of radical suffragists, discoveries of Eskimo customs, and the characteristics of boys' street gangs) is only raised in support of individual points and invariably refers to very recent events that Faris had read about.[15] In contrast, the discussions of the Congo refer to events that were between 10 and 17 years previous, almost invariably referred to things Faris had personally witnessed, and they appear in support of every major analytical proposition of the dissertation. Faris used the social psychology developed by Angell and Mead, along with the genetic or evolutionary-historical approach to social institutions that he gained from Thomas's and Cooley's sociology, to make sense of the strange lack of punishment among Congolese natives, the apparently unlimited hostility displayed toward outside social groups, and the psychological effects of cruel treatment.

"The Mental Capacity of Savages" is the other key document from this early period in Faris's career, documenting his shift toward a sociological interpretation of his experiences.[16] It was originally composed as a talk that helped land Faris his University of Chicago sociology professorship. The article is aimed at refuting the older "Spencerian" view of "primitive man" by drawing upon Faris's first-hand observations "based on a residence of several years among the tribes of the Upper Congo River, with particular reference to the people living around the mouth of the Bosiri [Busira] River, almost exactly on the equator," and on the basis of the growing critical psychological and anthropological literature from Franz Boas, Dewey, Thomas, and Angell (Faris, 1918a, p. 603).

Faris (1918a, p. 604) noted that the Bantu people among whom he resided "are the sort of people to whom the older and familiar generalizations were meant to apply," but before he refuted these items one-by-one, the real analytical center of the article is his outline of six sources of error that help explain how such an erroneous view could have formed. For Faris (1918a, p. 604), "the most obvious force operating to tip the scales of sober judgment" is (1) "race prejudice"; and the other sources of error are (2) unwarranted generalization from particular incidents; (3) the assumption that the investigator views the matter exactly as the person under observation does (William James's "the psychologist's fallacy"); (4) the "mythopeic error" of not recognizing that, when people are asked about customary practices, they tend to invent an explanation rather than to confess ignorance; (5) the investigator's ignorance of the character of

DANIEL R. HUEBNER   141

native languages; and (6) the opposite error of relying on language structure
alone to explain mentality.

In the course of this discussion, Faris related a fascinating anecdote that he
apparently meant to puncture the easy assumptions of racial or civilizational
superiority of his audience by, himself, playing the devil's advocate:

> In a good-natured debate one day I was giving arguments for the superiority of the white man
> over the black, and instanced the fact that in a territory containing twenty million natives the
> absolute authority was exercised by the Belgians, who numbered less than a thousand. The
> reply was immediate.
>
> Give us breech-loading guns and ammunition, and within a month there will not be one of the
> thousand left alive here.
>
> "But," says the white man [Faris], "that is the point. The white men invented and made their
> guns and ammunition."
>
> Sir, do you know how to make a gun and ammunition?
>
> Well, no, not yet, but I could learn to make them in a factory.
>
> Certainly you could, if they would teach you, but so could we. (Faris, 1918a, pp. 604–605)

Note the "immediacy" of the response, and the astute logic of Faris's (recol-
lected) Congolese interlocutor who saw that domination was not based on racial
superiority but on oppression maintained by a monopoly of weapons and education. This anecdote adds an even sharper edge to Faris's 1900 missionary report
back home, which included explicit remarks about how the people regarded their
colonial treatment as "oppression" and "hate the State but cannot offer any
resistance" (quoted in Williams, 2006a, p. 10).

Faris's most pointed criticisms were for supposedly scientific writers who still
"copied with an uncritical credulity" the "isolated anecdotes from travelers" and
assume that no special training is needed to accurately observe and report on the
"facts of social life" (Faris, 1918a, p. 606). This is especially obvious when
reporting on "native religion," according to Faris (1918a, p. 606), because
"Western observers" are likely to think of religion in terms of doctrines, beliefs,
and theologies, and to report on native religion in a way that, by systematizing
and attempting to explain them in such terms, becomes "misleading." In a later
review, Faris wrote that Durkheim's *Division of Labor in Society* similarly
"accepts as accurate the crude misconceptions of the 1880s concerning the life of
primitive man as set forth in the books of those who were no more competent to
describe them than a botanist would be to write a treatise in his field without ever
having seen a plant" (quoted in Murray, 2013, p. 197).

Faris's most elaborate refutations of the sources of error relate to language, a
topic upon which he displayed his in-depth specialist knowledge. He provided a
detailed morphological analysis of the language of the "people of the equatorial
Congo," which is "complete and developed to a degree surprising to those whose
conception has been derived from writings of the Spencerian variety" (Faris,
1918a, p. 609).[17] This level of detail on the language was required, according to
Faris (1918a, p. 612), in order to show that it would be impossible to draw "any
conclusive argument of a lack of mental power or ability on account of the lack of

linguistic development." Each of the ways that Faris characterized the language likewise points back quite directly to his missionary experiences. The features of the language he highlighted and the terms he used match closely with the professional comparative linguistic work of W. H. Stapleton (1903) to which Faris had contributed while in the Congo. Faris also gave examples of sentences, oratory narratives, and proverbs to illustrate these various features, which bear the traces of having been first worked out as part of his study of native proverbs and translation of the bible during his time as a missionary (Faris & Dye, 1904; Faris & Dye, 1905).

In the course of exposing sources of error, Faris (1918, pp. 606–608) also proposed a novel counter-analysis of Western culture, clearly meant as a humorous device to expose how absurd the unwarranted assumptions and generalizations are. He posited a fictional "Eskimo psychologist" or "primitive psychologist" from "Polaris Scientific Institute" who, using the same error-ridden assumptions as writers on "primitive mentality," proposed that white people believe chairs, golf balls, and collar buttons to be inhabited by spirits because they are seen to curse or pray to them, and hypothesizes that English-speaking people have only vague, undefined notions of "tailhood" or "spinality" because they call the "feathers of a chicken," "the caudal appendage of a dog," and "the steering gear of a fish" all by the same word "tail" (which was, itself, based in an anecdote that Faris related of using the wrong Lonkundo word to describe a chicken's tail while in the Congo).

This device of getting his audience to be amused or disgusted by the unwarranted assumptions that could be drawn about their own culture and mental capacities became key to his attempts to refute racial prejudices in many of his published works by getting the audience to experience what it is like to be the racialized object of other people's ethnocentric knowledge. Discussions such as this one reveal how Faris (1937a, pp. 165–166) sought not only to pursue an ethnographic sensibility but also to construct rhetorical strategies to encourage readers to "take the role of the other" in the Meadian language he often used. In his later published reviews of others' work on "primitive society," among many other topics, Faris was quite explicit in lamenting authors' "regrettable omission" of Mead's relevant work, arguing that it makes "invaluable and wholly unique contributions" to scholarship (Huebner, 2014, p. 187).

The remaining part of Faris's article then addresses each of the assumptions of the Spencerian view one-by-one from his own observations among Congolese natives. He recounted that he participated in a hippopotamus hunt that showed natives didn't have especially keen eyesight; he witnessed debates about proper directions among natives that showed they didn't have "compasses in their heads"; he wrote year-long contracts with Congolese servants and workmen that showed they were not impetuous or overly emotional; he witnessed the nine-month cultivation required to raise and harvest cassava, the principle breadstuff, that revealed people were not improvident or without a sense of ownership; although there were no formal educational drills, native children could perform mathematical calculations; their habitual observation of complex taboos showed the inhibition and mastery of impulses that is supposed to be

DANIEL R. HUEBNER

"one of the best indexes of mentality"; and the wearing of Western clothes, attempts to acquire guns, and efforts to build houses did not reveal a native impulse to imitate, but rather rational pursuits in which they saw certain advantages (Faris, 1918a, pp. 612–615).[18]

Largely on the basis of these insights, Faris, along with fellow Chicago-trained sociologist L. L. Bernard, became a leading sociological critic of "instinct" theories in the 1920s, especially as theories of instinct were used to explain supposed "racial characteristics" and promote the standardization of educational practices (Huebner, 2015, p. 179; Murray, 2013, pp. 165, 181). And he developed his critique of "imitation" into further influential work in which Faris (e.g., 1937a, pp. 79–80) emphasized Mead's "taking the role of the other" as a better explanation of supposedly imitative behaviors. In opposition to "appealing to native African endowment" to explain behavior, Faris (1918a, pp. 608, 618) proposed that a "hypothesis" had recently been forming to "think of the human mind as being, in its capacity, about the same everywhere," and he proposed to treat all of these conflicting claims as hypotheses that could now be put to "careful, painstaking, scientific experiment and inquiry" in light of modern social psychological principles.

Sociological Field Expeditions to the Congo – 1932, 1949

Faris had apparently been considering and discussing plans for an expedition to the Congo as early as 1914. Consider the final paragraph of "The Mental Capacity of Savages":

> If an expedition could be made to the equatorial Congo in charge of one who could speak the language readily and who was also trained in psychology technique, and if records could be obtained of mental and physical ability of, say one thousand or fifteen hundred properly distributed individuals, it would be possible to be far more positive on the general question [of the "mental capacity of savages"] than we are at the present time. Some thought of organizing such an expedition has recently been indulged in, and the plans were outlined in detail in the early part of 1914, but the outbreak of the war [World War I] postponed everything. When peace comes, it may be that funds can be secured and the expedition conducted, and if so it would be possible to write in much more certainty concerning the mind of primitive man. (Faris, 1918a, p. 619)

As the President of the US National Research Council, James Angell (Faris's dissertation chair) proposed a study in almost identical words at the 1920 American Philosophical Society meeting, and it seems clear that Angell and Faris had talked about such an expedition ("American Philosophical Society," 1920, p. 598).[19] Faris subsequently solicited funding to conduct research from the National Research Council by 1924, but without success. He was then approached by Leonard Outhwaite, Director of the "Race Relations" program at the Laura Spelman Rockefeller Memorial Foundation in 1925, who was also interested in funding an American anthropological field expedition in Sub-Saharan Africa (Stanfield, 2011, p. 92). Although he and Outhwaite reportedly agreed on a plan, Faris encountered family health problems and university administrative delays that repeatedly prevented him from departing

144   *Colonial Violence and the Chicago School*

on such an extended undertaking, the possibility of which he again raised in 1927.

Faris's eventual 1932 journey to the Congo and Sudan was sponsored by a "Mental and Social Science Fellowship" from the philanthropic Julius Rosenwald Fund and the University of Chicago to study "the cultural phases of the native African population, particularly with respect to the changes that have taken place due to contact which has recently been made with western European civilization."[20] From the first account of plans for such an expedition to its fruition, there are 18 years of war, health problems, administrative duties, and other roadblocks, during which time the situation in the Congo had changed tremendously. In early 1932 as part of his preparation, Faris was talking with scholars such as anthropologist Melville Herskovits, who advised him on travel and outfitting arrangements and put him in touch with the London-based International Institute of African Languages and Cultures (IIALC, now the International African Institute) of which Faris became a member. Partly through his early sociology publications, and partly through the further connections developed around this 1932 expedition, Faris had come to be known as an "Africanist" scholar displaying a specialist's depth of understanding and making important contributions to "our knowledge of the civilizations of Africa and the background of Negroes in this country [i.e., the United States]."[21] And the connections Faris developed through the IIALC were likely important in fostering his travels into the British colonies of Sudan and, in 1949, Uganda.

Faris's follow-up and more deliberate attempt to study the culture and people of the Congo occurred in a period in which the professional methodological idea of ethnographic re-study was just emerging. Faris would have been a founder of this approach, had he systematically published results of his research; and even so, his multiple published articles that directly address the notion of restudying the same culture as it changes give him a good claim to innovation. Some anthropological textbooks in the 1930s were beginning to discuss the need for multiple studies of the same cultures and places, for methodological reasons (to check the validity of findings), historical reasons (to document processes of social change over time), and additional knowledge (to investigate further aspects not covered in a previous study) (Holmes, 1956). If we accept Faris's reinterpretation of his missionary experiences in 1897–1904 as ethnographic observations, as they are treated in his dissertation and subsequent sociology publications, then his 1932 investigation to deliberately document social change in the Congo predates even the earliest of these re-studies.[22] Faris made no systematized methodological claims for his re-study in published work – there are, for example, no claims about increased reliability by repeated observations or controlling for the "personal factor," as later scholars would make. Still, his "Culture and Personality Among the Forest Bantu" (Faris, 1934c), which is the primary published outcome of his 1932 expedition, discusses the "assumptions" with which he approached his study, and concludes that the results of the field expedition "bear out the assumptions and hypotheses concerning the relation of culture and personality." He noted that "this is what usually happens," because "keep[ing] one's mind open is so difficult that few of us succeed" and "whether what was found was previsaged can be

DANIEL R. HUEBNER

determined only by others less interested" (Faris, 1934c, p. 11). Faris focused primarily on documenting the features and possible social or social-psychological mechanisms of change, revealing a unique way in which the Chicago School focus on social process could study the nature of comparative-historical social change (Murray, 2013, p. 186). In his view, "it is hardly too much to say that nowhere in the history of the world has there occurred so great a change over so large an area in so short a time" (Faris, 1934c, p. 4).

CONCLUSION

In addition to contributing to the historiography of Symbolic Interactionism by reintroducing Ellsworth Faris's missionary experience and compiling the first attempt at a comprehensive bibliography of Faris's work, the present study invites us to reconsider the relevance of the field's history to contemporary scholarship. Despite being a discipline "marked by a high degree of reflexivity about its objects, methods, and theoretical reference points," sociology tends to address its disciplinary history in terms of a relatively narrow set of "canonical" authors, primarily in textbooks and classical theory classes (Silver et al., 2022, pp. 287–289). In recent work on the "colonial origins of modern social thought," for instance, Steinmetz (2023) has argued that the discipline exhibits "historical amnesia" around its relation to colonialism that is reproduced today in the preconscious disciplinary categories and commonsense interpretations with which we approach the study of social practice. The parochial "Eurocentrism" of the sociological tradition is, in his view, not only something we inherit from canonical figures and theories, because it is also reproduced by the disciplinary amnesia that limits our understanding of how some of the ideas we now treat as abstract and universally applicable were formulated to conceptualize colonial encounters. In Steinmetz's (2023) view, we need a kind of reflexivity best accomplished by a "historical sociology of sociology" that uses the strangeness of our discipline's past to interrogate the assumptions it reproduces and to reveal how our own thought is socio-historically embedded.

In this regard, decolonial scholarship overlaps in some of its goals with pragmatist and Symbolic Interactionist approaches to the discipline's history. For example, Silver et al. (2022, pp. 306–307) identify an emerging pragmatist alternative to expanding, reinterpreting, or historicizing the canon that seeks to "dissolve" the problem of the canon by deliberately studying historical works for the conceptual skills and habits that they can help us cultivate in our own theorizing. Drawing from Steinmetz, Werron (2024) likewise recently argued that the discipline needs to expand our approach to the authors and perspectives we examine in order for a historical sociology of sociology to live up to its "heuristic" potential to educate us. In his view, such a renewal of social theory as a "global" genre can bring new excitement (and disorder) to its discussions, as well as potentially prepare us better for the uncertain demands of the future, if for no other reason, then because we live in a complex pluralistic society the understanding of which benefits from multiple perspectives. Neither of these recent approaches focuses extensively on the earlier articulations of a "sociology of sociology," but we can also note that Symbolic Interactionists have long been pioneers in the self-reflexive study of the discipline's social practices (e.g., Curtis & Petras, 1972; Reynolds & Reynolds, 1970).

It would be, at best, presumptuous to ventriloquize what Faris "would have said" about the contemporary problems we care about, or to elevate him as a historical figure with the "right" answers. Faris's ways of examining colonialism do not fully interrogate how processes of forced migration, appropriation, and exploitation helped to constitute the social differences studied by contemporary sociology, nor how even prior to the late nineteenth-century "Scramble for Africa," these territories had already been drawn into the impacts of colonialism through enslavement and other transnational processes. He did not have a framework of phases or types of colonialism, nor did he develop a notion of postcolonial or decolonial politics. In a sense, Faris is not critical enough to be remembered as a critic of empire, but he is perhaps also not secular and metrocentric enough to be remembered for studies of nationally bounded, modern social processes. Instead, following the lead of decolonial and pragmatist scholarship, the usefulness of such a historically particular figure is to challenge the naturalness of our commonsense story of the discipline. And following Symbolic Interactionist concerns to examine mundane interactions of people in social contexts, we can note that Faris does not have to be a central "canonical" author for us to learn from the ways he was an active social thinker responding to his experiences and contexts in informative ways.

Reexamining the work of Faris with a focus on the influence of his colonial experiences fills in our understanding of a transitional period in the professionalization of American sociology by helping to reveal the comparative-historical relations within which the social processes of colonialism were translated into now-classic sociological terms and distinctions. Faris is instructive in this regard precisely because he is difficult to square with the kinds of methodological and conceptual boundaries we draw in present-day sociology. He went to the Congo with clear intentions of gaining religious conversions, and he never had a crisis of religious faith, even though he grew skeptical of Fundamentalist interpretations of his denomination and about whether the agents of the Belgian colonial state were agents of progress. And just as with the French colonial sociologists Steinmetz studied, Faris made contributions to sociological thought that not only sought to conceptualize the colonial situation he wrote about, but also influenced the construction of concepts still in use today, even though his works have largely been forgotten.

Focusing on how Faris developed ideas that helped build early conceptual foundations of Symbolic Interactionism and the canon of American social theory can give us a specific, nuanced sense of the historical contexts and experiences that shaped them. Concepts important to this tradition, including social attitude, social control, self, symbolic language, and primary group, were not only popularized within a framework bounded by the American nation-state but also formed central parts of Faris's approach to understanding international colonialism. In this regard, Faris is unique especially in centering the violence, punishment, social control, and ethnocentrism of colonialism as constitutive problems to be worked out with sociological concepts. His encounter with colonial violence brought into question assumptions of natural racial inferiority that so often rationalized the civilizing process. And Faris sought to analyze difference where others might have simply ignored it or encompassed it with universalizing terms, so perhaps the colonial violence that Faris witnessed was so shocking or the somewhat involuntary way in which he was brought into controversies around colonial brutality made it impossible to dismiss the topic without continually wrestling with it intellectually and morally.

Faris's embrace and integration of pragmatist social psychological ideas as a graduate student was clearly generative of the perspective from which he approached the analysis of colonial encounters throughout his sociological career. Still, the acute tensions of missionaries with the colonial government and the sheer scale and brutality of state-sponsored violence may well have veiled the ways his missionary efforts depended upon and interacted with colonialism. Whether such radical forms of dominance and inequality are missing from the conceptual foundations of Symbolic Interactionism has long been a concern, and recent scholarship has begun to reexamine these issues historically (e.g., Athens, 2013). As scholarship on Robert E. Park and others has begun to show, the displacement of colonialism in early American sociology is not simply a matter of the supposed ignorance of those scholars (Balon & Holmwood, 2022; Lyman, 1992; Magubane, 2013). This growing literature, to which the present study seems to contribute, returns to the particular ways colonialism was addressed in the work of earlier scholars whose work we continue to build upon in order to reopen our taken-for-granted concepts to critical scrutiny.

ACKNOWLEDGMENTS

I would like to thank several colleagues who have helped me think through topics related to this study, helped with access to primary document materials, or answered my questions about these documents, including Andrew Abbott, Robert Burroughs, Sarah Daynes, and Dean Pavlakis, and the staff at the Disciples of Christ Historical Society, Fisk University Special Collections and Archives, Northwestern University Archives, University of Chicago Special Collections Research Center, and University of North Carolina Greensboro Special Collections and Archives. Thank you to the participants of a 2022 Social Science History Association session and to my colleagues and students who participated in a 2023 UNCG Working Papers Series on this topic from which the paper benefited.

NOTES

1. While reviewing materials for the revision of this study, I became aware of unpublished work by independent scholar Lionel Lacaze (n.d. [c. 2017]; n.d. [c. 2021]) that addresses topics closely related to the present study. I wish to draw attention to this valuable research which, in addition to laying out overlapping historical evidence about

148   *Colonial Violence and the Chicago School*

Faris's missionary and sociological work, also includes information from first-hand interviews and other sources addressed primarily to reconstructing Faris's life and forgotten influence in sociology.

2. Faris spent much of his waiting time in 1896–1897 in the public library at Cincinnati researching the Congo and preparing a recommendation as to the location of the new station to be built (Browning, 1952, p. 14), evidence of which includes newspaper articles he published with geographical information about central Africa (Faris, 1895a, 1895b). A complete listing of Faris's publications is included in an appendix bibliography to this project.

3. The settlement (also written "Bolengi") is now an outlying village of the city of Mbandaka, Democratic Republic of the Congo. The Baptist missionaries at Bolenge had been among the most vocal in protesting colonial abuses, so the colonial policy preventing new stations from being built led the Disciples of Christ to locate in an existing hotbed of protest (Williams, 2006b, p. 59; Lagergren, 1970).

4. Lonkundo is the designation that Faris used to refer to the local language spoken around the Bolenge station in his early letters back to the US (also referred to as "Lunkundo" or "Lonkundu"). This language and the people who speak it are considered in contemporary cultural linguistics to be a part of the Mongo (or Mongo-Nkundu) language group, a division of the larger Bantu language family. Especially later in his career, Faris referred generally to his experiences among the "Forest Bantu" people.

5. The history of the Disciples of Christ Congo Mission has been extensively researched, especially by church historians, and additional information may be found in Williams (2006a, 2006b), Yates (1967), Yocum (1945), Browning (1952), and Dye (1909), among others.

6. For citations to works by Ellsworth Faris, see the appendix bibliography to this study.

7. Faris was referred to by a Lonkundo name by the local people, "Bakola," which he used in publications in that language, a fact confirmed by Frederick Starr (1908, p. 39; 1909, p. 176), and in published editions of Roger Casement's diaries (Ó Síocháin & O'Sullivan, 2003, p. 323). The fact that Starr repeatedly misspelled Faris's name "Farris" suggests that they did not know one another well in this period. Starr's own account of translating Lonkundo sayings indicates that he relied upon Royal Dye for the materials and language instruction (Starr, 1909, p. 176).

8. The Congo reform movement has been called the first international humanitarian campaign in history (Clay, 2016; Hochschild, 1998; Pavlakis, 2016), drawing in part upon models of activism that had been pioneered in the international abolitionist movement against slavery. Congo reformers made major new innovations in the production and distribution of visual depictions of atrocities (primarily photographic cards and lantern slides taken by missionaries to generate public outcry) and international legal concepts (including the notion of "crimes against humanity" and calls for international investigative tribunals pioneered by African American lawyer and journalist George Washington Williams), both innovations that have become part of the repertoire of international human rights discourse since this time (Carton, 2009; Grant, 2014; Hochschild, 1998, pp. 102–107; Jacobsen & Daniel, 2014; Lyman, 1992; Sliwinski, 2006; Thompson, 2007; Twomey, 2012).

9. A copy of Twain's *King Leopold's Soliloquy* located in the archives of the Disciples of Christ Historical Society in Bethany, West Virginia was owned by Edward A. Henry who marked the text with Faris's name on two pages: (1) next to the passage from Faris's diary that Twain had anonymized (page 18), and (2) beside three of the nine photographs that form a collage photographic plate (inserted between pages 40 and 41) documenting people who had had their hands cut off by state-sanctioned soldiers, which may indicate that these were incidents known to Faris. Other sources assert that the photographs were taken by Alice Seely Harris, W. D. Armstrong, and perhaps others (but almost certainly not by Faris), and that one of the photographs that Henry marked is of Epondo, who Faris certainly did know (Grant, 2014; Jacobsen & Daniel, 2014; Sliwinski, 2006; Thompson, 2007; Twomey, 2012). The caption to the plate reads: "The pictures get sneaked around everywhere" – a line that also appears in the text, put into the mouth of Twain's

DANIEL R. HUEBNER 149

fictionalized King Leopold who laments the "incorruptible *kodak*" camera, "the only witness I have encountered in my long experience that I couldn't bribe" (Twain, 1905, p. 40). E. A. Henry was a fellow student with Faris at the University of Chicago and his longtime friend. He also became a librarian and expert in ancient biblical history at the University of Chicago, where he reviewed a couple works for the *American Journal of Sociology* when Faris was editor, and he was affiliated with Edward S. Ames's Disciples of Christ church and Disciples Divinity House, both of which Faris was involved in. It seems likely that Faris talked with Henry about his experiences in the Congo and may have been the source for Henry's attributions in the text.

10. Faris's letters quoted by Morel – to Belgian colonial authorities, to Casement, and to fellow missionaries – were subsequently published by the British Foreign Office as part of their *Further Correspondence Respecting the Congo Free State* (Faris, 1905a, b, c, d). Faris is mentioned in one other place in the *Further Correspondence* of the British Foreign Office: a revealing letter from Acting Consul A. Nightingale (who succeeded Casement) to Henry Petty-Fitzmaurice, 5th Marquess of Lansdowne (the British Foreign Secretary), dated December 19, 1904. Nightingale (1905) responded to a point from a previous dispatch in which it was apparently reported that Faris had been "dismissed by his [missionary] Society." Nightingale wrote that he had inquired about this and found that there was "no truth in such a silly report" for the simple fact that Faris had "not severed his connection" with the mission even after he left. Noteworthy here is both the contemporary account of perceived reasons for Faris leaving the Congo and the very fact that Faris was referred to, in intimate detail and directly by name, in a letter to the highest-ranking British foreign affairs official.

11. I am unable to find an American publication that published Faris's remarks or an original manuscript of those remarks, despite the *Neue Zürcher Zeitung* article reporting that Faris had "a detailed message going through the American press" ("*geht durch die amerikanische Presse eine ausführliche Mitteilung*") ("Grausamkeiten" 1904). It is possible that the correspondent saw a draft that Faris was circulating in otherwise unsuccessful attempts to get it published. There is other supporting evidence regarding this notice that comes, ironically, from a propagandizing organization seeking to discredit reports of atrocities, called the "Federation for the Defense of Belgian Interests Abroad." This Federation published a newsletter in which they criticized the *Neue Zürcher Zeitung* report – in parallel English, French, and German columns – noting that Faris was the same missionary who had previously recorded the retraction of the well-publicized "Epondo" case, and speculating that Faris may have been dismissed as a missionary owing to his interference in this case or perhaps because of an ongoing personality dispute with his fellow missionaries. They speculated that perhaps he was more interested in accumulating charges against the colonial state that would ingratiate him with his superiors than in uncovering the truth. They repeatedly insinuated that his statement was thoroughly suspect and biased. And after all, they noted, the practices in the Congo were "merely imitating the methods in use in other colonies, inter alia in British possessions," and the companies "carry on business there in the ordinary course usual in all colonies" (Hermann, 1905). This publication supplies additional information that makes it clear Ellsworth Faris was, indeed, the person they understood to be the author of these remarks, that he was already known to people concerned with the Belgian Congo, and that Faris's report was seen as a potentially serious blow to public opinion about the colony that its defenders needed to attempt to discredit.

12. Although later TCU sociology professor (and contributor to Symbolic Interactionism) Austin L. Porterfield claimed that Faris had been his direct predecessor and taught the first sociology courses at TCU, Cain (2005, p. 33) reports that there are no courses with that title or course description, even though some appear to have been "'sociological' in thrust." Faris's controversy did not go unnoticed nationally, as one of the leading journals of mainline American Protestantism, *The Christian Century*, included an editorial (unattributed, but likely written by Herbert L. Willett of the University of Chicago) expressing support for Faris and mocking his critics as more concerned with "heresy hunting" than

with matters of "the living and vital gospel for the present" ("A Heresy Hunt in Texas," *The Christian Century* 27 [January 6, 1910], p. 5).

13. Faris's son later recalled that a "trivial accident" had played an important role in this appointment in sociology: Faris had been invited by the sociology club at Chicago to give a talk on "The Mental Capacity of Savages" (which would be published as Faris [1918a]), but the student in charge had forgotten to get the announcement in the university calendar, so the faculty hastily rounded up professors from various departments and members of the administration to serve as a "small but important audience" (Faris, 1970, p. 31). The audience was "favorably impressed by the talk and well-disposed to the appointment of Faris at the time of Thomas's departure," according to R. E. L. Faris.

14. The chapter was immediately reproduced in a reader on "primitive and ancient legal institutions" and had some influence at the time on sociological approaches to criminology. It is also the earliest contribution to be included in Faris's compiled essays *The Nature of Human Nature*, which further supports the notion that this piece was foundational in reformulating his missionary experiences as puzzles to be explained sociologically. He contributed related published reviews of work cited in his dissertation, Heinrich Oppenheimer's *The Rationale of Punishment* (Faris, 1914e), and of his mentor Charles R. Henderson's *The Cause and Cure of Crime* (Faris, 1915b), both for the *International Journal of Ethics*.

15. Faris was particularly taken by the work of Vilhjalmur Stefansson's (1913) explorations of Eskimo customs, which would remain a repeated point of reference in his publications. As is discussed below, Faris imagined what an "Eskimo psychologist" might say about white Euro-American society.

16. Faris wrote in the article that the title was meant to reflect the language used in the literature on primitive mentality. When he included this article in his *The Nature of Human Nature*, he altered the title to "The Mental Capacity of Preliterates" to reflect his own preferred, supposedly non-judgmental, terminology.

17. Faris described the language's device of "alliterative concord" that distinguishes Bantu languages from virtually all others; use of diminutive and augmentative prefixes and inflections; verb prefixes to indicate direct and indirect objects; "fundamentally different" tense and modal inflections from those in Indo-European languages; relative lack of adjectives and pronouns; agglutinate words; and onomatopoeic particles supplied by listeners to complete expressions of action (Faris, 1918a, pp. 609–612). Murray (2013, pp. 177–178) argues that Faris's "prolonged field experience in a functioning primitive society" and especially his defense against the "theory of primitive mind" through "a morphological analysis of Bantu languages" might have appealed to pioneering linguistic anthropologist Edward Sapir, whom he brought into the University of Chicago department on a scholarship.

18. On this point, Faris noted that native Congolese people were likely to accuse white men of just the same emotionality that writers on primitive mentality accused them of: "The white man comes into the tropics with exaggerated ideas of the importance of getting things done on schedule. When people do not move as fast as he wishes he often loses control of himself and raves and fumes quite like a spoiled child. The African would be able to insist that it is the white man who has no control of himself" (Faris, 1918a, p. 613).

19. They may, for instance, have had in mind the interest expressed in 1912 by the recently formed Phelps-Stokes Fund in funding a survey into the condition of "negro education," which was almost immediately used to promote surveys of the conditions of native education in colonial Africa by Hampton Institute sociologist Thomas Jesse Jones (Jerónimo, 2015, pp. 111–112).

20. "Statement of Offer" dated December 16, 1931 (Box 411, Folder 5, Julius Rosenwald Fund Archives, 1917–1948, Franklin Library Special Collections and Archives, Fisk University, Nashville, TN). At the time of Faris's 1932 expedition, the International Missionary Council's Department of Social and Industrial Research was also sponsoring a major expedition to Central Africa to investigate conditions relating to copper mines and Christian missions, headed by J. Merle Davis, Director of the Institute for Social and Religious

DANIEL R. HUEBNER

Research (ISRR), and Charles W. Coulter, a Yale-trained sociologist at Ohio Wesleyan University. This is noteworthy for at least two reasons. First, the groups could easily have crossed paths with one another: Coulter (1935) even published some of the results of his work in the *American Journal of Sociology* that Faris edited. Second, the sponsoring ISRR was financially endowed by the Rockefeller Foundation "to apply to religious phenomena the methods of social research without the distorting influence of ecclesiastical or theological bias" or "to combine the scientific method with the religious motive" (Brunner, 2021, pp. 420–421; Zurlo, 2015, pp. 187–188). The ISRR also funded the Pacific Coast Survey of Race Relations headed by Robert Park, the "Middletown" community studies of Helen and Robert Lynd, and the bombshell "Hocking Commission" report that advocated a radical reorientation of American Protestant missions, among its nearly 50 major studies (Gross, 2008, pp. 69–70; Yu, 2002, p. 28; Zurlo, 2015). The studies of the ISRR exhibited what has been called a "missionary social science" in that they combined the moral and practical concerns of missionary ameliorative efforts with professional academic social science (Brunner, 2021, p. 421). Indeed, historical studies have stressed the complicated missionary entanglements of even the most avowedly secular social scientists who were involved in the ISRR-funded studies, and how Christian religious discourses helped shape these social scientific projects (Brunner, 2021; Yu, 2002, Zurlo, 2015).

21. Letter from Melville J. Herskovits to Ellsworth Faris, 23 October 1939 Box 7, Folder 28, Melville J. Herskovits (1895–1963) Papers (Northwestern University Archives, Charles Deering McCormick Library, Evanston, IL). From their correspondence, it is clear that Herskovits served as a liaison to the IIALC, helping to coordinate submissions from North America to the Institute's journal *Africa*, including a planned paper from Faris after his 1932 expedition that never materialized because of ill health and other commitments.

22. Early "individual re-studies," in which the same community is studied again by the same ethnographer to investigate socio-cultural change, include Helen and Robert Lynd's 1937 *Middletown in Transition* study of Muncie, Indiana; Robert Redfield's 1950 *A Village That Chose Progress* of Chan Kom village in the Yucatan; Margaret Mead's 1956 *New Lives for Old* study of a Manus village in Papua New Guinea; and Raymond Firth's 1959 *Social Change in Tikopia* study in the Solomon Islands – all originally studied in the late 1920s (Hammersley, 2016; Holmes, 1956, p. 10).

REFERENCES

Alatas, S. F. (2006). *Alternative discourses in Asian social science: Responses to Eurocentrism*. Sage.

Alatas, S. F. (2021). Deparochialising the canon: The case of sociological theory. *Journal of Historical Sociology, 34*(1), 13–27.

Alatas, S. F., & Sinha, V. (2017). *Sociological theory beyond the canon*. Palgrave Macmillan.

Athens, L. H. (Ed.). (2013). *Radical interactionism on the rise. Studies in symbolic interaction* (Vol. 41). Emerald Publishing Limited.

Balon, J., & Holmwood, J. (2022). Race, nation and empire; the forgotten sociology of Herbert Adolphus Miller. *Journal of Classical Sociology*. (Online First October 4, 2022).

Barkawi, T., & George, L. (2017). The international origins of social and political theory. *Political Power and Social Theory, 32*, 1–7.

Bhambra, G. K. (2014). *Connected sociologies*. Bloomsbury Academic.

Bhambra, G. K., & Holmwood, J. (2021). *Colonialism and modern social theory*. Polity.

Bhambra, G. K., & Holmwood, J. (2022). Editorial: Writing (and righting) the 'classics': A symposium on Gurminder K. Bhambra and John Holmwood's *Colonialism and Modern Social Theory*, Polity 2021. *Journal of Classical Sociology, 22*(4), 377–381.

Blasi, A. (2017). The impact of Robert E. Park on American sociology of religion. In P. Kivisto (Ed.), *The anthem companion to Robert Park* (pp. 225–242). Anthem Press.

Browning, L. [uncredited compiler]. (1952). Mr. and Mrs. Ellsworth Faris. In *They went to Africa: Biographies of missionaries of the disciples of Christ* (pp. 13–16). Missionary Education Department, The United Christian Missionary Society.

Brunner, M. P. (2021). From converts to cooperation: Protestant internationalism, US missionaries and Indian Christians and 'Professional' social work between Boston and Bombay. *Journal of Global History*, *16*(3), 415–434.

Cain, L. D. (2005). *A man's grasp should exceed his reach: A biography of sociologist Austin Larimore Porterfield*. University Press of America.

Carton, B. (2009). From Hampton '[I]nto the Heart of Africa': How faith in God and folklore turned Congo missionary William Sheppard into a pioneering ethnologist. In *History in Africa* (Vol. 36, pp. 53–86). Cambridge University Press https://doi.org/10.1353/hia.2010.0005

Clay, D. (2016). Transatlantic dimensions of the Congo reform movement, 1904–1908. *English Studies in Africa*, *59*(1), 18–28.

Comaroff, J., & Comaroff, J. (1986). Christianity and colonialism in South Africa. *American Ethnologist*, *13*(1), 1–22.

Congo Missionaries in Conference. (1904, June). In A. H. Baynes (Ed.), *The missionary Herald of the Baptist missionary society* (p. 306). Alexander & Shepheard, Ltd.

Connell, R. (1997). Why is classical theory classical? *American Journal of Sociology*, *102*(6), 1511–1557.

Connell, R. (2007). *Southern theory: The global dynamics of knowledge in social science*. Polity Press.

Coulter, C. W. (1935). Problems arising from industrialization of native life in Central Africa. *American Journal of Sociology*, *40*(5), 582–592.

Curtis, J. E., & Petras, J. W. (1972). The sociology of sociology: Some lines of inquiry in the study of the discipline. *Sociological Quarterly*, *13*, 197–209.

Dye, E. N. (1909). *Bolenge: A story of Gospel Triumphs on the Congo*. Foreign Christian Missionary Society.

Faris, R. E. L. (1970). *Chicago sociology, 1920-1932*. University of Chicago Press.

Ferguson, R. (2004). Introduction: Queer of color critique, historical materialism, and canonical sociology. In *Aberrations in black: Toward a queer of color critique* (pp. 1–30). University of Minnesota Press.

Go, J. (2013). Introduction: Entangling postcoloniality and sociological thought. *Political Power and Social Theory*, *24*, 3–31.

Go, J., & Lawson, G. (2017). Introduction: For a global historical sociology. In J. Go & G. Lawson (Eds.), *Global historical sociology* (pp. 1–34). Cambridge University Press.

Grausamkeiten im Kongo-Freistaate. (1904, November 2). *Neue Zürcher Zeitung*, *305*, 1.

Grant, K. (2014). The limits of exposure: Atrocity photographs in the Congo reform campaign. In H. Fehrenbach & D. Rodogno (Eds.), *Humanitarian photography: A history* (pp. 64–88). Cambridge University Press.

Gross, N. (2008). *Richard Rorty: The making of an American philosopher*. University of Chicago Press.

Gutiérrez Rodríguez, E., Boatcă, M., & Costa, S. (2010). *Decolonizing European sociology: Transdisciplinary approaches*. Ashgate.

Hammersley, M. (2016). Reflections on the value of ethnographic re-studies: Learning from the past. *International Journal of Social Research Methodology*, *19*(5), 1–14.

Hermann, C. (1905, January 18). Our correspondence. *La Vérité sur le Congo*, *16*, 46–48.

Hochschild, A. (1998). *King Leopold's ghost: A story of greed, terror, and heroism in colonial Africa*. Mariner Books.

Holmes, L. D. (1956). *The restudy of Manu'an culture: A problem in methodology*. Unpublished PhD dissertation. Northwestern University Department of Anthropology.

Huebner, D. R. (2014). *Becoming Mead: The social process of academic knowledge*. University of Chicago Press.

Huebner, D. R. (2015). Instinct, history of. In J. D. Wright (Ed.), *International encyclopedia of the social and behavioral sciences* (2nd ed., Vol. 12, pp. 175–180). Elsevier.

Jacobsen, Ó., & Daniel, J. (2014). *Danielsen and the Congo: Missionary campaigns and atrocity photographs*. Brethren Archivists and Historians Network.

Jerónimo, M. B. (2015). *The 'Civilising Mission' of Portuguese colonialism, 1870-1930*. Palgrave Macmillan.

Julius Rosenwald Fund Archives. (1917–1948). *Franklin library special collections and archives*. Fisk University.

DANIEL R. HUEBNER 153

Kivisto, P. (1999). Faris, Ellsworth. In J. A. Garraty & M. C. Carnes (Eds.), *American national biography* (Vol. 7, pp. 713–714). Oxford University Press.

Lacaze, L. (n.d. [c. 2017]). Ellsworth Faris: An outsider of the Chicago school? (From Waco to Chicago via Bolenge). Unpublished manuscript, 47 pages. https://www.academia.edu/33855036/ELLSWORTH_FARIS_AN_OUTSIDER_OF_THE_CHICAGO_SCHOOL_FROM_WACO_TO_CHICAGO_VIA_BOLENGE_1

Lacaze, L. (n.d. [c. 2021]). Ellsworth Faris and the Chicago school of psychosocial pragmatism. Unpublished manuscript, 20 pages. https://www.academia.edu/45007141/ELLSWORTH_FARIS_AND_THE_CHICAGO_SCHOOL_OF_PSYCHOSOCIAL_PRAGMATISM

Lagergren, D. (1970). *Mission and state in the Congo. A study of the relations between Protestant missions and the Congo Independent State authorities with special reference to the Equator District, 1885-1903* (Trans. Owen N. Lee) Studia Missionalia Upsaliensia, XIII. Gleerup.

Lyman, S. M. (1992). *Militarism, imperialism, and racial accommodation: An analysis and interpretation of the early writings of Robert E Park*. University of Arkansas Press.

Magubane, Z. (2013). Common skies and divided horizons: Sociology, race and postcolonial studies. *Political Power and Social Theory, 24*, 81–116. ("Postcolonial Sociology").

Magubane, Z. (2014). Science, reform, and the 'science of reform': Booker T. Washington, Robert Park, and the making of a 'science of society'. *Current Sociology, 62*(4), 568–583.

Melville, J. H. (1895–1963). *Papers*. Northwestern University Archives, Charles Deering McCormick Library.

Merton, R. K. (1968). *Social theory and social structure* (Enlarged ed.). Free Press.

Morel, E. D. (1904). *King Leopold's rule in Africa*. W. Heinemann.

Murray, S. O. (2013). *American anthropology and company: Historical explorations*. University of Nebraska Press.

Nightingale, A. (1905). No. 5. acting consul nightingale to the Marquess of Lansdowne.—(Received January 7, 1905.) [dated December 19, 1904]. In *Part IV. Further correspondence respecting the Congo free state* (p. 9). Printed for the use of the Foreign Office.

Odum, H. W. (1951). Ellsworth Faris. In H. W. Odum (Ed.), *American sociology: The story of sociology in the United States through 1950* (pp. 180–186). Longmans, Green.

Park, R. E. (1904, September 1). The case against the Congo government. *Christian-Evangelist*, 1121.

Pavlakis, D. (2016). *British humanitarianism and the Congo reform movement, 1896-1913*. Routledge.

Report of the Second Conference of missionaries of the protestant societies working in Congoland, January 28–31, 1904, Leopoldville, Stanley Pool, Congo State. Printed at "Hannah Wade" Press, B. M. S.

Reynolds, L. T., & Reynolds, J. M. (1970). *The sociology of sociology: Analysis and criticism of the thought, research, and ethical folkways of sociology and its practitioners*. David McKay Company.

Samarin, W. J. (1986). Protestant missions and the history of Lingala. *Journal of Religion in Africa, 16*(2), 138–163.

Second General Congo Missionaries' conference. Held at Leopoldville, January 28th to 30th, 1904. (July 1904). *The Missionary Herald of the Baptist Missionary Society, 330*, 359–360.

Silver, D., Guzman, C., Parker, S., & Döpking, L. (2022). The rhetoric of the canon: Functional, historicist, and humanist justifications. *American Sociologist, 53*, 287–313.

Síocháin, Ó, & O'Sullivan, M. (Eds.). (2003). *The eyes of another race: Roger Casement's Congo report and 1903 diary*. University College Dublin Press.

Sliwinski, S. (2006). The childhood of human rights: The kodak on the Congo. *Journal of Visual Culture, 5*(3), 333–363.

Stanfield II, J. H. (1985). *Philanthropy and Jim Crow in American social science*. Greenwood Press.

Stanfield II, J. H. (2011). *Historical foundations of black reflective sociology*. Left Coast Press.

Stapleton, W. H. (1903). *Comparative handbook of Congo languages*. "Hannah Wade" Printing Press, Baptist Missionary Society.

Starr, F. (1907). *The truth about the Congo: The Chicago Tribune articles*. Forbes & Company.

Starr, F. (1908). *A bibliography of Congo languages*. University of Chicago department of anthropology Bulletin V. University of Chicago Press.

Starr, F. (1909, May). Ethnographic notes from the Congo free state: An African miscellany. In *Proceedings of the Davenport Academy of Sciences* (Vol. 12, pp. 96–222). Davenport Academy of Sciences.

Stefansson, V. (1913). *My life with the Eskimo*. Macmillan Co.

Steinmetz, G. (2013). Major contributions to sociological theory and research on empire, 1830s–present. In G. Steinmetz (Ed.), *Sociology & empire: The imperial entanglements of a discipline* (pp. 1–50). Duke University Press.

Steinmetz, G. (2023). *The colonial origins of modern social thought*. Princeton University Press.

Sundkler, B. (2000). *A history of the church in Africa*. Cambridge University Press.

Suttles, G. D. (1976). Introduction to the paperback edition. In *The nature of human nature, and other essays in social psychology* (Abridged ed., pp. vii–xx). By Ellsworth Faris. University of Chicago Press.

Thompson, T. J. (2007). *Capturing the image: African missionary photography as enslavement and liberation* (Vol. 20). Yale Divinity School Library, Occasional Publication.

Turner, R. H. (1972). Introduction to the reprint of Faris: The nature of human nature. In *The nature of human nature, and other Essays in social psychology* (Pp. i–ix). By Ellsworth Faris. Brown Reprints in Sociology. Brown Reprints.

Twain, M. (1905). *King Leopold's Soliloquy: A defense of his Congo rule*. Warren Co.

Twomey, C. (2012). Framing atrocity: Photography and humanitarianism. *History of Photography*, *36*(3), 255–264.

Vinck, H. (1992). Charles Lemaire de passage à Mbandaka (1895 – 1900 – 1902). *Annales Aequatoria*, *13*, 67–124.

Wack, H. W. (1905). *The story of the Congo free state: Social, political, and economic aspects of the Belgian System of government in Central Africa*. G. P. Putnam's Sons.

Werron, T. (2024). Review essay: To build a future for social theory—What do we have to know about its past? *American Journal of Sociology*, *130*(2), 496–507.

Williams, P. A. (2006a). Disciples and 'Red Rubber': The disciples of Christ Congo mission (DCCM), the Congo free state, and the Congo reform campaign, 1897-1908. *Discipliana: The Quarterly Historical Journal of the Disciples of Christ Historical Society*, *66*(1), 3–18.

Williams, P. A. (2006b). Disciples of Christ at the equator—1897-1903: An essay on the history of Christianity in Congo. *Discipliana: The Quarterly Historical Journal of the Disciples of Christ Historical Society*, *66*(2), 55–71.

Yates, B. A. (1967). *The missions and educational development in Belgian Africa, 1876-1908*. PhD Dissertation. Columbia University.

Yates, B. A. (1987). Knowledge brokers: Books and publishers in early colonial Zaire. *History in Africa*, *14*, 311–340.

Yocum, E. E. (1945). *They went to Africa: Biographies of missionaries of the Disciples of Christ*. Missionary Education Department of the United Christian Missionary Society.

Yu, H. (2002). *Thinking orientals: Migration, context, and exoticism in modern America*. Oxford University Press.

Zimmerman, A. (2010). *Alabama in Africa: Booker T. Washington, the German empire, and the globalization of the new south*. Princeton University Press.

Zimmerman, A. (2013). German sociology and empire: From internal colonization to overseas colonization and back again. In G. Steinmetz (Ed.), *Sociology & empire: The imperial entanglements of a discipline* (pp. 166–187). Duke University Press.

Zurlo, G. A. (2015). The social gospel, ecumenical movement, and Christian sociology: The Institute of social and religious research. *The American Sociologist*, *46*(2), 177–193.

DANIEL R. HUEBNER   155

APPENDIX I: ELLSWORTH FARIS COMPREHENSIVE BIBLIOGRAPHY

[Items in brackets indicate additional relevant information or fragmentary information of materials that I have not been able to view].

(1) Ellsworth Faris Papers, 6 Volumes (c. 1910–1913). Hanna Holborn Gray Special Collections Research Center, Joseph Regenstein Library, University of Chicago.

(2) Faris, Ellsworth. 1894. "Lectures at Add-Ran." *Christian-Evangelist* ([date?]), p. 14.

(3) Faris, Ellsworth. 1895. "Africa." *Christian-Evangelist*, August 22, 1895, p. 533.

(4) Faris, Ellsworth. 1895. "Africa." *Christian Standard*, August 24, 1895, p. 814.

(5) Faris, Ellsworth. 1898. "Letter from Africa." *Christian-Evangelist*, March 10, 1898, p. 149.

(6) Faris, Ellsworth. 1898. "News from the Congo." *Christian Standard*, March 12, 1898, p. 334.

(7) Faris, Ellsworth. 1899. "Congo Letter." *Missionary Intelligencer* 12 (January 1899): 20.

(8) Faris, Ellsworth. 1899. "Bolengi, Africa." *Missionary Intelligencer* 12 (December 1899): 355–356.

(9) Faris, Ellsworth. 1899. [?]. *Christian-Evangelist*, November 16, 1899, p. 1468.

(10) Faris, Ellsworth. 1900. "Tidings from Africa: School Work at Bolengi." *Missionary Intelligencer* 13 (April 1900): 86–87.

(11) Faris, Ellsworth. 1900. "The Work in Africa." *Missionary Intelligencer* 13: 183.

(12) Faris, Ellsworth. 1900. "Bolengi, Africa." *Missionary Intelligencer* 13: 237.

(13) Faris, Ellsworth. 1901. "Africa: Bolengi." *Missionary Intelligencer* 14: 285–286.

(14) Faris, Ellsworth. 1902. "The Equatorial Congo: Missionary Work in Darkest Africa." Christian-Evangelist, January 9, 1902, p. 20.

(15) Faris, Ellsworth. 1902. "Is Higher Criticism Infidelity?" Christian Courier (quoted in the Christian Standard, "A Young Apologist," April 12, 1902, pages 532–533).

(16) Faris, Ellsworth. 1903. "Glad Tidings of Great Joy." Missionary Intelligencer 16: 124–125.

(17) Faris, Ellsworth. 1903. "Bolengi." Missionary Intelligencer 16: 272.

(18) Faris, Ellsworth. 1903. "Bolengi." Missionary Intelligencer 16: 401–403 [immediately followed by a short report of Bessie Homan Faris].

(19) Faris, Ellsworth. 1903. "Lolo [translation of 'The Parable of the Prodigal Son']." Pps. 237–238 in Comparative Handbook of Congo Languages.

By Walter Henry Stapleton. Stanley Falls, Congo Independent State: "Hannah Wade" Printing Press, Baptist Missionary Society, Bolobo, Congo Independent State.

(20) Faris, Ellsworth. 1904. "Bolengi." Missionary Intelligencer 17: 407–410.

(21) Faris, Ellsworth [Bakola], and Royal J. Dye. 1904. Bekolo Bi'ampaka ba Nkundo Bikolongo la nsako. Beki Bakola otakanyaka. Bolenge, Congo: Hannah Wade printing press, Baptist Missionary Society, Bolobo, Congo Independent State.

(22) Faris, Ellsworth [Bakola], and Royal J. Dye. 1905. Nsango ea ndoci eki Malako o kotaka. Bolengi, Foreign Christian Missionary Society, printed at the Congo Balolo Mission Press, Bongandanga, Upper Congo, Congo Independent State, Central Africa.

(23) Faris, Ellsworth. 1905. "Mr. E. Faris to Mr. Casement. [letter dated December 22, 1903]." Pps. 146–147 in Part III. Further Correspondence Respecting the Congo Free State. 1904. London, UK: The Foreign Office.

(24) Faris, Ellsworth. 1905. "Mr. E. Faris to Commandant Stevens. [letter dated October 20, 1903]." Pp. 147 in Part III. Further Correspondence Respecting the Congo Free State. 1904. London, UK: The Foreign Office.

(25) Faris, Ellsworth. 1905. "Statement by Mr. E. Faris [dated October 17, 1903]." Pps. 147–148 in Part III. Further Correspondence Respecting the Congo Free State. 1904. London, UK: The Foreign Office.

(26) Faris, Ellsworth. 1905. "Mr. E. Faris to Mr. W. Armstrong" [letter dated December 31, 1903]. Pp. 148 in Part III. Further Correspondence Respecting the Congo Free State. 1904. London, UK: The Foreign Office.

(27) Faris, Ellsworth. 1908. [Untitled letter to the editor]. Christian Century 25 (49) (December 5, 1908), p. 8 [reprinted in Christian Century 25 (51), December 19, 1908, p. 8].

(28) Faris, Ellsworth. 1909. "A Heroic Missionary." Christian-Evangelist, December 30, 1909, p. 1665.

(29) Faris, Ellsworth. 1909. [Unknown title, response to questions put by Rev. McPherson.] Christian Courier [unable to locate additional details].

(30) Faris, Ellsworth. 1910. "Infidels I Have Known." The Christian Century December 30, 1910: 11.

(31) Henry, Edward A. 1910 [untitled item quoting from a letter from Ellsworth Faris]. Campbell Institute Bulletin 7, No. 1 (October 1910): 3.

(32) Faris, Ellsworth. 1913. "Let's Change the Name for the Last Time." T. C. U. Grad [unable to locate additional details].

(33) Faris, Ellsworth. 1914. The Psychology of Punishment. Unpublished PhD dissertation, University of Chicago Department of Psychology, Chicago, IL.

(34) Faris, Ellsworth. 1914. "The Origin of Punishment." International Journal of Ethics 25(1): 54–67. [Reprinted in Primitive and Ancient Legal Institutions. Edited by Albert Kocourek and John H. Wigmore. Boston: Little, Brown, 1915.]

(35) Faris, Ellsworth. 1914. "Punitive Justice and the Social Consciousness [Abstract]." Psychological Bulletin 11(1): 46–47.

DANIEL R. HUEBNER

(36) Faris, Ellsworth. 1914. "Psychology of religion (practical) [Review of The Socialized Conscience by J. H. Coffin"; "The Reestablishment of Religious Conviction in the Religious World" by F. T. Mayer-Oakes; "The Winning of Religion" by F. T. Mayer-Oakes; "Pragmatism and Religion" by F. G. Morgan; "Prejudice, Education and Religion" by J. Morse; "Religion and Social Institutions" by J. D. Stoops; and "Moral and Religious Influences of Colleges" by E. C. Wilm. Psychological Bulletin 11(12): 463–466.

(37) Faris, Ellsworth. 1914. "[Review] The Rationale of Punishment by Heinrich Oppenheimer." International Journal of Ethics 25(1): 113–114.

(38) Faris, Ellsworth. 1914. "Negro Emotionalism in Religion." Campbell Institute Bulletin 10(4): 4–9.

(39) Faris, Ellsworth. 1914. "The Summer Meeting." Campbell Institute Bulletin 10(9): 1–3.

(40) Faris, Ellsworth. 1914. "Chamber of Philosophy." Campbell Institute Bulletin 11(2): 11.

(41) Faris, Ellsworth. 1914. "Chamber of Philosophy." Campbell Institute Bulletin 11(3): 3.

(42) Faris, Ellsworth. 1914. "A Christian in a state university." Christian-Evangelist (date?), p. 816.

(43) Faris, Ellsworth. 1915. "The Psychology of Punishment [Abstract]." Philosophical Review 24(2): 190–191.

(44) Faris, Ellsworth. 1915. "[Brief review] The Cause and Cure of Crime by C. R. Henderson." International Journal of Ethics 25(2): 271.

(45) Faris, Ellsworth. 1915. "[Brief review] What Men Live By: Work, Play, Love, Worship by Richard C. Cabot." International Journal of Ethics 25(2): 272.

(46) Faris, Ellsworth. 1915. "[Brief review] A Historical Introduction to Ethics by Thomas Verner Moore." International Journal of Ethics 25(4): 560.

(47) Faris, Ellsworth. 1915. "The Possibilities of the Campbell Institute." Campbell Institute Bulletin 11(4): 2–4.

(48) Faris, Ellsworth. 1915. "Chamber of Philosophy." Campbell Institute Bulletin 11(4): 11.

(49) Faris, Ellsworth. 1915. "Chamber of Philosophy." Campbell Institute Bulletin 11(5): 5.

(50) Faris, Ellsworth. 1915. "Chamber of Philosophy." Campbell Institute Bulletin 11(6): 6.

(51) Faris, Ellsworth. 1915. "Chamber of Philosophy." Campbell Institute Bulletin 11(7): 11.

(52) Faris, Ellsworth. 1915. "A New Plea for Union." Campbell Institute Bulletin 11(9): 2–3.

(53) Faris, Ellsworth. 1915. "Chamber of Philosophy." Campbell Institute Bulletin 11(9): 8.

(54) Faris, Ellsworth. 1915. "The Summer Meeting." Campbell Institute Bulletin 11(9): 10.

(55) Faris, Ellsworth. 1915. "Chamber of Philosophy." Campbell Institute Bulletin 12(2): 22–23.

(56) Faris, Ellsworth. 1915. "Chamber of Philosophy." Campbell Institute Bulletin 12(3): 38.

(57) Faris, Ellsworth. 1916. "[Review] Life and Human Nature by B. Fuller." Psychological Bulletin 13(7): 275–276.

(58) Faris, Ellsworth. 1916. "Chamber of Philosophy." Campbell Institute Bulletin 12(4): 62–63.

(59) Faris, Ellsworth. 1916. "Chamber of Philosophy." Campbell Institute Bulletin 12(7): 108–109.

(60) Faris, Ellsworth. 1916. "Chamber of Philosophy." Campbell Institute Bulletin 13(1): 4.

(61) Faris, Ellsworth. 1916. "Chamber of Philosophy." Campbell Institute Bulletin 13(2): 18.

(62) Faris, Ellsworth. 1916. "Chamber of Philosophy." Campbell Institute Bulletin 13(3): 51–52.

(63) Faris, Ellsworth. 1916. "Business by Mail—A Suggestion for a Constitutional Amendment." Campbell Institute Bulletin 13(4): 66–67.

(64) Faris, Ellsworth. 1917. "The Campbell Institute: Questions and Answers." Pages 44–52 in Progress: Anniversary Volume of the Campbell Institute on the Completion of Twenty Years of History. Edited by Herbert L. Willett, Orvis F. Jordan, and Charles M. Sharpe. Chicago: Published for the Campbell Institute by Christian Century Press.

(65) Faris, Ellsworth. 1917. "Anger, Resentment, and Retribution [Abstract summarized by Edward L. Schaub]." Journal of Philosophy, Psychology, and Scientific Methods 14(15): 413–414.

(66) Faris, Ellsworth. 1917. "Chamber of Philosophy." Campbell Institute Bulletin 13(6): 94–95.

(67) Faris, Ellsworth. 1917. "Chamber of Philosophy." Campbell Institute Bulletin 13(7): 115–116.

(68) Faris, Ellsworth. 1917. "Do I Hear a Second?" Campbell Institute Bulletin 13(7): 116.

(69) Faris, Ellsworth. 1917. "Chamber of Philosophy." Campbell Institute Bulletin 13(8): 127–128.

(70) Faris, Ellsworth. 1917. "Chamber of Philosophy." Campbell Institute Bulletin 13(10): 157–158.

(71) Faris, Ellsworth. 1917. "Faris Speaking at Camp Cody: University Professor Represents Extension Department Among the Soldiers." Iowa City Press Citizen (November 28, 1917): 2.

(72) Faris, Ellsworth. 1918. "The Mental Capacity of Savages." American Journal of Sociology 23(5): 603–619. [Later retitled "The Mental Capacity of Preliterates."]

(73) Faris, Ellsworth. 1918. "[Review] The Secret of Personality by George Trumball Ladd." American Journal of Sociology 24(2): 221–222.

(74) Faris, Ellsworth. 1919. "The State Program of the Iowa Child Welfare Research Station." Proceedings of the National Conference of Social Work 46: 33–36.

DANIEL R. HUEBNER   159

(75) Faris, Ellsworth. 1919. "The Psychology of Language [Review of Psychological Aspects of Language" by G. C. Brandenburg; "Psychologie du langage" by H. Delacroix; and "Convergences des développements linguistiques" by A. Meillet]. Psychological Bulletin 16(3): 93–95.

(76) Faris, Ellsworth. 1919. "Stoning the Prophets." The Christian Century 36(13) (April 10, 1919): 12–13. [Apparently originally in The Christian Courier.]

(77) Faris, Ellsworth. 1920. "[Review] The Psychology of Nationality and Internationalism by W. B. Pillsbury." International Journal of Ethics 30(3): 339–340.

(78) Faris, Ellsworth. 1921. "Are Instincts Data or Hypotheses?" American Journal of Sociology 27(2): 184–196.

(79) Faris, Ellsworth. 1921. "The Sociology of Peace." Unity 87(16): 248–251.

(80) Faris, Ellsworth. 1921. "Ethnological Light on Psychological Problems." Publications of the American Sociological Society 16: 113–120.

(81) Faris, Ellsworth. 1921. "Africa, Religions of." Pps. 7–9 in A Dictionary of Religion and Ethics. Edited by Shailer Mathews and Gerald Birney Smith. New York: Macmillan.

(82) Faris, Ellsworth. 1921. "Australia, Religions of." Pps. 37–38 in A Dictionary of Religion and Ethics. Edited by Shailer Mathews and Gerald Birney Smith. New York: Macmillan.

(83) Faris, Ellsworth. 1921. "Parents, Religious Duties to." Pp. 324 in A Dictionary of Religion and Ethics. Edited by Shailer Mathews and Gerald Birney Smith. New York: Macmillan.

(84) Faris, Ellsworth. 1921. "[Review] Is America Safe for Democracy? by William McDougall." American Journal of Sociology 27(2): 240–243.

(85) Faris, Ellsworth. 1921. "[Review] Primitive Society by Robert H. Lowie." American Journal of Sociology 27(2): 243–244.

(86) Faris, Ellsworth. 1921. "[Review] Source Book in Anthropology by A. L. Kroeber and T. T. Waterman." American Journal of Sociology 27(2): 244–245.

(87) Faris, Ellsworth. 1921. "A Problem in Theological Engineering." The Scroll 17(9): 212–215.

(88) Faris, Ellsworth. 1922. "[Review] Educational Sociology by David Snedden." The School Review 30(9): 707–709.

(89) Faris, Ellsworth. 1923. "[Review] Primitive Society: The Beginnings of the Family and the Reckoning of Descent by Edwin Sidney Hartland." American Journal of Sociology 28(4): 483–484.

(90) Faris, Ellsworth. 1923. "[Review] Principles and Methods of Physical Anthropology by Rai Bahadur Sarat Chandra Roy." American Journal of Sociology 28(4): 485–485.

(91) Faris, Ellsworth. 1923. "'Student Cheaters Neglect Obligations to Group'– Faris." Daily Maroon (April 18, 1923): 1, 3.

(92) Faris, Ellsworth. 1924. "Social Evolution." Pps. 211–242 in Contributions of Science to Religion. Edited by Shailer Mathews. New York: D. Appleton.

(93) Faris, Ellsworth. 1924. "The Problem and Method in Social Psychology [Abstract]." Psychological Bulletin 21: 107.

(94) Faris, Ellsworth. 1924. "The Ethnological Bases of Racial Cooperation." Address to the Women's International League for Peace and Freedom, May 1924. Manuscript in the Anita McCormick Blaine Correspondence and Papers, Box 765, Division of Library, Archives, and Museum Collections; Wisconsin Historical Society, Madison, WI.

(95) Faris, Ellsworth. 1925. "The Subjective Aspect of Culture." Publications of the American Sociological Society 19: 37–46.

(96) Faris, Ellsworth. 1925. "The Concept of Social Attitudes." Journal of Applied Sociology 9(6): 404–409.

(97) Faris, Ellsworth. 1925. "[Review] Instinct: A Study in Social Psychology by L. L. Bernard." American Journal of Sociology 30(5): 600–602.

(98) Faris, Ellsworth. 1925. "Pre-Literate Peoples. Proposing a New Term." American Journal of Sociology 30(6): 710–712.

(99) Faris, Ellsworth. 1925. "[Review] Social Psychology by Floyd Henry Allport." American Journal of Sociology 30(6): 719–722.

(100) Faris, Ellsworth. 1925. "Three Fields of Sociological Investigation Here, Says Faris." Daily Maroon (April 28, 1925): 1–2.

(101) Faris, Ellsworth. 1926. "The Nature of Human Nature." Proceedings of the American Sociological Society 20: 15–29. [Reprinted in Burgess, Ernest W., ed. 1926. The Urban Community: Selected Papers from The Proceedings of the American Sociological Society 1925. Chicago: University of Chicago Press. Pages 21–37.]

(102) Faris, Ellsworth. 1926. "What Constitutes a Scientific Interpretation of Religion?" Journal of Religion 6(3): 236–242.

(103) Faris, Ellsworth. 1926. "The Concept of Imitation." American Journal of Sociology 32(3): 367–378.

(104) Faris, Ellsworth. 1926. "[Review] The Laws of Social Psychology by Florian Znaniecki." American Journal of Sociology 31(4): 531–533.

(105) Faris, Ellsworth. 1926. "[Review] The Psychology of Human Society by Charles A. Ellwood." American Journal of Sociology 32(2): 305–307.

(106) Faris, Ellsworth. 1926. "[Review] Psychologies of 1925. Powell Lectures in Psychological Theory." American Journal of Sociology 32(2): 309–311.

(107) Faris, Ellsworth. 1926. "[Review] Psychologies of 1925. Powell Lectures in Psychological Theory." Religious Education 21(4): 427–428.

(108) Faris, Ellsworth. 1926. "[Review] Social Psychology by Knight Dunlap; An Introduction to Social Psychology by L. L. Bernard; Outlines of Abnormal Psychology by William McDougall; Problems of Personality: Studies Presented to Dr. Morton Prince, Pioneer in American Psychopathology by C. MacFie Campbell, H. S. Langfeld, William McDougall, R. A. Roback, E. W. Taylor; The Meaning of Psychology by C. K. Ogden; Brains of Rats and Men: A Survey of the Origin and Biological Significance of the Cerebral Cortex by C. Judson Herrick." American Journal of Sociology 32(3): 482–486.

(109) Faris, Ellsworth. 1926. "Pictures and Imitative Behavior." Pps. 87–105 in Proceedings of the Fourth National Motion Picture Conference, under the auspices of the Federal Motion Picture Council in America, Inc. Chicago, IL: [privately mimeographed].

(110) Faris, Ellsworth. 1926. "Wild Students I Have Known." Daily Maroon (December 17, 1926): 10.

(111) Faris, Ellsworth. 1927. "Remarks on Race Superiority." Social Service Review 1(1): 36–45.

(112) Faris, Ellsworth. 1927. "The Church as a Prophet of Unity." Journal of Religion 7(3): 277–283.

(113) Faris, Ellsworth. 1927. "The Natural History of Race Prejudice." Pps. 89–94 in Ebony and Topaz: A Collectanea. Edited by Charles S. Johnson. New York: Opportunity Publishing Co.

(114) Faris, Ellsworth. 1927. "The Superiority of Race: Some Considerations in Approaching the Study of Racial Difference." Preliminary Paper Prepared for Second General Session, July 15–29, 1927, of the Institute of Pacific Relations. Honolulu: Institute of Pacific Relations.

(115) Faris, Ellsworth. 1927. "Topical Summaries of Current Literature: Social Psychology in America." American Journal of Sociology 32(4): 623–630.

(116) Faris, Ellsworth. 1927. "[Review] The Nature of the World and of Man by H. H. Newman." American Journal of Sociology 32(4): 645–646.

(117) Faris, Ellsworth. 1927. "[Review] General Theory of Value: Its Meaning and Basic Principles Construed in Terms of Interest by Ralph Barton Perry." American Journal of Sociology 33(2): 283–285.

(118) Faris, Ellsworth. 1928. "The Sect and the Sectarian." Papers and Proceedings of the American Sociological Society 22: 144–158. [Reprinted in: (1) Personality and the Social Group. Edited by E. W. Burgess. Chicago: University of Chicago Press, 1929; (2) American Journal of Sociology 60(6) (supplement: The Early and the Contemporary Study of Religion, 1955, edited by Everett C. Hughes): 75–89.]

(119) Faris, Ellsworth. 1928. "The Sociologist and the Educator." American Journal of Sociology 33(5): 796–801.

(120) Faris. Ellsworth. 1928. "Attitudes and Behavior." American Journal of Sociology 34(2): 271–281.

(121) Faris, Ellsworth. 1928. "Social Attitudes and Character." Pps. 296–306 in Building Character: Proceedings of the Mid-West Conference on Parent Education, February 1928. Chicago: University of Chicago Press.

(122) Faris, Ellsworth. 1928. "Religious Education and the Community." Religious Education 23: 718–19.

(123) Faris, Ellsworth. 1928. "Rethinking the Tasks of the Church." Religious Education 23: 943–947.

(124) Faris, Ellsworth. 1928. "Introduction." In Suicide. By Ruth Shonle Cavan. Chicago: University of Chicago Press.

(125) Faris, Ellsworth. 1928. "[Review] The Polish Peasant in Europe and America by William I. Thomas and Florian Znaniecki." American Journal of Sociology 33(5): 816–819.

162   *Colonial Violence and the Chicago School*

(126) Faris, Ellsworth. 1928. "[Review] The American Race Problem: A Study of the Negro by Edward Byron Reuter." Annals of the American Academy of Political and Social Science 140 (The American Negro): 337–338.

(127) Faris, Ellsworth. 1928. "[Review] Introduction to Social Psychology by L. L. Bernard." Psychological Bulletin 25 (2): 118–20.

(128) Faris, Ellsworth. 1928. "Sociology and Anthropology." University of Chicago Record, New Series, Vol. 14, No. 3 (July 1928): 189–191.

(129) Faris, Ellsworth. 1929. "Racial Attitudes and Sentiments." Southwestern Political and Social Science Quarterly 9(4): 479–490.

(130) Faris, Ellsworth. 1929. "Some Phases of Religion that are Susceptible of Sociological Study." Papers and Proceedings of the American Sociological Society 23: 342–343. [Later reprinted in 1955 as: "Some Phases of Religion That Are Susceptible of Sociological Study." Edited by Everett C. Hughes. American Journal of Sociology 60(6): 90.]

(131) Faris, Ellsworth. 1929. "The Verbal Battle of the Races." Social Service Review 3(1): 19–29.

(132) Faris. Ellsworth. 1929. "Current Trends in Social Psychology." Pps. 119–133 in Essays in Philosophy by Seventeen Doctors of Philosophy of the University of Chicago. Edited by T. V. Smith and William Kelley Wright. Chicago: Open Court Publishing.

(133) Faris, Ellsworth. 1929. "Implications of Behaviorism for Character Development." Religious Education 24: 117–121.

(134) Faris, Ellsworth. 1929. "Does the Community Determine Character?" Religious Education 24: 408–409.

(135) Faris, Ellsworth. 1929. "On the Fundamental Tendencies of Children." Religious Education 24: 808–812.

(136) Faris, Ellsworth. 1929. "The Junior-College Survey Course in Sociology and Anthropology." Pps. 234–243 in The Junior-College Curriculum. Proceedings of the Institute for Administrative Offices of Higher Institutions, 1929, Vol. 1. Edited by William S. Gray. Chicago: University of Chicago Press.

(137) Faris, Ellsworth. 1929. "The Cave Man within Us [review of The Story of Superstition by Philip F. Waterman, The History of the Devil: The Horned God of the West by R. Lowe Thompson, and Rope and Faggot: A Biography of Judge Lynch by Walter White]." The New Republic (May 8, 1929): 337–338.

(138) Faris, Ellsworth. 1929. "[Review] The Religion Called Behaviorism by Louis Berman." American Journal of Sociology 34(6): 1207.

(139) Faris, Ellsworth. 1929. "[Review] Social Psychology Interpreted by Jesse William Sprowls; Introduction to Social Psychology by Radhakamal Mukerjee, Narendra Nath Sen-Gupta; An Outline of Social Psychology by J. R. Kantor; Social Psychology: The Psychology of Political Domination by Carl Murchison." American Journal of Sociology 35(2): 304–308.

(140) Faris, Ellsworth. 1929. "[Review] The Decroly Class by Amelie Hamaide and Jean Lee Hunt." American Journal of Sociology 35(2): 313–315.

DANIEL R. HUEBNER 163

(141) Faris, Ellsworth. 1930. "Borderline Trends in Social Psychology." Publications of the American Sociological Society 25: 36–42.

(142) Faris, Ellsworth. 1930. "Building a Christian Society." Pps. 104–114 in Building a Moral Reserve or, The Civic Responsibilities of the Christian Citizen. Outline Bible-Study Courses of the American Institute of Sacred Literature, Volume 28. By Shailer Mathews, Andrew C. McLaughlin, Harold D. Lasswell, William W. Sweet, Ellsworth Faris, Samuel C. Kincheloe, Frank J. Loesch, and Georgia L. Chamberlin. Edited by Georgia L. Chamberlin. Chicago: University of Chicago Press for the American Institute of Sacred Literature.

(143) Faris, Ellsworth, Ferris Laune, and Arthur J. Todd, eds. 1930. Intelligent Philanthropy. Chicago: University of Chicago Press.

(144) Faris, Ellsworth. 1930. "Research and the Religious Education Association." Religious Education 25: 491–493.

(145) Faris, Ellsworth. 1930. "Nature and Significance of the Mores." Religious Education 25: 500–506.

(146) Faris, Ellsworth. 1930. "Discipline in the Modern Family." Religious Education 25: 911–914.

(147) Faris, Ellsworth. 1930. "Building a Christian Society." The Institute [American Institute of Sacred Literature journal] 14: 130–136.

(148) Faris, Ellsworth. 1930. "Foreword." Pps. v-vii in The Child's Emotions: Proceedings of the Mid-West Conference on Character Development, February 1930. Chicago: University of Chicago Press.

(149) Faris, Ellsworth. 1930. "[Review] Social Psychology of International Conduct by George Malcolm Stratton." American Journal of Sociology 35(5): 833–834.

(150) Faris, Ellsworth. 1930. "[Review] Social Psychology by Bernard C. Ewer." American Journal of Sociology 35(5): 853–854.

(151) Faris, Ellsworth. 1930. "[Review] Science and Personality by William Brown." American Journal of Sociology 35(5): 846.

(152) Faris, Ellsworth. 1930. "[Review] Encyclopaedia of the Social Sciences, Vol. I, Aaronson-Allegiance by Edwin R. A. Seligman, Alvin Johnson." American Journal of Sociology 35(6): 1112–1113.

(153) Faris, Ellsworth. 1930. "[Review] The Evolution of War: A Study of its Role in Early Societies by Maurice R. Davie." American Journal of Sociology 35(6): 1114–1116.

(154) Faris, Ellsworth. 1931. "The Concept of Social Attitudes." Pps. 3–16 in Social Attitudes. Edited by Kimball Young. New York: Henry Holt.

(155) Faris, Ellsworth. 1931. "[Review] The Story of Punishment—A Record of Man's Inhumanity to Man by Harry Elmer Barnes." International Journal of Ethics 41(2): 261–263.

(156) Faris, Ellsworth. 1932. "The Primary Group: Essence and Accident." American Journal of Sociology 38(1): 41–50.

(157) Faris, Ellsworth. 1932. "Foreword." Pps. Xiii–xvii in American Social Psychology: Its Origins, Development, and European Background. By Fay Berger Karpf. New York: McGraw-Hill.

(158) Faris, Ellsworth. 1932. "[Review] Race Psychology: A Study of Racial Mental Differences by Thomas Russell Garth." Social Service Review 6(2): 341–343.

(159) Faris, Ellsworth. 1933. "Research Projects and Methods in Educational Sociology." Journal of Educational Sociology 6(9): 564–566.

(160) Faris, Ellsworth. 1933. "Standpoint and Method of Sociology in the Study of Personality and Social Growth." Pps 1–24, Appendix C, in Fourth Conference on Research in Child Development, The University of Chicago. Chicago, Illinois, June 23–24, 1933. Washington, DC: Committee on Child Development, National Research Council.

(161) Faris, Ellsworth. 1933. "Studies Pigmies: Dr Faris Writes of Vast Changes in Native Tribal Life." Daily Maroon 33, No. 91 (April 11, 1933): 1, 3.

(162) Faris, Ellsworth. 1934. "Too Many PhD's?" American Journal of Sociology 39(4): 509–512.

(163) Faris, Ellsworth. 1934. "Native Education in the Belgian Congo." Journal of Negro Education 3(1): 123–130.

(164) Faris, Ellsworth. 1934. "Culture and Personality Among the Forest Bantu." Publications of the American Sociological Society 28: 3–11.

(165) Faris, Ellsworth. 1934. "[Review] Methods in Sociology by Charles A. Ellwood." American Journal of Sociology 39(5): 686–689.

(166) Faris. Ellsworth. 1934. "[Review] The Dynamics of Therapy in a Controlled Relationship by Jessie Taft." American Journal of Sociology 39(6): 861–862.

(167) Faris, Ellsworth. 1934. "[Review] The Art of Conference by Frank Walser." American Journal of Sociology 40(1): 124–125.

(168) Faris, Ellsworth. 1934. "[Review] The Evolution of Human Behavior by Karl J. Warden." American Journal of Sociology 40(2): 268.

(169) Faris, Ellsworth. 1934. "[Review] Emile Durkheim on the Division of Labor in Society by George Simpson." American Journal of Sociology 40(3): 376–77.

(170) Faris, Ellsworth. 1934. "[Review] China's Geographic Foundations: A Survey of the Land and Its People by George Babcock Cressey; The Chinese: Their History and Culture by Kenneth Scott Latourette." American Journal of Sociology 40(3): 379–380.

(171) Faris, Ellsworth. 1935. "Preface." American Journal of Sociology, Index to Volumes 1–40, 1895–1935: iii–iv.

(172) Faris, Ellsworth. 1935. "The Sociology of Religious Strife." Journal of Religion 15(2): 207–219.

(173) Faris, Ellsworth. 1935. "Two Educational Problems." Journal of Educational Sociology 9(1): 40–46.

(174) Faris, Ellsworth. 1935. "Religious Social Attitudes [Review of Intolerance by Winfred Ernest Garrison]." Journal of Religion 15(1): 86–88.

(175) Faris, Ellsworth. 1935. "[Review] An Introduction to Pareto: His Sociology by George C. Homas and Charles P. Curtis Jr." American Journal of Sociology 40(5): 667.

DANIEL R. HUEBNER 165

(176) Faris, Ellsworth. 1935. "[Review] Education of Primitive People by Albert D. Helser." American Journal of Sociology 40(5): 685.

(177) Faris, Ellsworth. 1935. "[Brief review] Races, Nations and Jews by Joseph Tenebaum." Journal of Religion 15(3): 374.

(178) Faris, Ellsworth. 1935. "Roger Clarke – A Modern Missionary." The Scroll 31(5): 137–140.

(179) Faris, Ellsworth. 1936. "An Estimate of Pareto." American Journal of Sociology 41(5): 657–668.

(180) Faris, Ellsworth. 1936. "Of Psychological Elements." American Journal of Sociology 42(2): 159–176.

(181) Faris, Ellsworth. 1936. "Small, Albion Woodbury." Pp. 221–222 in Dictionary of American Biography, Vol. 9. Edited by Dumas Malone. New York: Charles Scribner's Sons.

(182) Faris, Ellsworth. 1936. "Editorial Note." American Journal of Sociology 41(6): 803.

(183) Faris, Ellsworth. 1936. "[Review] Mind, Self, and Society by George H. Mead, edited and with introduction by Charles W. Morris." American Journal of Sociology 41(6): 809–813.

(184) Faris, Ellsworth. 1936. "Rejoinder." American Journal of Sociology 42(3): 391–392.

(185) Faris, Ellsworth. 1936. "Editorial." Journal of Educational Sociology 9: 514.

(186) Faris, Ellsworth. 1937. The Nature of Human Nature, and Other Essays in Social Psychology. New York: McGraw-Hill.

(187) Faris, Ellsworth. 1937. "The Social Psychology of George Mead." American Journal of Sociology 43(3): 391–403.

(188) Faris, Ellsworth. 1937. "Official Communication and Report." American Sociological Review 2(3): 409–412.

(189) Faris, Ellsworth. 1937. [Untitled letter to the editor]. American Journal of Sociology 42(4): 561.

(190) Faris, Ellsworth. 1937. "[Review] Primitive Behavior: An Introduction to the Social Sciences by William I. Thomas." American Journal of Sociology 43(1): 166–171.

(191) Faris, Ellsworth. 1937. "[Review] What Man has Made of Man: A Study of the Consequences of Platonism and Positivism in Psychology by Mortimer Adler." American Journal of Sociology 43(3): 492–493.

(192) Faris, Ellsworth. 1937. "[Review] The Higher Learning in a Democracy: A Reply to President Hutchins' Critique of the American University by Harry D. Gideonse." American Journal of Sociology 43(3): 497–498.

(193) Faris, Ellsworth. 1938. "The Promise of Sociology." American Sociological Review 3(1): 1–12.

(194) Faris, Ellsworth. 1938. "Assimilation." Social Process in Hawaii 4: 6–11.

(195) Faris, Ellsworth, Wilson Gee, and Harold A. Phelps. 1938. "Report of the Committee on Membership." American Sociological Review 3(1): 97–99.

(196) Faris, Ellsworth. 1938. "The Nature of Human Nature [Letter to the Editor]." American Journal of Sociology 43(4): 635.

(197) Faris, Ellsworth. 1938. "Report of the Committee of Presidents of Regional Sociological Societies." American Sociological Review 3(1): 95.

(198) Rice, Stuart, E. W. Burgess, Dorothy Swaine Thomas, Harold A. Phelps, and Ellsworth Faris. 1938. "Report of the Research Planning Committee." American Sociological Review 3(1): 96.

(199) Faris, Ellsworth. 1938. "[Review] Religion and Medicine of the Ga People by M. J. Field." Journal of Religion 18(1): 117–118.

(200) Faris, Ellsworth. 1938. "Journalism—Not Sociology [Review of Middletown in Transition: A Study in Cultural Conflicts by Robert S. Lynd and Helen Merrell Lynd]." Journal of Higher Education 9(4): 229–230.

(201) Faris, Ellsworth. 1938. "[Review] Personality: A Psychological Interpretation by Gordon W. Allport." Annals of the American Academy of Political and Social Science 198 (Present International Tensions): 239–240.

(202) Faris, Ellsworth. 1939. "Sociology and Human Welfare." Social Forces 18(1): 1–9.

(203) Faris, Ellsworth. 1940. "Religion and Social Attitudes." Pps. 35–46 in Faith of the Free. Edited by Winfred Ernest Garrison. Chicago: Willett, Clark & Company.

(204) Faris, Ellsworth. 1940. "Seven Pillars of Family Strength." Living 2(3): 69–76.

(205) Faris, Ellsworth. 1940. "The Retrospective Act." Journal of Educational Sociology 14(2): 79–91.

(206) Faris, Ellsworth. 1940. "[Review] Frustration and Aggression by John Dollard, Leonard W. Doob, Neal E. Miller, O. H. Mowrer, and Robert W. Sears." American Journal of Sociology 45(4): 595–598.

(207) Faris, Ellsworth. 1942. "[Review] Corporal Punishment: A Social Interpretation of Its Theory and Practice in the Schools of the United States by Herbert Arnold Falk." American Journal of Sociology 48(2): 298.

(208) Faris, Ellsworth. 1942. "[Review] Foundations for a Science of Personality by A. Angyal." American Sociological Review 7(2): 276–278.

(209) Faris, Ellsworth. 1942. "[Review] Frustration and Regression by Roger Barker, Tamara Dembo, and Kurt Lewin." American Sociological Review 7: 140–141.

(210) Faris, Ellsworth. 1943. "The Role of the Citizen." Pps. 118–142 in American Society in Wartime. Edited by William F. Ogburn. Chicago: University of Chicago Press.

(211) Faris, Ellsworth. 1943. "[Review] Desert Saints: The Mormon Frontier in Utah by Nels Anderson." American Journal of Sociology 48(4): 522.

(212) Faris, Ellsworth. 1943. "[Review] Principles of Anthropology by Eliot Dinsmore Chapple and Carleton Stevens Coon." American Sociological Review 8(2): 240–241.

(213) Faris, Ellsworth. 1944. "Prospects for a World Without Intolerance." American Journal of Sociology 49(5): 457–464.

(214) Faris, Ellsworth. 1944. "Robert E. Park. 1864–1944." American Sociological Review 9(3): 322–325.

(215) Faris, Ellsworth. 1944. "The Mores and the Color Line." Typescript of speech delivered at the A. M. A. Institute of Race Relations, Fisk University, Nashville, Tennessee, July 3–21, 1944. Pps. 1–6.

(216) Faris, Ellsworth. 1944. "Contrasting Racial Policies in Colonial Africa." Typescript of speech delivered at the A. M. A. Institute of Race Relations, Fisk University, Nashville, Tennessee, July 3–21, 1944. Pps. 1–4.

(217) Faris, Ellsworth. 1944. "Frank Interpretation [Review of Personality and Social Change: Attitude Formation in a Student Community by Theodore M. Newcomb]." Journal of Higher Education 15(3): 170–171.

(218) Faris, Ellsworth. 1944. "[Review] Conscience and Society: A Study of the Psychological Prerequisites of Law and Order by Raynard West." American Journal of Sociology 50(3): 252–253.

(219) Faris, Ellsworth. 1944. "[Review] A Realistic Philosophy of Religion by A. Campbell Garnett." American Sociological Review 9(3): 338–339.

(220) Faris, Ellsworth. 1945. "The Beginnings of Social Psychology." American Journal of Sociology 50(6): 422–428.

(221) Faris, Ellsworth. 1945. "Nothing on Higher Education [Review of The Condition of Man by Lewis Mumford]." Journal of Higher Education 16(2): 110–111.

(222) Faris, Ellsworth. 1945. "[Review] The Concept of Dread by Soren Kierkegaard, translated and with introduction and notes by Walter Lowrie." American Journal of Sociology 50(5): 401–404.

(223) Faris, Ellsworth. 1945. "[Review] Sociology of Religion by Joachim Wach." American Journal of Sociology 50(5): 404–405.

(224) Faris, Ellsworth. 1945. "[Review] The Philosophy of Bertrand Russell by Paul Arthur Schilpp." American Journal of Sociology 50(5): 407–408.

(225) Faris, Ellsworth. 1945. "To the Editor, the 'American Journal of Sociology' [Letter to the Editor]." American Journal of Sociology 50(6): 549.

(226) Faris, Ellsworth. 1945. "Some Professors' Opinions [Review of New Perspectives on Peace by George B. de Huszar]." Journal of Higher Education 16(8): 449–450.

(227) Faris, Ellsworth. 1945. "Another Theory of Higher Education [Review of Education for Responsible Living by Walter Brett Donham]." Journal of Higher Education 16(9) 497–498.

(228) Faris, Ellsworth. 1945. "With Malice Toward None." University of Chicago Magazine 38, No. 1 (October 1945): 8–9.

(229) Faris, Ellsworth. 1946. "Some Results of Frustration." Sociology and Social Research 31(2): 87–92.

(230) Faris, Ellsworth. 1946. "Is the 'Melting Pot' Obsolete? [Review of One America: Our Racial and National Minorities by France J. Brown and Joseph S. Roucek]." Journal of Higher Education 17(1): 52.

(231) Faris, Ellsworth. 1946. "In Praise of the Doctorate." University of Chicago Magazine 38, No. 9 (July 1946): 10–13.

(232) Faris, Ellsworth. 1948. "In Memoriam: William Isaac Thomas, 1863–1947." American Journal of Sociology 53(5): 387.

(233) Faris, Ellsworth. 1948. "W. I. Thomas (1863–1947)." Sociology and Social Research 32(4): 755–759.

(234) Faris, Ellsworth. 1948. "[Review] Father of the Man by W. Allison Davis and Robert J. Havighurst." American Journal of Sociology 53(5): 401–402.

(235) Faris, Ellsworth. 1948. "[Review] Opiate Addiction by Alfred R. Lindesmith." American Journal of Sociology 54: 169–170.

(236) Faris, Ellsworth. 1949. "[Review] The New Congo by Tom Marvel." American Journal of Sociology 54(6): 577–579.

(237) Faris, Ellsworth. 1949. "Sin, Sex, and Segregation [review of Killers of the Dream by Lillian Smith]." The Christian Century (December 7, 1949): 1457.

(238) Faris, Ellsworth. 1949. "Secularism and God's Design." The Scroll 46(2): 361–366.

(239) Faris, Ellsworth. 1949. "Congo Revisited." The Scroll 46(10): 494–500.

(240) Faris, Ellsworth. 1951. "The Ivory Tower." Southwestern Social Science Quarterly 31(4): 231–242.

(241) Faris, Ellsworth. 1951. "[Review] This is Race: An Anthology Selected from the International Literature on the Races of Man by Earl W. Count." American Journal of Sociology 56(4): 388–389.

(242) Faris, Ellsworth. 1951. "[Review] Social Behavior and Personality: Contributions of W. I. Thomas to Theory and Social Research by Edmund H. Volkart." American Sociological Review 16(6): 875–877.

(243) Faris, Ellsworth. 1952. "[Review] Religion Among the Primitives by William J. Goode." American Journal of Sociology 57(4): 394–395.

(244) Faris, Ellsworth. 1952. "[Review] Types of Religious Experience, Christian and Non-Christian by Joachim Wach." American Sociological Review 17(2): 253–254.

(245) Faris, Ellsworth. 1953. "[Review] The Social System by Talcott Parsons." American Sociological Review 18(1): 103–106.

(246) Faris, Ellsworth. 1953. "Rejoinder." American Sociological Review 18(3): 323.

(247) Faris, Ellsworth. 1953. "Presidential Advice to Younger Sociologists." Edited by Samuel A. Stouffer (transcript of a recorded brief messages from former Presidents of the American Sociological Society). American Sociological Review 18(6): 599–600.

(248) Thompson, Edgar, Stuart A. Queen, and Ellsworth Faris. 1953. "Minutes of the Business Meeting of the Society." American Sociological Review 18(6): 676–677.

(249) Faris, Ellsworth. 1958. [Untitled reminiscence of E. S. Ames]. The Scroll 49, No. 4 (Spring 1958): 18–19. [Written as much as a decade earlier and collected by the editor of The Scroll with others for publication at a later date.]

ETHNOMETHODS OF INCREASING THE BELIEVABILITY OF EXTRAORDINARY CLAIMS: STRATEGIES FOR THE PRESENTATION OF SELF

David Aveline and Brant Downey

Mount Royal University, Canada

ABSTRACT

This chapter is based on the results of a larger project on people's beliefs in ghosts and their claims to have encountered them. Thirty-eight such people were interviewed in depth upon their assumed paranormal encounters. Primarily using Goffman's work on self-presentation and Mead's ideas on the past, as well as his concept of the generalized other, *we examine the transcripts for "ethnomethods" used by the claimants telling of their experiences with ghosts as strategies for increasing or assuring the believability of their claims. Ten such methods were identified. These ethnomethods are likely to arise when the claimant, in evoking the concept of the generalized other, interprets the perception of their extraordinary claims as false, highly fanciful, or dubious.*

Keywords: Paranormal; interview data; clairvoyance; alternative realities; Canada

INTRODUCTION

But if he will not hear thee, then take with thee one or two more, that in the mouth of two or three witnesses every word may be established. —Matthew 18: 16 (The King James Bible)

Essential Methods in Symbolic Interaction
Studies in Symbolic Interaction, Volume 60, 169–186
Copyright © 2025 David Aveline and Brant Downey
Published under exclusive licence by Emerald Publishing Limited
ISSN: 0163-2396/doi:10.1108/S0163-239620250000060009

If a person mentioned casually to friends that (s)he had eggs for breakfast, (s) he would no doubt be believed without evidence. Eggs are a time-honored breakfast staple and they have been eaten as such billions of times in the last several decades alone. This same taken-for-granted acceptance might also occur for routine claims such as "I took the bus to work today" or "I went to bed early last night." There is nothing peculiar about such activities and to disbelieve someone claiming them would be highly unusual. As Harold Garfinkel (1967) well illustrated with his *breaching experiments* decades ago, to question the ordinary, the everyday, or the mundane would likely meet with shock, bewilderment, or anger. Indeed, society would cease to function if every simple claim was disbelieved in lieu of irrefutable evidence. In contrast, people are less likely to believe the extraordinary, the highly unlikely, and the impossible (e.g., "I flapped my arms and flew to school this morning").[1] In fact, if claimants did insist that impossible events actually took place, others might think them fanciful, deceitful, or mentally ill.

Garfinkel's micro-sociology is suggestive of the approach we use in this paper. We re-examine data from transcripts of interviews with 38 people who firmly believed that they encountered ghosts and ground them in some key aspects of symbolic interaction. We look at George Herbert Mead's (1929, 1934) concepts of the *generalized other* and the self's symbolic interpretation of the past, Erving Goffman's (1956, 1959) concepts of self-presentation and avoidance tactics, and Scott and Lyman's (1968) concept of *accounts*. First we look at this theoretical background, then the method we use, and then an application of original findings that overlap with the aforementioned symbolic interactionist ideas (although not fully reduceable to them). In so doing, we look at 10 "ethnomethods" used by people who firmly believe that they have encountered ghosts. These methods serve as strategies for increasing or assuring the believability of their extraordinary claims.

THEORETICAL BACKGROUND

As a rule, when people make fantastic claims, we are skeptical. When we make those claims ourselves, we typically expect that same skepticism from others. We imagine what a typical community member might think of us, and the more inconceivable our claims, the more we expect not to be believed. In the language of George Herbert Mead, we take the role of "the generalized other," or "the attitude of the whole community," (1934, p. 154) and are consequently influenced – mentally, symbolically – by social meanings held in high esteem by this group. Furthermore, because we take the generalized other into account with virtually all that we say and do in social life, this awareness of imminent doubt toward the fantastic emerges a priori. Through a process of interpretation based on past interactions with others (Blumer, 1969), we develop expectations of which types of claims might be believed as a matter of course and which types might not. Thus, if we do believe that we have witnessed a highly extraordinary event – "a unicorn in the garden" as James Thurber put it – we may well anticipate that we will not be taken seriously in the telling.[2] "No one is going to believe this one" we might think, or "they're all going to think I'm crazy."

This anticipation of judgment is compatible with Scott and Lyman's (1968) analysis of accounts, defined as socially approved statements made to defend actions or claims that are widely regarded as untoward. For example, a fight at a traffic light between two motorists may later be justified as "he deserved it." A combination of vitamins and herbs consumed in secret by a competitive athlete might also later be justified as "not breaking the rules." For Scott and Lyman, *justifications* are one of the main ways that accounts are provided, and they are identifiable by the challenging of expected disapprovals. In the interview data we analyze, one pattern reveals respondents reporting that others had also seen a ghost in question, implying that their claim is more credible than a sighting by a solitary person. In this way, potential rebuttals by skeptics are contested, perhaps even before they are made. In short, the respondents justified their claims and any accusations of eccentricity are dismissed as unfounded. The 10 "appeals" discussed later in this paper may be viewed as extensions of this basic idea proposed by Scott and Lyman.[3]

Goffman (1959) suggested in his dramaturgical analysis that we would all like to be taken seriously and, as a result, we put much effort into our presentations of self for the purpose. Whether in the form of gestures, props, or words, we use what is available to us to put forth a favorable image. Specifically, Goffman mentions "dramaturgical circumspection" or the "exercise of foresight and design in determining in advance how best to stage a show [...] and exploiting the opportunities that remain" (1959, p. 218). Because we wish to appear as competent actors and avoid embarrassment, we are motivated to provide evidence of our capabilities during face-to-face interactions. If we play our parts well, our audiences will see us in the ways in which we intend. Regarding encounters with ghosts, we will suggest how Goffman's approach sheds light on strategies used to increase the likelihood of the believability of extraordinary claims. In other words, we discuss the *ethnomethods* used in the construction of claims to maximize the likelihood that an audience will take them as true.

Before doing so, one more theoretical point related to George Herbert Mead is needed. Goffman's strategic "exercise of foresight" points to a temporal dimension of the self, which is also evident in Mead's work. In "The Nature of the Past" (1929, p. 238), Mead highlights the symbolic interplay between our past and present lives and proposes that the past "is an overflow of the present." By this, he means, that we privilege some aspects of the past over others based on our current situation. "We have assurances of the reality of past events because they connect in a believable way with the reality of events in the present," as Maines et al. (1983, p. 164) put it.

People who encountered ghosts in the past notice events in the present that validate their experience, and when they are confident enough to tell their story to others, many are simply reporting on something that is, to them, undeniable. Specifically, those who have encountered ghosts regard their experience as connected to an "implied objective past" (Maines et al. (1983, p. 164). This connection creates a narrative that emphasizes their sincerity and increases the possibility that, at the very least, audiences will not cast them as deceitful. In effect, those who make the claim that they have indeed encountered ghosts recognize, implicitly, that they neither share a past nor have a past in common with those who have not experienced such encounters (Katovich & Couch, 1992).

Furthermore, linking the claim of encountering ghosts to a past that cannot be denied (or an obdurate occurrence) creates an impression that convictions associated with encountering ghosts do not resemble, in any shape of form, a Machiavellian attempt to say whatever is deemed necessary to convince a skeptical, scientifically grounded observer. Some respondents, for example, recalled their encountering ghosts within the contexts of their self-defined clairsentience; their "psychic gifts" not only made their encounters possible but were used in the present to understand the "implied objective past." As Mead observed, "the past is the sure extension which the continuities of the present demand" (1929, p. 238). The various strategies used when reporting supernatural encounters are elaborated in detail below and may be considered in relation to Mead's ideas on the intersection of past and the present.

METHOD AND SAMPLE

This chapter emerged from a larger research project conducted by Aveline (2022, 2023) in Canada upon people who believe that they had come across ghosts. Briefly, he conducted in-depth interviews with a convenience sample of 38 people who reported such encounters. A few only thought this is what they saw but most were rigid in their beliefs that they had come across a ghost.[4] A questionnaire for gathering demographic information and a semi-structured schedule of questions were used to gather data. The questions were kept as general as possible while still focusing on the issues. This allowed the respondents to tell their stories in their own ways as they recalled them. The first question, for example, was "Can you tell me about the last time you encountered a ghost?" The interviews were audio-taped and took place in relaxed settings. Aveline transcribed all interviews himself and coded their emergent themes.[5] The respondents ranged from 19 to 87 years of age with a mean of 48 years, 60% were female, all but 6 were born in Canada and all but 6 again defined themselves as Caucasian or White. The remainder were either Indigenous or Latino. As a whole, they were a highly educated and professionally trained group. Thirty reported at least some university and 14 had a bachelor's degree or higher. There was also a police officer, a physician (general practitioner), a nurse, and a journalist – occupations suggesting rigid training in empirical observation, deduction, and analysis. Finally, there were eight people who defined themselves as sensitives, empaths, or clairvoyants. They all referred to these qualities as "gifts" and believed that they were born with them. In total, the sample claimed to have come across 212 specific ghosts and 21 other entities (e.g., orbs of light, goblins, angels, demons, etc.).[6]

Many respondents appeared relieved to have the opportunity to tell their stories. Some had done so before but they said that they selected their confidants carefully since they feared being judged as frivolous or mentally ill. They appeared to know

DAVID AVELINE AND BRANT DOWNEY

intuitively that their stories would be viewed skeptically. Because there is no empirically verifiable evidence of the existence of ghosts, and because such existence would defy the laws of physics, the claim that one has seen one let alone interacted with one remains dubious. As Aveline's research (2022, 2023) showed, there were usually no other witnesses to ghostly encounters as well as no photographs, no audio-recordings, and no physical evidence of any kind. In general, the only "evidence" that ghosts exist is that lone individuals say that they saw them, and despite their insistence that this is what they encountered, there is no opportunity for verification, thus rendering their claims unfalsifiable. A story of a ghost remains a fantastic claim and it is therefore up to the claimants to convince others that what they came upon was a true encounter.

ETHNOMETHODS FOR INCREASING THE BELIEVABILITY OF EXTRAORDINARY CLAIMS

The respondents' accounts were rich with methods intended to increase the believability of their claims. After a careful examination of the transcripts, 10 types emerged. They may be divided into three categories. First were two *Sacrificial Ethnomethods* which dared ill fate if the claimant were making false statements. Two such methods emerged – (1a) *Appeal to the Sacred* and (1b) *Appeal to Profound Loss*. Second were *Internal Ethnomethods* which referred to self-reflections by the claimant. The implication is that a claim should be believed because of the actions or qualities of the claimant. Four such methods were identified as: (2a) *Appeal to Mental Competence*, (2b) *Appeal to Hypersensitivity*, (2c) *Appeal to Self-Coherence*, and (2d) *Appeal to Analytical Process*. Third were *External Ethnomethods* referring to circumstances outside the individual claimant. Here, there were also four types: (3a) *Appeal to the Hearer's Self-Esteem*, (3b) *Appeal to Corroboration*, (3c) *Appeal to Verification*, and (3d) *Appeal to History*. The three categories and their respective types are shown in Table 1 together with examples.

SACRIFICIAL ETHNOMETHODS ($N = 2$)

I swear to God

Appeal to the Sacred and Appeal to Profound Loss

Often, when people add statements to extraordinary claims intended to increase their believability, many either evoke the sacred or dare fate with a profound loss should they be lying. They will "swear to God" that they are telling the truth, they might cross their hearts and "hope to die," or they may say that they will "swear on a stack of bibles." Indeed, similar declarations have long been formalized and given a structural legitimacy in legal proceedings, swearing-in

Table 1. Ten Ethnomethods for Increasing the Believability of Fantastic Claims.

Category	Type	Example
1 Sacrificial appeals	1a Appeal to the sacred	"May God strike me dead if I am lying"
	1b Appeal to profound loss	"I swear on my mother's life"
2 Internal appeals	2a Appeal to mental competence	"I am a sane person"
	2b Appeal to hypersensitivity	"I am clairvoyant"
	2c Appeal to self-coherence	"I judge myself as a competent observer"
	2d Appeal to analytical process	"I considered other possibilities but then rejected them"
3 External appeals	3a Appeal to the Hearer's self-esteem	"You are obviously an intelligent person"
	3b Appeal to corroboration	"My father also saw the ghost"
	3c Appeal to verification	"The neighbors have long thought there was a ghost in the house"
	3d Appeal to history	"I did research and found that there was a murder in the house long ago."

ceremonies and the like. Others in stressing their commitment to the truth might tell us that they swear on their mothers' graves or the lives of their children. The implication of these accompanying statements is that the claimants are so committed to the accuracy of their accounts that they are willing to place themselves in positions of great vulnerability in that if they are lying, they will either lose something precious or suffer eternal damnation. *Appeal to the Sacred* (1a) evokes the wrath of a deity or another supernatural being, or it symbolically bears witness against a sacred object such as the Qur'an, the Holy Bible, or the Cross of Jesus, thus risking blasphemy. *Appeal to Profound Loss* (1b) dares fate with the loss of something precious.

While sacrificial ethnomethods have their origins deep within history and have long carried with them fears that hellfire will reign mercilessly upon those who bear false witness, they have all but lost their religious impact in a secularized culture.[7] Still, vows to deities are often used and thrive in two respects. They are declared formally as oaths during solemn occasions (see Kadoch, 2006) and informally as part of everyday language. In this latter sense, "I swear to God" is typically less of a solemn declaration to a deity as it is a linguistic hold over used to communicate that one is telling the truth.[8] Because it has long been used as a solemn declaration to a deity, it continues as such symbolically regardless of religious belief due to its embeddedness in culture. In this sense, it has typically come to mean, "I declare that I am telling the truth" and, because of its history, it likely still carries with it some degree of impact as an ethnomethod for the purpose.

Surprisingly, despite their widespread use in culture, sacrificial appeals were not the typical interjections of the 38 respondents – only a few made such declarations. Several, for example, began sentences with oaths such as "I swear I heard footsteps" or "I swear I heard a noise" and one other swore on her mother's life that she was telling the truth. Despite their rarity within the sample, however, sacrificial appeals are nevertheless bonafide ethnomethods for increasing claim believability.

INTERNAL ETHNOMETHODS (N = 4)

I consider myself very logical

Appeal to Mental Competence

In Gogol's (1972) short story, *Diary of a Madman*, first published in 1835, there are elements to the main character Poprishchin's narrative (e.g., talking dogs) that give credence to the title. Poprishchin's madness is judged tautologically by his narrative – in effect, he is mad because his diary is that of a madman, and his diary is that of a madman because he is mad. With this same reflexivity, and because of the sheer incredulity of their claims, people who tell fantastic tales are often thought to be insane or disingenuous. The claim defines the claimant. Because, as Mead would say, claimants are aware that such impressions are what the generalized other might have of them, they may be motivated to counteract them at the onset. This appeared to be what one respondent, Diane was trying to do with the following announcement[9]:

> Before we get going, I think I should tell you a little bit about myself so you know that *I am not a lunatic.*[10] ... *I went to university* for journalism and then *I worked as a jou*rnalist. . . for quite some time. And then I started working for non-profits. I still continue to do this until this day. So, I consider myself *very logical, a clear thinker, and I solve problems*, so everything has to make sense for me and so these things that have been happening don't make any sense which drives me a little batty sometimes. (Diane, 57 years old)

Among other attributes, Diane wanted to establish that she is "very logical," "a clear thinker," and "not a lunatic." In so doing, she made appeals to her own mental competence and, thus, presented herself as a qualified observer of reality. Interestingly, she also suggested that she will be telling a story that *does not make sense to her*, thus placing herself in the dual position of narrator and critic of her own narrative in solidarity with the hearer. The implication is that "we" as collaborators have to make sense of what happened.

Another respondent, Leonora, also appealed to her own mental competence with her critique of paranormal reality television shows as follows[11]:

> I am *a science-oriented person*. There are definitely things we don't know yet and to be discovered. Having said that, there are these shows that have ghost investigators with their supposed instruments and *I am a skeptic* of those shows. I watch them and I go yeah, well, they can do a lot of things with cameras and sound effects and whatever (Laugh) ... *That show is not going to prove it to me*. (Leonora, 57 years old)

176   *Ethnomethods*

Leonora thus suggested that the experiences she describes in her ghost story are the observations of someone who is a "science-oriented person" and, thus, a rational thinker. They are also the observations of someone who is a skeptic and, thus, not taken in by creative camera work and sound effects. In both cases, the respondents were communicating that they are not prone to flights of fancy but instead look at evidence and facts without prejudice. They know how to distinguish between fantasy and reality. As a result, they implicitly suggest that the hearer should regard their story as "pre-vetted" by their abilities to discern fact from fiction.

Appeal to Hypersensitivity

Eight respondents said in some way that they were clairsentient. They were "psychics," "empaths," or "sensitives," claiming special abilities beyond that of the general population. They could see ghosts while others could not, they could sense their presence or feel their emotions if they were nearby. They believed themselves to have "gifts" which others who had not yet "opened their minds" do not. Being clairvoyant, however defined or labeled, appeared to be a highly salient part of their identities. As two respondents also claimed, ghosts were aware of their abilities and regularly approached them for help (e.g., asking them to give a message to someone), regarding them as special agents among the living. All eight respondents made it known during their interviews that they are clairsentient and did so at the onset of the interviews. In so doing, they were making appeals to hypersensitivity, saying that their claims are the experiences of someone with greater abilities to detect truth or reality than regular others and should thus be measured with a different yardstick. The following are examples:

I don't see ghosts . . . *I feel them. I have sensory perception.* . . . Some of these skills develop and change and shift over time, and as they become more open. They come in different ways. *I am one of these people that is developing*, so it is shifting now. (Olivia, 56 years old)

I figured out why I didn't want to be around people, even as a child. It was because *I could feel their energy*. I just didn't know how to *control* it. *I'm an empath* and I didn't know that back then. (Victoria, 54 years old)

For me, *sensing ghosts is a pressure feeling*. I feel like I am being squeezed. I am *in someone else's energy* and the air is getting thicker and I feel dense. . . . I could *just feel a sense of what their energy is*, you know, whether they were happy or sad. (Tanya, 48 years old)

Olivia, Victoria, and Tanya all suggested that their data were derived in ways other than through the five senses. The implication is that their stories are bona fide products of the gift of clairsentience and, thus, should be judged on the same (or an even greater) level as empirically verified observations.

Appeal to Self-Coherence

Because people who make fantastic claims usually believe that others might be skeptical, they may be likely to make statements about their own competence as reporters of what took place or their commitment to a story's accuracy. An appeal to self-coherence is thus an inventory of one's own reliability as a

DAVID AVELINE AND BRANT DOWNEY

measuring instrument, or a reflexive analysis of one's own abilities as such (Budd, 2016). The following from a man who regularly saw the ghost of his mother is one example:

Well, I'm in my bed. *I was wide awake.* I couldn't sleep and (my mother's ghost) came to me but you know like I say *I was awake.* She was at the end of my bed and she said to me, when we're done, would you like to go for coffee. . . . She had a happy smile on her face and we chatted. She was there and *I saw her as plain as day.* After a while she went away and I went to sleep. (Adam, 61 years old)

Here, Adam mentioned twice that he was "wide awake" and thus able to assess the situation with full alertness. He was confident in his ability to distinguish between waking states and sleep states of consciousness. He could see his mother's ghost "as plain as day," thus not as a shadow or a flash of light. As such, he was declaring himself as a competent observer of the situation he encountered.[12] Other respondents similarly made appeals to their own self-coherence, interjecting their accounts with phrases such as "I could see it right in front of me." That statement, like Adam's insistence that he "was wide awake," invokes Mead's generalized other in the sense of the widely agreed upon, rigid distinction between sleeping and being awake, with the latter linked publicly to clarity and certainty about what is real and what is imagined.

In addition, these appeals appeared either productive in that they were intended to add credibility to the story (e.g., "I could see every detail"!) or pre-emptive in that they were intended to stop credibility from lessening (e.g., "I had not been drinking"). One seems to build verisimilitude; the other stops that which has already been built from falling away. While many appeals to self-coherence such as "I was wide awake" could be regarded as either productive or pre-emptive, there does appear to be an ideal-type dichotomy of such statements as Weber (Gerth & Mills, 1946) might have said. In any case, it is likely that the more incredible the respondents believed their own stories to be, the more likely they would be to interject appeals to self-coherence. It was as if they regularly performed self-diagnostics and reported on their findings.

Appeal to Analytical Process

As people give fanciful accounts of events, they may well be aware that their hearers are puzzled and trying to make sense of their words at each turn. If they tell of ghosts looming in their bedrooms at night, the hearers might think that they were dreaming. If they say that a door slammed in an adjacent room, it must have been the wind. Scratches heard in the wall are from mice, creaking stairs are from a lack of moisture in the wood, and howls in the distance are the cries of wild animals. Aveline (2022), in his *autoethnographic* reflections of his initial biases in the research process, wrote the following:

As I listened to the stories, I found that with many of them my mind would go immediately to supposed logical explanations that fit into my own sense of what is real – or, in Schutzian terms, explanations compatible with the paramount reality as I defined it.[13],[14]

178   *Ethnomethods*

In other words, to make sense of a situation that appears to defy the laws of physics, we may comb the annals of our own past experiences for more plausible explanations which might lessen our sense of cognitive dissonance. Those explanations then become *what really must have happened.* As Aveline further suggested, many respondents seemed to know this and wanted to get ahead of him and discredit any other explanations that they thought he might consider. They did this by documenting their own thought processes. The following are examples with the documentations in italics:

> Well, the experience happened around 1994 or 1995. I was sleeping, and at first, *I thought it was a dream.* But then *I thought about it a bit more*, and I was aware of what might be classified as ghosts or spirits and what have you. So, I believe there was some kind of encounter. (George, 55 years old)

> It looked like a woman who had on one of those old dresses down to the ground coming in at the waist and then going out, and it looked like it came up to the neck and she had her hair tied in a bun. . . . *I thought I was dreaming. Like I'm sleepy, I'm dreaming, that can't be real.* . . . I went back to bed and I got into bed and I was really sleepy so I just went to sleep and *I kind of thought I must have imagined it.* . . . But I think I was alert enough. (Xaviera, 49 years old)

> I was in a women's shelter. One night I woke up. *I thought I was dreaming.* There was a big man sitting in a chair. . . . He was staring at the floor slumped over a little bit but he was staring at the floor and I was lying there and *I kept thinking this was only a dream, only a dream, only a dream*, and all of a sudden a woman who was in the next bed and she had her little girl with her and her little girl was about five or six, a really cute little thing, she sat up in bed and she was looking at me and she said can you take me to the washroom please, so I got up and I went to the bathroom, and we're in the bathroom and she said I asked you to take me because I was scared of the man. She saw him too. (Florence, 56 years old)

George, Xaviera, and Florence were thus making appeals to the thoroughness of their own analyses. As if evoking Occam's Razor, they considered any rational explanations such as having been sleeping or dreaming and rejected them in favor of actual ghostly encounters. It was as if they were saying that they knew what hearers would be thinking because they had originally thought (and then rejected) the same thing. They were, in effect, saying, "I am way ahead of you here" or "do not worry, I have done the analytical work for you." Such a conclusions suggest a repeated revisiting of the ghostly event and interpreting it as "what really must have happened" in the sense of Mead's "implied objective past" (Maines et al., 1983; Mead, 1929). Encounters with potential skeptics in the present lead to their recollections of earlier attempts to mentally grapple with the original events and ultimately coming to see them as undeniably real.

EXTERNAL ETHNOMETHOD2 ($N = 4$)

Did you see the lady?

Appeal to the Hearer's Self-Esteem

"Flattery will get you everywhere," as early film star Mae West quipped. Flattering the audience is an age-old tactic used by salespeople, politicians (Covazza & Guidetti, 2018), and lawyers alike to gain favor. Ziemke and Brodsky (2014)

DAVID AVELINE AND BRANT DOWNEY

found that when lawyers flattered jury members or ingratiated themselves to them during closing arguments, their credibility increased and their clients were less likely to be found guilty. If people can be made to feel that they are among an elite group who understand concepts that others might miss due to their shortcomings, they have created in them a personal investment in acceptance of what is being said. Certainly, being made to feel special when privy to particular information has emerged as a key concept in conspiracy theory research (van Prooijen & Douglas, 2018). Appeal to the hearer's self-esteem, however, was the least used ethnomethod among the sample. Two respondents suggested that they were pleased to be able to tell their stories to an academic. Norman (age 73) told Aveline that he was anxious to tell his story to "someone like you" and Kenneth (age 55) said that it was encouraging to see a sociologist interested in the material. While these comments were flattering, they were most likely not meant as flattery, nor were they meant to produce a sense of ingratiation. In other words, they did not seem to be mentioned to increase believability in the stories or to manipulate the hearer in any way. Nevertheless, even though there were no true examples here, appeal to the hearer's self-esteem remains an ethnomethod that may be used for the purpose.

Appeal to Corroboration

If one person witnesses an unusual event, we have only that person's word to go by. If two people see the same event and their reports are sufficiently congruent, believability likely increases. Presumably, it would further increase with a third person, a fourth, and so on (Walton & Reed, 2008). Once the number of witnesses reaches into the thousands, even impossible events may be declared factual by decree.[15] While most respondents were the sole witnesses to the ghosts they reported seeing, there were several who mentioned (or brought with them) others who saw them as well. In this respect, there were two types of reports: ones where two or more witnesses are present at the story's telling and ones where one person mentions that one or more others was present when the event occurred. Neville and his father Frank provide an example of both in that they told a story together and named others who were witnesses as well. They and two other family members visited a church graveyard in an isolated rural area one afternoon and saw a young girl dressed in "period clothing" (later explaining this as "from the 19th century") sitting with a dog. Neville described the event as follows:

> We walked around looking at the gravestones and the church, which was not around anything. There were no other cars in the parking lot at all. My Dad (Frank) saw a young female in period clothing sitting on a bench, and there was a large dog with her. . . . my girlfriend and I walked by her and she was looking at us with a smile on her face. I think I said hi to her and she just looked at me, smiled and nodded, she didn't say anything. I know that for a fact, she didn't say anything to me. And the dog didn't seem to move, he just looked. He didn't have any restless movements of anything, he just look at us. It was very eerie. It was an eerie experience more after the fact, just the strangeness of it. (Neville, 51 years old)

His father Frank agreed with him on several points, adding that he even recalled exchanging a few words with the girl. They then said that the girl and her dog suddenly vanished and there was nowhere where they could have gone.

180   *Ethnomethods*

Another respondent, Derek, named a second witness when he told a story of a time when he attempted to rid a house of a ghost:

> I called out the ghost and I said you're here. Show yourself now. And she stood there, the (owner of the house) right next to me and we watched him come out from behind the headboard. We both saw him. He walked right out from behind the headboard, and he was a six-foot tall, skinny white, looking like a tall Caspar – black eyes, black mouth, black nose. And we were talking to him and saying you don't belong here. (Derek, 61 years old)

As he concluded, the ghost eventually got the message, rose and disappeared through the ceiling. Both he and the house owner witnessed this, as he claimed. While only he was telling the story (in contrast to Neville and Frank who were both present), the naming of a corroborating witness would supposedly make his story more believable than that of a single individual's interpretation. "She saw him too," he said, rendering the testimony of the named witness available as an additional resource.

Appeal to Verification

The *bandwagon effect* is a well-known phenomenon whereby people are more likely to believe something if it is also believed by many others as "popular opinion" (Kiss & Simonovits, 2014). This may well apply when people believe that they have encountered a notorious ghost. Wendell told a story of when he and his wife were checking into the *Fairmount Banff Springs Hotel* in Alberta:

> As soon as we checked in, we got our bags and we went into the elevator. There was an elevator operator there who looked very old and rather odd. He was wearing dishevelled clothing which looked as though it was a style from a long time ago. I figured maybe this was some gimmick that the hotel had done where they put their staff in period clothing. He had his back to us. So, I started talking to him and said something like nice day isn't it. He answered in a very surly tone "not so nice." I looked at my wife and we both looked at each other and thought that was kind of strange. And then he added, "not so nice because this hotel has to put up with the likes of you." We were both shocked at this and I thought this was really beyond just being in character to entertain the guests and was insulting. And then, as soon as we got to the floor he stepped out, turned the corner and was absolutely gone. We were both stunned. (Wendell, 41 years old)

The hotel receptionist later told them that they probably ran into "Sam the Bellhop" – the ghost of a former employee from the 1950s who had been spotted many times by other guests in many locations in the hotel (Carter, 2015). While it may be true that hotels exaggerate stories of ghosts to boost occupancy rates (Inglis & Holmes, 2003), the claim that one has seen a ghost that many others have seen before would likely carry greater weight in the narrative than that involving an unknown ghost. Appeal to Verification may appear similar to Appeal to Corroboration but there is a marked difference. While the latter claimants name or bring with them other witnesses who were present when the event took place, the former refers to the experiences of others as told to them after the fact. Appeal to Corroboration says, "we saw the same thing at the same time," Appeal to verification says, "other people told me they saw the same thing at other times." One is an eyewitness report; the other is hearsay.

DAVID AVELINE AND BRANT DOWNEY

In general, if one can convince hearers that others have also seen a particular ghost, they might well increase the believability of their claim. As it happened, several respondents mentioned that neighbors, boarders, or others were also witnesses to what they encountered as follows:

> I was walking my dog and still not really believing that I had seen a ghost, but I was talking to some neighbours one time who had been in the neighbourhood a long time and I said oh, by the way, did this house ever have a reputation for being haunted? Oh, yeah, there is supposedly a ghost in there and I said, really? I said, male or female? And they said female. . . . This was a neighbour who had never volunteered the information before I asked. (Leonora, 57 years old)

> We moved into a lovely little house. We were told by a neighbour that a man had built the house and he passed away only a couple of years before and he loved his house. And so, he made himself known to the neighbours in a number of ways. He would turn on things, turn off things. (Alice, age 57)

Leonora and Alice felt that they had received verification of their suspicions. Gregory, a physician, provided another example, recalling a time when he was closing up his clinic one late afternoon. His colleagues and all of the staff were gone and he was sure he was alone. As he walked down the hallway, he noticed an elderly woman sitting in one of the examination rooms:

> So, I got up and I walked down the hall, and in room number two, I saw a lady sitting in a chair. I just walked by and this lady was sitting akimbo in a chair and she had this very strange posture. Her head was down, and I couldn't really see her face but her head was down and I could tell she was very old and her hair was white, greyish white. . . . so I walked by and looked and I took about two steps, and immediately I thought oh, what's wrong with that lady? She obviously looks like she was in a lot of pain. And so, I'm thinking oh, probably sciatica, . . . I get to the end of the hall and I think wait a minute, why is that lady sitting in that room? . . . I'd better go and see that lady. I walk back and go in the room and there's nobody there. . . . But I could still see this person so vividly in my mind. It is almost like that, I hate to say it, it's almost like that movie "The Ring" with hair hanging down. She was super creepy. She was gone. (Gregory, 37 years old)

The next day, because of a leg injury, Gregory kept his appointment with a massage therapist in the same building on a different floor:

> I went to my massage therapist and I was sitting in a room. I had injured my leg and it was sore and I said can you work on my leg and she said okay. This was before the day started and she said you will never guess what happened to me. You'll never guess what I saw here yesterday? She said, "did you see the lady? Immediately the hair on the back of my neck stood up and I said what lady"? Did you see the white-haired lady"? I said, yeah, in room two. She said yeah, I've seen her downstairs, twice. (Gregory, 37 years old)

Thus, according to Gregory's account, the same ghost was seen by another individual, not to mentioned it being described similarly as old and female. The implication with all of these examples is that while one person may have been imagining things, two or more others give greater verisimilitude. In Gregory's case, Mead's theory of the past well applies. The massage therapist's account ("what I saw here yesterday") brings his own ghost sighting the day before closer to a certainty in the present. The past and present connect convincingly for him.

182   *Ethnomethods*

Appeal to History

When a house is said to have ghosts, it is considered haunted. For many people, this means that the ghosts are not mere entities who happen to be present but they do something – they "haunt" a house, suggesting agency and intentionality. This further suggests a history behind the haunting – or at least a history for those defining the ghosts as real and actively doing haunting. In this sense, several respondents said that they "did research" on their houses or other locations to see if they could determine the identities of the ghosts or the reasons they were present. The following are examples:

> My wife and I took a trip to (name of town) because this woman was having experiences in her home. She has a three-year-old son and she was convinced he was scratched. It was a black shadow man and she wanted to get rid of him. I did a lot of investigating and research to figure out what was going on with that house. I found the original death certificate of the people that lived there originally in the 1950s because the house was built then. (Xaviera, 49 years old)

> (The ghost was) probably between three and five years old. . . . We had just moved in and I saw her and I thought oh wow, why is there a four-year-old in the house? It seems a little weird. So, I started to make inquiries and I found out from my neighbours that her father brutally murdered her in that house and I was like oh, no. That explained why I could see her. (Henry, 36 years old)

Xaviera suggested that the "black shadow man" might have been connected to the house's past history and Henry suggested that the ghost he saw was that of a murdered child from long ago. The implications are that what they encountered is connected with real and historical events and thus, must thus be regarded as true as opposed to mere fiction. While there is a conflation of historical events with their present claims, and while the connections might well be assumed more than verified, the idea is that if the ghosts can be connected to real past events, they too should also be regarded as real.

DISCUSSION

So far, we have discussed a variety of strategies used in narrative constructions in the form of ethnomethods geared toward increasing the believability of fantastic claims. Depending upon how claimants anticipate the degree of skepticism from their hearers, they may use one or more for the purpose.[16] The selection of method(s), however, was only one aspect of strategy. The transcripts revealed three additional dimensions to their use: *placement*, *scope*, and *direction*. First, there was a decision about the placement of an ethnomethod(s) within a narrative. They may be in the form of *pre-announcements* (Campion & Langdon, 2004; Maynard, 1997) placed before the main story (e.g., "What I am about to tell you is genuinely what I saw"), *post-announcements* placed afterward ("I swear that this is what I saw"), or they may be injected into the story at any point, thus as *inter-announcements*. As for scope, an ethnomethod might pertain to a specific part of a narrative or the entire thing. For example, when Diane (age 57) said as a pre-announcement that she was "not a lunatic" and "went to university," she implied that the hearer should keep these factors in mind throughout her narrative. When Derek (age 61) said "we both saw him," referring to he and another person as dual witnesses to the presence of a ghost, he was referring to a specific part of his narrative. Consequently, ethnomethods may be sweeping or specific, depending on a claimant's intentions. As for direction, ethnomethods appeared as either *productive*, intended to bring about or increase believability (e.g., "My father also saw it") or *pre-emptive* as attempts to prevent unwanted reactions or interpretations (e.g., "I know it sounds crazy but it's true"). Productive statements build believability; pre-emptive ones stop the loss of believability.[17] Thus, there were at least four dimensions (see Table 2) to the respondents' strategies, each building upon the others toward the construction of a believable narrative. This construction was therefore multidimensional and multi-tiered.

Strategies to reduce skepticism have several implications. First, we must ask where the expectation of disbelief comes from. For one thing, the use of ethnomethods seem peculiar to the fantastic or the improbable. Unless there are idiosyncrasies surrounding a claimant, mundane claims such as "I had a salad for lunch today" need no bolstering because, in everyday life, they are accepted on faith. To claim that someone made 11 holes in one in a golf game, however, or indeed, saw a ghost in a graveyard, is a fantastic claim. We generally know this because we take the perspective of the *generalized other* (Mead, 1934). Claimants, in considering the reception of their claims, imagine how they might be received by people in general and construct their narratives in what they consider the most believable way possible. Garfinkel (1967) stated that we operate under the assumption of a *reciprocity of perspectives* believing that the world would look the same to anyone who occupies a given space at a given time. Similarly, as Mead argued, if we believe that what we have seen sounds impossible, we might expect through a perception of the reaction of a typical community member, that others believe the same.

The generalized other, however, is not a monolith. Any claim about reality, no matter how "obvious" it seems, will inevitably have some disagreement whether by only a handful of people or millions.[18] When it comes to belief in ghosts, the world is divided and deadlocked. Whether by socialization, culture, or otherwise, there are sizable populations in North America and around the world who firmly believe that ghosts exist. According to one poll (Ipsos, 2021), 46% of Canadians have such beliefs and, according to another (Chapman University Survey of

Table 2. Four Dimensions of Narrative Construction.

	Dimensions of Strategy	Number
1	Ethnomethods	10+ choices (see Table 1)
2	Placement	Pre-announcements/Post-announcements/Inter-announcements
3	Scope	Entire narrative/Part(s) of narrative
4	Direction	Increase believability/Stop loss of believability

American Fears, 2018), the proportion is even higher in the United States with 58% of Americans believing that ghosts can haunt houses and other places. There are thus two principle clusters of the generalized other – one potentially affirming, the other sharply skeptical. As Tanya (age 48) and others suggested, one must know one's audience before making one's claim. It would seem, therefore, that if one is telling a story of a ghostly encounter to firm believers (thus "preaching to the choir"), using ethnomethods to produce or maintain believability would be thought unnecessary. If told to skeptics, however, they would be thought of as essential.

Goffman (1959) referred to these considerations as "proper scheduling of one's performances" (p. 138) where individuals consider relevant factors of various audiences and structure their claims accordingly. This may also involve two types of ceremonial rules – *deference* and *demeaner* (Goffman, 1956). Deference usually involves showing signs of appreciation during interactions, for example, the eagerness of one respondent to tell his story to a sociologist – positively expressed as "someone like you" mentioned earlier. Deference also includes avoidance rituals. As Tanya noted, "You choose who you hang around [with]. You have to be very picky." Demeaner, as Goffman explained, refers to a ritualized attention to "deportment, dress, and bearing, which serve to express to those in his immediate presence that he is a person of certain desirable and undesirable qualities" (1956, p. 489). Accordingly, statements quoted earlier such as "I know it sounds crazy but it's true" or "I went to university" demonstrate the reflexivity and discretion associated with someone vigilantly attentive to demeanor. Individuals interpret their past in ways that makes sense according to their present situations, in the latter case, the rational confidence of a university educated person telling a story to a researcher.

CONCLUSION

In this sense, ethnomethods become targeted strategies rather than automatic add-ons to extraordinary claims. In general, however, it would seem in the ideal that the greater the perception of skepticism, the greater the likelihood that ethnomethods will be used. Even so, because the skeptical generalized other looms powerfully in the backdrop of any fantastic tale, ethnomethods might nevertheless appear as buffers to its scrutiny.

NOTES

1. For example, in 1991, North Korean officials claimed that Leader Kim Jong-Il made 11 holes in one in his first-ever round of golf (Jones, 2017).

2. In an essay in the *New Yorker* in 1940, James Thurber characterized the dilemma of an unbelievable claim as "The Unicorn in the Garden" (Nichols, 2017). No one would ever believe anyone claiming to have seen one.

3. In addition to presenting credible "accounts," witnesses to the supernatural may be viewed as striving to establish awareness contexts that allow for open and honest conversations with others. As our interview data swill show, witnesses are often hesitant to talk

about their experiences with those who lack their perspective of the topic (See Glaser & Strauss, 1964 for the origins of this theory).

4. Aveline's research was driven by the Thomas Theorem which states that "If men (people) define situations as real, they are real in their consequences" (Thomas & Thomas, 1928, p. 572). Thus, for people who define ghosts as real, they are real entities and will have some effect – good or bad – upon their lives.

5. Aveline chose to do this arduous task purposely to allow him to be as close to the data as possible.

6. The respondents referred to and described 212 individual ghosts. Other more amorphous or vague references to ghosts – e.g., "That house was full of ghosts" – were not counted.

7. For example, in the Jewish tradition, the solemnity of oaths to God is explained in *Numbers 30:2* as "vow(ing) a vow to the Lord, or swear(ing) an oath to bind (one's) soul with a bond."

8. Similarly, the oft used phrase "I'll kill you" is rarely meant literally.

9. All respondents mentioned here are given pseudonyms and any identifying information has been removed.

10. Through this paper, we have written the relevant parts of quotations in italics to emphasize them.

11. For example, *Ghost Hunters* (2004–2016), *The Dead Files* (2011–2023), and *Paranormal State* (2007–2011).

12. "As plain as day" is an oft used meaning that something is obvious, or that there is no doubt that something is real.

13. Alfred Schutz (1970) referred to the taken-for-granted world as the *paramount reality*.

14. Aveline added that as soon as he was able to suspend such thoughts and see the world as the respondents described it, he went from outsider to insider in the research process.

15. On October 13, 1917, in Fatima, Portugal, thousands of people saw the sun "dance" and zigzag across the sky – something astronomically absurd. Nevertheless, this event was declared factual 13 years later in 1930 by the Catholic Church and became known as the "Miracle of the Sun" (Bennett, 2012).

16. Given that this research is far from exhaustive, there may be other ethnomethods used in the telling of fantastic accounts pertaining to ghosts, unlikely events, or other wild claims. Thus, further research is needed.

17. Of course, an ethnomethod may be both productive and pre-emptive rendering unidirectionality an ideal-type dichotomy.

18. Even the seemingly universal idea that the Earth is round has sufficient disagreement, leading to the emergence of *Flat Earth Societies* everywhere (Erlaine, 2020).

REFERENCES

Aveline, D. (2022). "I saw him clearly through my eyelids": Strategies for dealing with discordant realities and the phantasm in qualitative research. *Studies in Symbolic Interaction, 53*, 47–63.

Aveline, D. (2023). Anthropomorphism as symbolic interaction: The demographics of purgatory. *Studies in Symbolic Interaction, 57*, 101–116.

Bennett, J. S. (2012). *When the sun danced: Myths, miracles, and modernity in early twentieth-century Portugal*. University of Virginia Press.

Blumer, H. (1969). *Symbolic interaction: Perspective and method*. Prentice Hall.

Budd, K. W. (2016). Self-coherence: Theoretical considerations of a new concept. *Archives of Psychiatric Nursing, 219*, 75–81.

Campion, P., & Langdon, M. (2004). Achieving multiple topic shifts in primary care medical consultations: A conversation analysis study in UK general practice. *Sociology of Health & Illness, 26*(1), 81–101.

Carter, J. (2015). The Banff Springs – Most haunted hotel in Canada. https://anomalien.com/the-banff-springs-most-haunted-hotel-in-canada/

Chapman University Survey of American Fears. (2018, October 16). https://blogs.chapman.edu/Wilkinson/2018/10/16/paranormal-america.2018/

Covazza, N., & Guidetti, M. (2018). Captatio Benevolentiae: Potential risks and benefits of flattering the audience in a public political speech. *Journal of Language and Social Psychology, 37*(6), 706–720.

Erlaine, D. M. (2020). The culture of flat earth and its consequences. *Journal of Science & Popular Culture, 3*(2), 173–193.

Garfinkel, H. (1967). *Studies in ethnomethodology*. Prentice-Hall.

Gerth, H. H., & Mills, C. W. (1946). *From Max Weber: Essays on sociology*. Oxford University Press.

Glaser, B., & Strauss, A. (1964). Awareness contexts and cocial interaction. *American Sociological Review, 29*(5), 669–679.

Goffman, E. (1956). The nature of deference and demeanor. *American Anthropologist, 58*(3), 473–502.

Goffman, E. (1959). *The presentation of self in everyday life*. Doubleday.

Gogol, N. V. (1972). *Diary of a madman and other stories*. Penguin Books.

Inglis, D., & Holmes, M. (2003). Highland and other haunts: Ghosts in Scottish tourism. *Annals of Tourism Research, 30*(1), 50–63.

Ipsos. (2021, June 9). Ghost encounters: Nearly half of Canadians (46%) believe in supernatural beings; 13% have stayed at haunted hotel. https://www.ipsos.com/en-ca/news-polls/ghost-encounters-nearly-half-canadians-46-believe-supernatural-beings-13-have-stayed-haunted-hotel

Jones, S. (2017, October 11). Golf course where North Korea's leader scored 11 holes-in-one in first-ever round revealed for the first time. *Mirror*. https://www.mirror.co.uk/sport/golf/golf-course-north-koreas-leader-11325632

Kadoch, L. (2006). So help me God: Reflections in language, thought, and the rules of evidence remembered. *Law & Society*, 1. 2006 Annual Meeting.

Katovich, M. A., & Couch, C. J. (1992). The nature of social pasts and their use as foundations for situated action. *Symbolic Interaction, 15*, 25–47.

Kiss, A., & Simonovits, G.. (2014). Identifying the bandwagon effect in two-round elections. *Public Choice, 160*, 327–344.

Maines, D., Sugrue, N., & Katovich, M. (1983). The sociological import of G. H. Mead's theory of the past. *American Sociological Review, 48*(2), 161–173.

Maynard, D. (1997). The news delivery sequence: Bad news and good news in conversational interaction. *Research on Language and Social Interaction, 30*(2), 93–130.

Mead, G. H. (1929). The nature of the past. In J. Coss (Ed.), *Essays in honor of John Dewey* (pp. 235–242). Henry Holt & Co.

Mead, G. H. (1934). *Mind, self, and society*. University of Chicago Press.

Nichols, K. (2017). Case study #12: The unicorn in the garden. *Public Voices, 15*, 123–133.

van Prooijen, J. -W., & Douglas, K. M. (2018). Belief in conspiracy theories: Basic principles of an emerging research domain. *European Journal of Social Psychology, 48*(7), 897–908. Special Issue: Belief in Conspiracy Theories as a Social- Psychological Phenomenon.

Schutz, A. (1970). *On phenomenology and social relations*. University of Chicago Press.

Scott, M., & Lyman, S. (1968). Accounts. *American Sociological Review, 33*(1), 46–62.

Thomas, W. I., & Thomas, D. S. (1928). *The child in America: Behavior problems and programs*. Knopf.

Walton, D., & Reed, C. (2008). Evaluating corroborative evidence. *Argumentation, 22*, 531–553.

Ziemke, M. H., & Brodsky, S. L. (2014). To flatter the jury: Ingratiation during closing arguments, *Psychiatry, Psychology and Law, 22*(5), 688–700.

INDEX

Abduction, 56, 68, 72, 106
  value of statistical data for,
    113–116
Abductive analysis, 114–115
"Abductive method", 70
Academic career after Congo,
    134–137
Accidents of GTM, 67
Accounts, 170
"Acontextual description", 66
Active process, 55
American sociological theory, 122,
    124
Analytical process, appeal to, 177–178
Analytic induction, 69
Analytic interruptus, 52, 57
Analytic realism, 87–88
Anselm Strauss, 49
Anti-imperialist commitments, 132
Anti-racist commitments, 132
Apagoge, 70–71
Appropriation, 122–123
Artificial life, 18
Artificial settings, 9–10
Audio-visual recordings, 37, 40–41
Audio-visual technology, 10, 13–15
Authenticity, 94
Authoritarian position, 15
Autoethnographic reflections, 177
Avoidance tactics, 170
Awareness, 50, 53–54, 66

Balanced self, 98
Bandwagon effect, 180
Basics of Grounded Theory, 62–63
Basics of Qualitative Research (BQA),
    58–63
Becoming of self, 100–101
Belgian Congo, 138
Bessie Faris, 127

"Big data", 114
"Black box" approach, 112
"Blank mind", 59
"Bodycam", 85
Boys in White project, 52–54
Breaching experiments, 26, 29–30,
    38–39, 170
Buffer, 97–98

Canada, born in, 172
Casement report and aftermath,
    130–134
Causal identification, 111–112
Causal inference, 111–112
Causality, 111–112
Center for Research on Interpersonal
    Behavior (CRIB), 26–27
Chicago amalgam, 52–57
Chicago school, 54, 59, 122–123
  colonial experience impacts on
    Faris's academic career,
    134–145
  decolonial sociology, 122–124
  Ellsworth Faris and colonial
    Congo, 124–134
Classic grounded theory, 4–5,
    58
"Classic GTM", 51–52
Collective accomplishments, 34
Colonial Congo, 124–134
  casement report and aftermath,
    130–134
  Ellsworth Faris as missionary,
    124–127
  ethnologist and witness to
    atrocities, 127–130
Colonialism, 122–123, 132
Colonial ordering process, 129
Colonial sociology, 127–128
Colonial violence, 122

colonial experience impacts on
Faris's academic career,
134–145
decolonial sociology, 122–124
Ellsworth Faris and colonial
Congo, 124–134
Communication, 36
research approach, 80
Community, 94, 98
policing, 84
Comparative linguistic work, 127–128
Computer technology, 80
Concepts, 94
Conceptualization, 16
Concrete reasonableness, 55
Conditioning process, 110
Conditions, 110
Confrontational relationship,
97–98
Congo Reform Association, 131
Congo
academic career after, 134–137
sociological field expeditions to,
143–145
Constant comparative method, 69
Constant comparison, 60
Constructing theories, 59
Contemporary developments, 26
Contemporary symbolic inter-
actionists, 31–32
"Context-dependent", 66
Contextualize industrialization, 110
Contingency, 109–110
Continual Permutations of Action
(CPoA), 52, 55, 63
Conventional media, 88
Conversation, 15, 20, 36
Correlations, 112
Corroboration, appeal to, 179–180
Couch's laboratory experiments, 27
Counterfactual causality, 111–112
Counting methods, 15
Creative aspects of research, 51
Criminological theory, 107–108
Criminology, 114–115
Cultural forms, 26

Culture, 80
Cynicism, 107–108

Data, 51–52, 71, 106
collection sheet, 5
collection, 84, 96
data-grounded theory, 51
gathering, 60
materials, 82
mining, 114
Decolonial sociology, 122–124
Deduction, 56
Deference, 184
Demeaner, 184
Digital data, 80
Digital documents from social media,
90–91
Digital media, 89–90
Direction, 182–183
Directorial strategy, 18–19
Discipline-perspective dominance, 59
Discovery, 53–55, 57, 59, 66
Dispossession, 122–123
Distinctive approach, 15
Document analysis, 80, 87
Domination, 122–123
Dramatic realization, 12–13
Dramatization, 17
"Dramaturgical circumspection", 171
Dramaturgical studies, 10
Drugmusictalk, 95

Education, 135
Eggs, 170
Electronic technology, 80
Elementalism, 138
Ellsworth Faris, 124–134
Emergence, 13, 62–63, 108
Emotional responsiveness, 13–14
Empaths, 176
Empiricism, 5–6, 106, 108
"Enacted processes", 65
Enslavement, 122–123
Environments, 10–11
Epondo case, 132
Essences of GTM, 67

Index   189

Ethnocentrism, 38
Ethnographic approach, 40–41
Ethnographic content analysis (ECA),
    80–81
Ethnography, 99
Ethnologist, 127–130
Ethnomethods, 26, 68, 170–171
    external ethnomethod, 178–182
    for increasing believability of
        extraordinary claims,
        173
    for increasing believability of
        fantastic claims, 174
    internal ethnomethods, 175–178
    method and sample, 172–173
    sacrificial ethnomethods, 173–175
    theoretical background, 170–172
Existential self, 97–98
Experimental approach, 27, 32
Experimental design, 111–112
Experimental research, 27
Experimental subjects, 12
Experimentation, 26
External ethnomethods. *See also*
        Internal ethnomethods, 173
    appeal to corroboration, 179–180
    appeal to hearer's self-esteem,
        178–179
    appeal to history, 182
    appeal to verification, 180–181
    four dimensions of narrative
        construction, 183
Extraordinary claims, ethnomethods
        for increasing believability
        of, 173

Facebook, 84
    exchanges, 81
    group page, 82
Faris's academic career, colonial
        experience impacts on,
        134–145
    academic career after Congo,
        134–137

constitutive role of colonial
    experience in Faris's
    sociology, 137–138
Faris's earliest sociological
    publications, 139–143
sociological field expeditions to
    Congo, 143–145
Faris's earliest sociological
    publications, 139–143
Faris's remarks, 133–134
Faris's sociology, Constitutive role of
    colonial experience in,
    137–138
Fear set, 86
Fixed-effects models, 111–112
Force interaction, 17–18
Forcing, 62–63
Foreign Christian Mission Society
    (FCMS), 125

Garfinkel's breaching experiments,
    27
Garfinkel's experiments with social
    order, 28–31
Garfinkel's micro-sociology,
    170
Garfinkel's program, 40
Garfinkel's research, 28
Generalized other, 170–171,
    183–184
"Generating formal theory", 60–61
Genre, 14
Gonzo governance, 89
Grand theory, 67–68
Grounded theory (GT), 4–5, 49, 63,
    82, 99–100
    SI institutionalizes GT, 57–59
Grounded theory method (GTM),
    49
    Chicago amalgam, 52–57
    induction and abduction, 68–72
    pragmatism and, 61–63
    SA and, 63–64
    and SI, 59–61
    SI institutionalizes GT, 57–59
    and social justice, 65–66

varieties and essences of, 66–68
Group determination, 138

Hashtag (#), 90
Hearer's self-esteem, appeal to, 178–179
Hermeneutics, 68
Human construction, 18
Human variation, 108–109
Hypersensitivity, 176
Hypotheses testing, 20

Idea, 101–102
Identity, 94, 96, 98
Idioculture, 94, 98, 100–101
Imaginative groundwork, 10–11
Immaculate conceptualization, 71
Immediacy, 141
Impaired self, 96
Implicit, 51
Inarticulate operational rules, 51
Incongruity procedures, 40–41
Indeterminacy, 108
Indeterminate effects, 110
Induction, 68–72
Ineffable information or experience, 51
Information technology, 80
Innovative research, 37
Instagram, 84–85, 90
    comments, 81
Interaction, 94, 101
    elements of, 31, 35–36
Interactional dyads, 16
Interactionism, 3, 6, 27, 57, 105–107
Interactionists, 3–6, 110
    frameworks, 6
    optic, 95
Interactive process, 55
Inter-announcements, 182–183
Internal ethnomethods. *See also*
        External ethnomethods, 173
    appeal to analytical process, 177–178
    appeal to hypersensitivity, 176

appeal to mental competence, 175–176
    appeal to self-coherence, 176–177
International Institute of African
        Languages and Cultures
        (IIALC), 144
Interpretive approaches, 26
Interview, 172, 176
Interview data, 171

Jargonized GT, 58
Justifications, 171

Knowledge, 55
"Knowledge brokers", 127–128
Kuhn's Iowa School, 10

Laboratory environments, 12
Laboratory experiments, 26–27, 29, 33
Laboratory research, 3–4, 10–11
    NIS and qualitative research in, 18–20
    and premises of NIS in symbolic
        interaction, 14–16
    revisiting laboratory as
        provocative stage, 17–18
    and science of small group
        research, 11–12
    and sociological imagination, 12–14
    as space for qualitative inquiry, 21
Legal ramifications, 13
Lengthy conversations, 61

'Mainstream', 94
Maps, 63
Mass media, 80
Mead's pragmatic approach, 31–32
Mead's theory, 10, 181
Mechanistic causality, 111–112
Media, 88
    environment, 89
"Media logic", 80
Media research approach, 80

Index 191

Mental competence, appeal to, 175–176
Messy maps, 63
Metaphorical behavior setting, 33–34
Methodology, 3
#MeToo, 85, 90
  first-person accounts, 84–85
  movement, 84
  PDF data set, 85–86
  posts, 84–85
  on Twitter, 85
'Middle-range theory', 57
Milgram experiments, 13
Missionaries, 132–133
  Ellsworth Faris as, 124–127
Missions, 128–129, 134
Modernity, 122–123
Monographs, 36–37
Moral frameworks, 132
Moreness, 97
Multilevel regression models, 110–111
Multi-perspectival approach, 96
Multivariate regression models, 109–110
Musement, 71
Music, 5, 93, 96–97, 103
  authenticity, 101–102
  community, 98
  idioculture, 100–101
  interaction, 101
  as metaphor for society, 103
  music-atonce, 97
  pervasiveness of, 97–98
  scene, 98–100
  self and identity, 96–98
  sociology of, 94
  subcultural activities in, 95
  subculture, 94–96

Naturalism, 17–18
Naturalistic approach, 31
Naturalistic research, 26
Naturalistic settings, 9–10
Negotiation process, 19
Neo-positivism, 106–107

New Iowa School (NIS), 3–4, 10, 15, 26–27, 31, 36
  in laboratory, 18–20
  laboratory experiments, 34
  laboratory research, 17
  laboratory researchers, 12
  premises in symbolic interaction, 14–16

Observational research methods, 26–27
Online subcultural interaction, 95–96
Open-mindedness, 4–5

Paranormal reality television shows, 175
Partisan groups, 19
"Period clothing", 179
Phenomenology, 68
Philosophy, 135
Placement, 182–183
"Police body camera", 85
Police professionalism, 84
Poprishchin's madness, 175
"Popular opinion", 180
Portable document (PDF), 85
Positional maps, 64
Positivism, 51, 106, 108
  in sociology, 106
Positivistic approach, 15
Post-announcements, 182–183
Pragmatic-functionalist theory, 139
Pragmatism, 52, 54–55, 57, 107–109
  and GTM, 61–63
  and SI, 56
Pre-announcements, 182–183
Pre-emptive ethnomethod, 182–183
Primary group, 138–139
Primitive mentality, 142
Primitive society, 142
Probability, 108
Problematic situation, 56
"Problem finding", 56
Productive ethnomethod, 182–183
Profound loss, appeal to sacred and appeal to, 173–175

192 INDEX

Protestant missionaries, 128–129
Provocative stage, 14, 33–34
Provocative stage, revisiting
 laboratory as, 17–18
"Psychic gifts", 172
Psychics, 176
Psychoactive drugs, 26
Psychology, 135
#PublicCriminology, 90

Qualitative analysis, 82
*Qualitative Analysis for Social
 Scientists (QASS)*, 61–63
Qualitative data, 18, 113
Qualitative document analysis, 81
Qualitative inquiry, laboratory as
 space for, 21
Qualitative interactionist research,
 10
Qualitative media analysis (QMA), 5,
 79, 81–82
 conceptual significance of QMA in
  symbolic interactionism,
  87–88
 importance of QMA in symbolic
  interactionist research,
  88–91
 process of, 82–87
 steps of, 83
Qualitative methods, 80
Qualitative research, 9–10, 80
 in laboratory, 18–20
Qualitative researcher, 97–98
Quantification, 108
Quantitative approach, 15
Quantitative data, 50–51, 106–108,
 113–116
Quantitative measurements, 32
Quantitative results, 12
Quasi-experimental research, 27

"Race relations", 123, 143–144
Radical suffragists, 140
Readers, 6
Realization, 12–13
Reconciling agency, 55

"Regression fishing", 114
Relational maps, 64
Re-searching data, 19
Research methods, 102, 106, 113
Research process, 6
Research question, 83
Rigorous method, 60–61
Rigorous research methods, 32
Romanticism, 51

Sacrificial ethnomethods, 173, 175
 appeal to sacred and appeal to
  profound loss, 173–175
Scene, 94, 98
Science of small group research,
 11–12
"Science-oriented person", 176
Scope, 182–183
"Scramble for Africa", 125
Self, 96–98
 appeal to self-coherence, 176–177
 becoming of, 100–101
 self-presentation, 170
 sociology of music, 94
Sense of place, 98
Sensitives, 176
Sensitizing concepts, 94
Sentencing guidelines, 115
"Sexual misconduct", 87
Situational analysis (SA), 63–64
Sluggish imagination, 38
"Sober judgment", 140–141
Social attitudes, 138
"Social attitudes", 136
Social behavior, 10, 31
Social change, 144–145
Social co-construction, 56
Social consciousness, 135
Social contexts, 110–111
Social elements, 19
Social environments, 12–13
Social interaction process, 29, 106
Social justice, 65–66
Social media, 88
 algorithms, 90
 data, 90–91

Index　193

digital documents from, 90–91
platform, 90
post, 83
Social order
discovering forms and elements of
interaction, 31–36
disrupting social order, 28–31
experimenting with, 27–36
interactionist futures, 40–41
responses to Couch and Garfinkel,
36–40
"Social origins", 136
Social process, products of, 106
Social psychological research, 15
Social psychological researchers, 17
Social psychological studies, 14–15
Social psychology, 11, 135
Social scene, 99
Social-theoretic conceptions, 30–31
Social theory, 122
Social worlds/arenas maps, 64
Sociation, 34
elements of, 34–35
Society for Study of Symbolic Inter-
action (SSSI), 42
Sociological attitude, 26
Sociological field expeditions to
Congo, 143–145
Sociological imagination, 12–14
Sociological research, 50–51
Sociological theory, 26
Sociology, 5, 32, 106, 122, 135
of music, 94
positivism in, 106
Statistical analysis, 106–108, 110–111,
115–116
Statistical data, 106
value for abduction, 113–116
Statistical interaction effects, 109–110
Statistical methods, 106
Status passage, 60–61, 66
"Stone-Campbell Restoration
Movement", 124–125
Straight-edge subculture, 95
Strauss-Corbin approach, 66–67
Structural functionalist theory, 26

Subculture, 94, 96
Symbolic interaction (SI), 52, 57–58,
97–98
Chicago amalgam, 52–57
GTM and, 59–61
GTM and social justice, 65–66
induction and abduction, 68–72
pragmatism and GTM, 61–63
SA and GTM, 63–64
SI institutionalizes GT, 57–59
varieties and essences of GTM,
66–68
Symbolic interactionism, 3, 68, 96,
105–106, 122, 136–137
causality, 111–112
conceptual significance of QMA in,
87–88
contingency, 109–110
empiricism, positivism, 106–108
probability, 108
social context, 110–111
value of statistical data for
abduction, 113–116
variation, 108–109
Symbolic interactionists (SI), 9–10,
17–18, 31–33, 97, 102–103,
110
research, 26
research importance of QMA in,
88–91
model, 97–98
Symbolic interactionist theory,
115–116
Symbolic interaction, premises of NIS
in, 14–16
System of relevances, 28–29

Tacitly, 51
Technical equipment, 34
Technology, 80
Texas Christian University (TCU),
124–125, 134
Theoretical causality, 111–112
Theoretical sensitivity, 59, 61
"Theory-methods package", 56,
59–61

TikTok, 83–85, 90
  videos, 81, 84
Time, 53–54, 66
Twenty-Statement-Test (TST), 26–27, 31–32
Twitter, 83–84, 89–90
  #MeToo on, 85

United States, 126–127
University of California, San Francisco, The (UCSF), 50

"Variable analysis", 107–108
"Variables", 109–110
Variation, 108–109

Varieties, 66
Verification, appeal to, 180–181
Video-recordings, 34, 36

Web-scraping tools, 85–86
Western culture, 142
Witness to atrocities, 127–130
"Working group" format, 66
Written language, 138

X. *See* Twitter

YouTube, 85
  video, 81